THE ARCHITECTURE
OF BRITAIN

Doreen Yarwood

THE ARCHITECTURE
OF BRITAIN

CHARLES SCRIBNER'S SONS · NEW YORK

28749

Contents

PART TWO

CLASSICAL DOMINANCE

Preface

The text of this book presents a broad commentary on and description of architecture in Britain from Saxon times until the present day, relating the building activity to the life of the people and to their relationship with other countries of influence at the time. More than half the contents of the book is illustrative, in line drawings and half-tones. This pictorial coverage includes buildings of all types – ecclesiastical and secular, civic and domestic – as well as architectural and ornamental detail.

The line drawings were made by the author from her own photographic record. The author and publishers wish to thank J. M. Dent and Sons Ltd and the Royal Institute of Architects for permission to reproduce 451 from the *Works in Architecture of R. and J. Adam*; also the following for permission to reproduce the photographic illustrations in this book: H.M. The Queen for 187; Robert Adam for 40 and 168; Aerofilms and Aero Pictorial Ltd for 184 and 132; G. Douglas Bolton for 234; J. Allan Cash for 103; B. C. Clayton for 55 and 169; Country Life for 347; John Dunbar for 439; Noel Habgood for 518; A. F. Kersting for 166–7, 308, 322, 345, 362, 382, 468 and 521; Ministry of Public Building and Works for 83; Paul Popper Ltd for 182; Kenneth Scowen for 186; Edwin Smith for 104, 118, 121 and 344; Scottish National Buildings Record for 303; J. Valentine and Sons Ltd for 236; Warburg Institute for 364; John Watt, Scottish Field for 170; John Yarwood for 14, 32, 36–8, 47, 57, 60, 75–82, 93, 97, 101–2, 116, 119, 132, 135, 138, 140, 142, 144–5, 147, 150–1, 156, 161, 185, 192–3, 195, 205–7, 216, 218, 220, 233, 247–8, 257, 276, 374–6, 410, 416–17, 421–5, 431–4, 436–7, 440, 442–4, 452, 497, 500, 519–20, 565–7.

339, 341 and 384 are from the publisher's collection.

London 1975   Doreen Yarwood

PART ONE

THE MIDDLE AGES

CHAPTER ONE

Britain before the coming of the Normans: AD 450–1066

The centuries between the departure of the Roman legions and the arrival of William of Normandy were years in which the British race was formed from a mingling of the successive waves of invaders who assailed her shores. While the Roman occupation lasted, barbarian raids from the Continent were kept within bounds. But, from the time in AD 409 when the Roman emperor notified Britain that henceforth her towns must defend themselves, because Rome herself was threatened, the British Isles became an easy prey to invaders. The south and east coasts were constantly attacked from the Continent by the Germanic peoples – themselves being pushed westwards – in particular, Angles, Saxons and Jutes, who settled respectively in East Anglia, Mercia, Northumbria; Essex, Sussex, Wessex; Kent and the Isle of Wight. These waves of invaders percolated westward and northward, confining the earlier Celtic peoples more and more to the fringes of Britain: Cornwall, Wales, Scotland and Ireland.

The appearance of Britain steadily returned to what it had been before the coming of the Romans. Roads were overgrown, towns, pavements and buildings were broken or destroyed and a primitive, nomad life was resumed. The arts – literature, painting, sculpture, architecture – were lost and, for some time, destruction was general.

New cultural beginnings emerged with the tentative spread of Christianity. The movement had been seeping slowly into Romanised Britain, but this had been rudely halted and destroyed by the Saxon invasions of the fifth and sixth centuries. The new spread of Christian teaching and culture came from a different direction, from the Celtic fringe areas which had escaped the Saxon onslaught.

The *monastic* way of life had evolved in Egypt, where monks pursued solitary lives, hermits in caves and huts. The movement spread westwards and soon monks began to establish communities, still living in huts, but grouping these to form larger units. In fifth-century Ireland, St Patrick, himself a British Christian, son of a Roman provincial official, came from Gaul to convert the Irish. Monasteries were built and flourished there in the sixth and seventh centuries. From Ireland these monks went forth indefatigably to spread the gospel to Scotland, Wales and Cornwall, from whence the light of Christian arts and learning was disseminated slowly to the rest of Britain. St Ninian founded the Celtic monastery at *Whithorn* (Scotland) in, it is thought, about 400 AD and, in 563, St Columba left Ireland to found the Celtic monastery on the island of *Iona*. From here, later, the Celtic Church spread to Northumbria, where St Aidan established the monastery at *Lindisfarne*.

Isolated and, often, island sites were favoured by these Celtic monks who wished to lead the contemplative life. They constructed small buildings in stone or wood, according to the availability of materials. These structures were generally of one cell or room and were rectangular or round, bee-hive shapes, low and simply roofed. The bee-hive cells were separate buildings, but often inter-communicated. The most usual method of construction in Scotland and in England was in dry masonry, each course corbelled out to converge at the top to make a domed vault. Remains of these in Britain are fragmentary, but

1   *Escomb, Durham, 7th century*

2   *The chancel arch, interior, Escomb*

3   *Plan, Brixworth*

4   *Plan, Boarhunt, Hampshire, 11th century*

5   *Interior, Brixworth*

6   *Brixworth Church, Northants, c.680 also 10th and 11th century. Later spire*

6A *Hexham Abbey Church, Northumberland. Built of stone from Roman Camp at Corstopitum (Corbridge), c.674*

6B *Repton Church, Derbyshire, 10th century*

in Ireland there are a number of examples in more complete condition. In the ruins of monastic settlements can be found a larger church or chapel building with the monks' cells clustered around it. One such instance is on the island of Skellig Michael, where there are nine buildings comprising two oratories, six huts and the church.

Remains of Celtic stonework in Britain also include the tall *round towers* and *carved crosses*. Both of these are more common in Ireland, but some examples exist in Britain. The stone round towers (like the one at *Brechin*, Angus), were built on the monastic sites, mainly during the times of the Viking raids; they acted as refuges and storage places for valuables. They were tall, delicately tapering and were capped by a conical stone roof. They contained a belfry as a means of warning the community in times of danger and they had doorways set well above ground level, accessible only by wooden ladders which could be withdrawn when under attack. A port was provided which made it possible to overturn the ladder put up by an attacker. Inside were floors of wood connected by spiral staircases (27).

The carved standing stones and *high crosses* can also be found in Scotland and England. They were erected to mark a sacred site or a boundary, or might have been placed in commemoration of the dead. They vary in size and complexity of design; many are finely carved, the motifs of fret, plait and interlacing ornament being frequently employed as well as birds, animals, flowers and human figures (19, 22).

It was in AD 597, after nearly two centuries, that England again experienced the influence of the Christian Church from Rome. St Augustine, sent by the Pope, landed with his 40 Benedictine monks in Kent, to begin the re-establishment of Christianity in England. He built the first cathedral at Canterbury on the site remains of a Romano-British church. Like the early Christian churches in Rome, it was basilican in plan, with an apse, its nave flanked by aisles.

Anglo-Saxon Churches

Remains of Saxon building in England date from two different periods. The earlier work is seventh- and early eighth-century structures and the latter stems from the late ninth and the tenth century. Between these two periods took place the devastating Viking

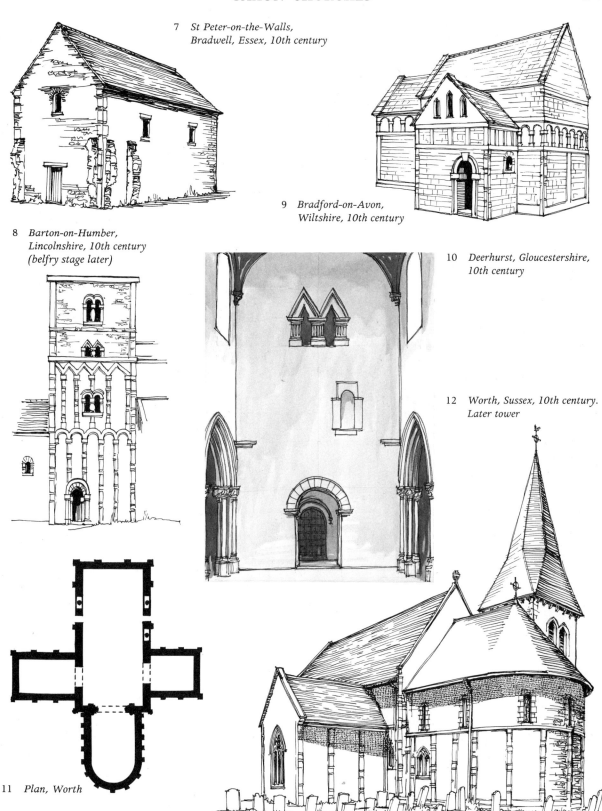

7 St Peter-on-the-Walls,
Bradwell, Essex, 10th century

9 Bradford-on-Avon,
Wiltshire, 10th century

8 Barton-on-Humber,
Lincolnshire, 10th century
(belfry stage later)

10 Deerhurst, Gloucestershire,
10th century

12 Worth, Sussex, 10th century.
Later tower

11 Plan, Worth

raids, which destroyed the bulk of early Saxon culture. The majority of Saxon building was in wood, or even timber with wattle-and-daub construction, but the more important churches and monasteries were built in stone. The work of the earlier period was centred in two areas; the southern one in Kent followed the Roman Christian line stemming from St Augustine, while the northern, in Northumbria, was centred around Hexham and Lindisfarne, with closer affinities with Celtic monasticism. The architecture of the seventh century, though its remains are not numerous and, in many cases, are fragmentary, clearly reflects this difference of approach.

The Canterbury school in the south created churches on basilican plan, as in Rome. Most examples were simpler than the prototypes, presumably because of the lesser experience of British builders. Instead of a row of columns supporting the arcaded wall which divided nave from aisles, there were plain walls broken only by an opening on each side which led to a series of chambers. An example of this type of design can be seen in the ruined *Church of Reculver* in Kent. The *Church of St Peter and Paul at Canterbury* was of this type with the Roman pattern of apsidal chancel and, at the opposite end of the nave, the narthex (13).

The Northumbrian churches, in contrast, were built in the simpler, Celtic design of tall, narrow, aisleless nave and rectangular chancel, like the small church at *Escomb* in Co. Durham (1, 2). Even the great, seventh-century monastic churches of *Jarrow* and *Monkwearmouth* were of this pattern. In 664, after the Synod of Whitby, Northumbrian monasticism pursued the lines of Roman Christianity and, by the end of the century, impressive northern churches were being built which were basilican in plan. Those at *Hexham* and *York* and at *Ripon* were of this type and, according to written records, they were large, complex structures. In *Hexham Abbey Church* the crypt of the Saxon building survives, the prime example in England from this early period. Constructed in 674 of large blocks of stone, it is designed in barrel-vaulted chambers after the pattern in Rome (6A).

The best example surviving of this early period of Saxon church building is *Brixworth* in Northamptonshire. Both geographically and architecturally it is placed half-way between the Kentish and Northumbrian designs. This is a remarkable structure for so early a building. Nearly 100 feet long, it is constructed of rag-stone and re-used Roman bricks. Originally an arcade separated the aisles from nave and choir, while the latter ended in a polygonal apse. Despite the walling-in of the arcades and loss of the aisles, the remains constitute a fine example of early Saxon work* (3, 5, 6, 23).

While Carolingian architecture was being established on the Continent under the flourishing empire of Charlemagne in the ninth century, Britain was suffering the savage and repeated raids of the Norsemen, who came plundering, burning and looting round the coasts. The Saxons were unprepared and ill-equipped to fight; monasteries especially were unprotected and offered tempting riches at little cost in battle. The destruction at Lindisfarne in 793 was followed by that at Jarrow in 794 and Iona in 795. These early raids were precursors of longer and more adventurous visits which increased in intensity until 850. By 865 a Danish invasion army had arrived and was only finally controlled under King Alfred later in the century.

The majority of Saxon architecture surviving in Britain dates from the tenth and early eleventh centuries, the so-called 'golden age' of Saxon art. These buildings are stone, rubble and brick churches, important enough to have been constructed in durable materials, but none of them are the larger, impressive structures which we know were built (and rebuilt after Viking depredations) at such monasteries as Ely and Malmesbury. In these years over 30 Benedictine monasteries were built in Britain but little, apart from foundations, of these remain, due to the tremendous building activity initiated by the Normans after the Conquest. They then rebuilt the churches and cathedrals from the foundations upwards, usually on the same site.

The Saxon building which exists, therefore, is of second rank; the smaller churches. There are a number of these in different parts of the country, but in no case is the structure entirely unaltered and, in some instances, only the tower, a doorway or fenestration remains from the original work.

An interesting feature of these churches is that they

---

* The church was badly damaged by Viking attacks. It was in the tenth and eleventh centuries that it was built up again and when the west end stair turret was added, the side aisles with lean-to roof removed and the arcades blocked. The spire is fourteenth-century.

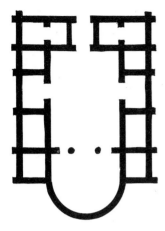

13 *Plan, Reculver, Kent*

14 *St Benet, Cambridge*

15 *Earl's Barton,
Northamptonshire, early
11th century*

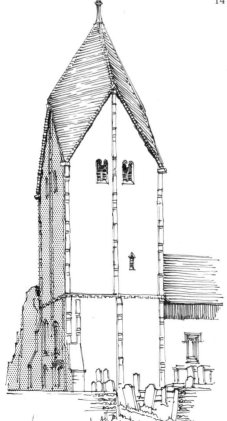

16 *Greensted, Essex, 10th century*

17 *Sompting, Sussex, early 11th century*

appear to have developed hardly at all, either in plan or structure, from those churches erected in the seventh century. A number of them are still very simple, merely a long, narrow, high nave or nave and chancel. Such churches have no aisles, no apse, no transepts. The best of these small churches is that dedicated to *St Lawrence* at *Bradford-on-Avon*, near Bath. This has a nave and chancel; its walls, some two and a half feet thick, are of large blocks of local stone, well cut and closely fitted. The chancel arch is typically narrow and the tiny, high nave is pierced by doorways on the other three sides. The small windows are set high in the otherwise unbroken walls (9). Other examples of the simple nave and chancel or single chamber church include those at *Boarhunt*, Hampshire (4) and *Bradwell*, Essex (7).

Many Saxon churches were built on the basilican plan with an apsidal-ended chancel, but these were rarely aisled; *Wing Church*, Buckinghamshire has a polygonal apse. The cruciform plan was unusual; two examples survive partly unaltered, that of *St Mary in Castro* in Dover Castle and *Worth Church* in Sussex. At Worth the chancel is apsidal; inside, the church is remarkably Saxon in appearance (11, 12, 20). The interior of *Deerhurst Church*, Gloucestershire retains its tall west wall, pierced by a small doorway and windows; the aisle arcades are later, Medieval, work (10, 21).

Characteristic of Saxon building style are the church *towers*, of which several survive. The one at *Earl's Barton* in Northamptonshire is the best known. It is an ornamented tower (15, 18, 29) with the typical stone pilaster strips in vertical line and chevron pattern. Several possible explanations have been put forward to account for these stone strips, which are also to be seen in the towers at *Sompting Church*, Sussex (17, 26), which retains its helm roof, *Barton-on-Humber Church*, Lincolnshire (8), *Barnack Church*, Northamptonshire, *Monkwearmouth Church*, Durham, *Dunham Magna Church*, Norfolk and *St Benet's Church*, Cambridge (14), as well as on the walling of *Worth Church* and *Bradford-on-Avon*, for example (9, 12). The strips are not of any structural significance and are probably only for decoration, though it has been suggested that the treatment is evocative of timber prototypes and represents a simulation of the wood and plaster structure. It seems more likely that it is the Saxon version of the Mediterranean blank wall arcading or a primitive attempt to portray the Carolingian neo-Roman treatment. At Bradford-on-Avon the simple arcading round the exterior walls is reeded, like classical pilasters.

Other characteristics of Saxon work which differentiate it from the later Norman structures are the long-and-short work, the unbuttressed, thinner walling and the window and doorway design. This so-called *'long-and-short work'* occurs where a tall, squared stone of up to four feet high is set vertically and this alternates with a flat stone slab set horizontally into the wall. This is a common construction for quoins, as in Earl's Barton, Barnack and Barton-on-Humber towers (8, 15).

Saxon *window openings* were round or triangular-headed, set singly or in pairs (21, 25, 29). They were often double splayed, that is, they had a narrow opening which splayed inwards and outwards. Earlier examples were generally set in the centre of the wall, later versions nearer the outer face, then, commonly, splayed inwards only. In the double window style, the two lights were often divided by a shaft or turned baluster (28), which supported the impost. This was a long rectangular block of stone, carried through the whole thickness of the wall, while the baluster was set nearer to the outer face (20). Some windows had narrow, round mouldings over the arch.

Belfry openings were cut straight through the wall thickness and were subdivided into two or more openings, each of which was covered by a round arch. A shaft or pilaster separated the openings. Shafts could be turned in baluster form with horizontal decorative bands or they were octagonal, oblong or square in section. *Capitals* were generally cubical, or, later, scalloped, while a few had volutes* (24, 26).

Doorways, like windows, were round or triangular-headed. Some examples were plain, others had simple mouldings or voussoir blocks. A number were finished with Roman bricks (23). Doorways were narrow in proportion to their height. At Earl's Barton, vertical pilaster strips are taken round the arch while the arch mouldings are set inside them. Square blocks form the imposts (18).

Few Saxon *crypts* survive in good condition though many of the larger churches possessed them. Apart

---

* All of these display crude derivations from classical, Byzantine and Carolingian work, as well as pre-dating Romanesque cushion capitals.

18 Tower doorway,
Earl's Barton Church

19 Celtic Cross, Scotland,
10th century

20 Window opening,
Worth Church

21 Window opening,
Deerhurst Church

22 Saxon cross, 8th century

23 Doorway, Brixworth Church

24 Saxon capital

25 Saxon window using Roman
bricks

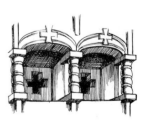

26 Sompting Church

27 Stone round tower, Ireland

28 Saxon baluster shaft

29 Tower window, Earl's
Barton Church

from the seventh-century one at *Hexham* (6A and page 6), there are traces of a basilican crypt at Brixworth Church and a tenth-century one at *Wing Church*. Here, under the polygonal-ended chancel, is an octagonal chamber with an ambulatory round it under the apse above. At *Repton Church* there is a square, tenth-century crypt with four columns supporting a stone vault (6B).

After the Viking raids, the Saxons, in the tenth and eleventh centuries, used more permanent *building materials* than previously. They re-used Roman stone from ruined buildings, and took Roman bricks for quoining and arch turning though, as at Brixworth, their skill was not sufficient to radiate brick voussoirs of the arches (23, 25). The Saxons quarried their own stone, such as Barnack stone in Northamptonshire, as well as different rag-stones, while in the chalk areas of the country they used flint for building. The majority of Saxon building was still of wood, of which almost nothing survives. One interesting exception is at the village church of *Greensted* in Essex, where remains of the tenth-century nave wall timbers still exist. This little church was built from the trunks of large oak trees, split and roughly hewn. They were set upright, close together and let into a sill at the bottom and a plate at the top, to form nave walls. They were fastened with wood pins. These timbers still form the nave walls of the little church, although they had to be removed in the nineteenth century, shortened and set into a brickwork plinth, because of decay at the foot. The church was originally nearly 30 feet long and 17 feet wide. A later tower, spire and roof have been added (16). It is interesting to compare this example at Greensted with the stave churches of Norway. In Essex the design is dictated by the availability of the limited length of the oak timbers whereas, in Norway, the structure is taken from tall pine trees.

The Saxons dug *earthworks* to protect their important homes and village groups, particularly after the commencement of the Viking raids. The chief hall or house was of timber with surrounding huts of timber and wattle-and-daub.* A wood palisade enclosed these and the whole site – planned on top of a natural hill or artificial mound – was surrounded by a circular ditch or two concentric ditches. The earth from these provided the mound or, alternatively, a bank beyond the ditch. Sometimes a double palisade was constructed with space for cattle

between the two. Water filled the ditches which could be spanned with removable planks.

The Saxons lived in small communities. They built *homes* in most parts of the country of timber and wattle-and-daub, though in areas where stone was readily available it was used for walling. The common style of building was one used widely, even in Medieval times, and it can still be seen in England and in areas on the Continent from where it originated. This is the *cruck* form of house, built in bays. Each bay was about 16 feet wide and the number of these varied according to the wealth and importance of the owner. The bay divisions were marked by crucks or forks of massive timbers, in pairs. These crucks were bent tree trunks, meeting at the top in gable shape to support a ridge pole which ran horizontally along the ridge of the roof of the whole building. Smaller timbers between, called rafters, helped to hold up the roofing, which was of thatch or wood shingles. Such a building lacked head-room, as the walls and roof were in one curved piece. Inside, the great room or hall was divided into living and sleeping space for the family, servants, farm workers and animals. Such halls were for the *thegn* or lord (30). The majority of people lived in small huts of straw and branches, covered in turf, bracken, mud and heather, much as their prehistoric ancestors had done. Such huts could be abandoned and rebuilt if the inhabitants were harried to another part of the country by invaders and barbarian raids.

Cruck houses continued to be built in Britain throughout the Middle Ages. Then they were of half-timber and in the fourteenth and fifteenth centuries the roofs were raised and vertical walls inserted in order to give head-room. A number of examples from this time, still showing the cruck construction, can be seen in Britain (32).

Stone structures were built by the people of the tenth and eleventh centuries in the north of the country, in Scotland, Orkney and Shetland and in

---

* A type of construction where a row of vertical stakes or large branches are interwoven horizontally by smaller branches and reeds. Mud is plastered on one or both sides and dried out in the sun. A structural method used throughout the Middle Ages. In later times laths replaced branches and surfaces were plastered and painted on top of the mud. Hair or straw could be mixed with the mud to give greater strength and durability.

30 *Anglo-Saxon hall: a conjectural restoration*

32 *Medieval cruck construction, Weobley*

31 *Dry-stone structure, Gallarus Oratory, Dingle, Ireland, 7th century or later*

Ireland. The cruck shape was built in stone, as can be seen in the corbelled *Gallarus Oratory*, near Dingle in Ireland (31). The Norsemen also brought their form of house building with them and immigrant farmers interpreted this in stone from the ninth century onwards. In northern Scotland, Orkney and Shetland they built *long-houses*. These were low, long buildings with stone walls infilled with turf. Roofing was of thatch and timber weighted down, as Norwegian houses have been in country areas almost up till modern times, by heather ropes and stones. There was a door at each end of the long-house and windows in the lower roof slopes. A stone wall encircled the building, which was shared, like the southern, Saxon home, by family and livestock.

CHAPTER TWO

The Norman Conquest: Romanesque architecture 1066–1160

The Norman invasion of England, the last of its kind, was a princely conquest, led by Duke William of Normandy, who succeeded with a small army of only about 6000 men. In this it was unlike the earlier invasions by Saxons and Danes. These had been migrations of peoples, attracted by a rich, pleasant land, where they hoped to settle, farm and raise communities. Successive invaders who had come since the fifth century, when the Roman legions had left the British Isles undefended, had been unable totally to subdue the native peoples and weld them into one kingdom.

William was of different mould. He was of Viking stock, descendant of those Northmen (Norsemen) who had given their name to the part of north-west France to which they had come more than 150 years earlier from Scandinavia. They had retained their energy and fighting spirit; they had adopted the Latin culture, the French language and succeeded in combining their abilities in the arts of war and colonisation with those of administration and advanced political thinking. Being established in Normandy, these Norman aristocrats then turned their attention to Britain and Sicily.

Having conquered Harold's army, William proceeded unhesitatingly to subdue and unite his new colony and make it Norman. He parcelled out the land in estates to his Norman followers, so replacing the English aristocracy with one of his own. He then initiated the tremendous building programme to erect castles and fortified homes as strongpoints, to resist attempts at rebellion, and cathedrals and churches in support of the Christian religion which the Normans

had wholeheartedly embraced since early in the tenth century. These structures were, like the character of their builders, massive, ruthless, direct; they were only sparingly decorated. Stone had been readily available in Normandy and Norman builders were better masons than the Saxons though, for many years, most of the work was in wood, for speedy construction.

Many of the Saxon *towns* had been developed on Roman sites and, in turn, the Normans were attracted by similar suitable places to establish centres for defence and trade. These included towns such as Lincoln, York, Chester, Bath, Norwich, Southampton. London, from the days of Roman Londinium, was always the major city. One of the earliest stone buildings of William's reign was the keep of the Tower of London, now called the White Tower, erected as a sign of his dominance of the capital. Towns were small, buildings, even churches, were of wood, with thatch roofing and wattle walling. Most of them had gardens or open ground nearby. The streets were narrow and often steep so that excess water flowed down to the watercourse. Open drains ran down the centre while the passageways on either side were cobbled and sloped towards the drain. Cattle and pigs were driven over the cobblestones in streets which were dirty and dark.

The Romanesque style of architecture

The easiest way to define and to recognise an architectural style is by reference to its component parts and details. The style itself is a combination of all these parts, handled in such a manner as to present an overall scheme of specific character. Since each style owes something to others which have gone before, it may share components with these but yet, in totality, be something different and novel. This is so with Romanesque building. It is recognisable by its general and detailed characteristics where it appears in all parts of Europe, but its guise varies considerably from one area to another.

The two chief forms comprise the one developed in central Europe and that to be seen in the north and west. The former, as the name Romanesque suggests, springs from Roman classical design. It is in the central and southern areas such as northern Italy, south-east France, southern Germany and Spain that most examples of Roman building survive. From these, more numerous in the eleventh century than now, the Romanesque masons developed their own designs, using the round arch, the classical columns and capitals, arcading, tunnel vaults and the basilican church plan with its division into nave and aisles, its central timber roof and apsidal termination behind the high altar. These builders used the foliated motifs as well as animals, birds, human figures and devils. Their decoration was rich and vigorous, their façades and porticoes sculptured all over in biblical themes.

The strongest influence on Romanesque architecture in the north and west was the Norman style of work. Established in Normandy during the tenth century, the Normans brought their building methods and designs to Britain, also to southern Italy and Sicily, creating in these two widely dissimilar areas buildings of like character but adapted to the needs of the indigenous peoples.

Carolingian influence is apparent in Romanesque building design. This, characterised in its round and triangular-headed arches, simple shafts and brickwork patterning, had penetrated into Anglo-Saxon work. It also can be traced in Norman building but of stronger note is the pattern established in Normandy itself.

Here, in Caen, we can still see the two great churches of Duke William, the *Church of St Étienne* (L'Abbaye-aux-Hommes) and the *Church of La Trinité* (L'Abbaye-aux-Dames). St Étienne, built in 1066–77, illustrates the quality of northern Romanesque grouping in its masses and towers. The west front shows a strong vertical emphasis, with its twin, tall towers (capped by Gothic spires) flanking the plain

façade, broken only by unenriched round-headed windows and doorways. La Trinité, founded in 1062 by William's queen, Matilda, of Bayeux tapestry fame, has retained its original pattern even better. This is a massive, very Romanesque building, with a monumental façade of twin western towers in arcaded stages and, in between, a gabled centrepiece with deeply recessed round-headed doorway below; there is a square tower over the crossing, crowned by a stumpy spire. The interior is well preserved. It has a long nave with barrel-vaulted aisles and a fine apse covered by a groined vault. The nave is divided horizontally, on a northern pattern, into arcade, triforium and clerestory (35).

These two churches, though partly altered, display most clearly the structural pattern which the Normans brought to England. The buildings are massively constructed with very thick walling, especially at base, tall façades, little decoration, the round arch used for all openings and columns and piers solid and heavy with the plainest of capitals. Where decoration is used it is in abstract form – the chevron, the billet, the cushion. Unlike the central European models, the only Roman features used here are the arcade and round arch. The capitals are sternly formal, there is no sculpture, no richly ornamented portals. The Norman concept of Romanesque architecture, designed to suit the northern light and climate, as well as its religious needs, was for plainer, larger window area, solid, undecorated wall surfaces and an interior which is grouped to define and control the spatial qualities of the building. An important feature here was the Norman introduction of the tall, vertical shafts which extended from floor to wooden ceiling in the nave and choir. These divided the interior into bays and articulated the whole into compartments, creating a sense of progression from west doorway, up the aisle to eastern altar. This was a new concept and one which provided the basis for later Medieval building. The visual impact of the masses of solid walling is everywhere apparent. Even though these are pierced by arcades the effect is of carefully balanced power and weight (39).

Most Norman building in England before 1080 was in wood. This was the quickest means of erecting the secular buildings, in particular, which were needed to control and administer the country. After the initial rush to put up temporary castles, houses, churches and monasteries, the Normans settled down to constructing the great stone cathedrals, abbey churches and castles which still exist as testimony to their building skill, initiative and energy.

The earlier work had much in common with the corresponding structures in Normandy, but, just before the end of the century, the architectural style evolved from its early form into what may be termed High Romanesque: the zenith of its achievement. This is seen in the rediscovery of how to vault a tall, wide nave or hall with the groin and rib vaults, also in the increase of decoration on arch mouldings, capitals and columns. These features are still massive, strong and simple and the decoration is geometrical, but the deeply incised zig-zags, chevron cuts and cubiform capitals lend animation to the solidity of exterior portals and interior arcades not previously seen in Norman architecture. Towers especially were arcaded, generally in blind form, but imparting a plasticity which was new. The two great Norman buildings of this era in Britain are Durham Cathedral and the keep of the Tower of London. In a number of respects, Norman building in Britain was now moving ahead of its counterpart in northern France. Rib vaulting is the prime innovation and Durham is the prototype. In Normandy wooden ceilings remained the usual covering during the eleventh century.

It is especially interesting for students of Norman architecture in Britain to compare this version of northern Romanesque with the Norman work in their other kingdoms of *southern Italy* and *Sicily*. Here too, the Normans implanted their own style of work but, as in Britain, the buildings developed a somewhat different character from their Normandy prototypes. The south of Italy is now a region of poverty. In the tenth and eleventh centuries Apulia, its capital in Bari, became wealthy and powerful under Norman rule.

The great cathedral churches here – Trani, Troia, Bitonto, Molfetta, Canosa, as well as Bari itself – have the same Norman characteristics of power and solidity as in Normandy and Britain (38). Because of the brilliant sunlight, window openings are much smaller and the impression of immense areas of solid masonry walling is even more notable. The walls are equally thick but roof pitches are lower since it is unnecessary to throw off snow and heavy rains. Unlike the long, English naves, Italian ones are short and wide. Due to the width, roofing has to be of timber. Façades have the typical Norman form of tall,

twin towers but cupolas cover the crossing instead of a tower as in Britain while, inside, triforia are rare, the Italian fashion for a solid wall between nave arcade and larger clerestory windows above being adhered to. These differences are of surface character, the general impression being of the same fundamental source of style as in Britain and Normandy. The differences stem entirely from climatic variations and the people's temperament and needs.

The feature which creates the greatest difference between Apulian Norman Romanesque and the northern interpretation is the decoration. In Apulia, and even more in the Sicilian Norman kingdom, at Palermo, Cefalù and Monreale, for example, the craftsmen were Greek, from Byzantium, and the Saracenic influence from the Arabs was strong. Instead of English incised zig-zags, round arches and cubiform capitals, there are Saracenic arches, mosaic facing to walls and apses and a wealth of sculpture on capitals and portals based on plant and geometrical motifs. The sculpture is vigorous and the mosaics emit a rich glow of colour and gold to the darker interiors.

In Normandy *masons* had used chiefly their local Caen stone for important buildings. They introduced this material into England, transporting it from Normandy, for fine work on quoins, capitals and especially interiors. Caen stone is white and easy to carve. It was imported all through the Middle Ages but, because of the cost and effort of transportation, the Normans turned more to local materials for other building. They worked Bath stone, limestone, sandstones and rag-stones. Chalk and flint were included in walling. Such materials were used for cathedrals, churches, castles and monasteries. Most of the building in Britain was of the nearest convenient material and this, most commonly, was wood, wattle-and-daub, thatch with, possibly, stone foundations and bases.

Early Romanesque masonry by the Normans in England was massive. Fearful of collapse in the great buildings erected, masons built walls up to 24 feet thick at base. In general, they overestimated the thickness necessary for safety, though, since this work had wide joints and the mortar was poor and thin, the collapse of towers and roofs was not unknown. Windows were small, partly in order not to weaken the wall and partly for defence reasons. In castles and houses, the lowest row of windows was

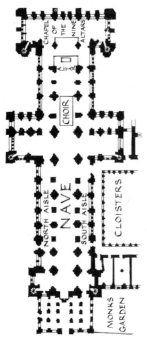

34   *Durham Cathedral,*
12th century.
Central Tower,
15th century

33   *Plan, Durham Cathedral*

35   *Church of La Trinité, Caen, Normandy, 1063–1125*

36   *Nave capital, Hereford Cathedral*

37   *West doorway capitals, Rochester Cathedral*

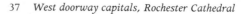

above first-floor level.

Twelfth-century work was less massive. The masonry was by now fine jointed and more often carved in incised line or three-dimensional decoration. The knowledge and art of the mason increased and improved, enabling him to build with thinner walling and yet maintain stability. The Normans were prodigious builders and the quantity of work which they produced was immense. Even discounting the loss of all structures not of stone and the disappearance and alteration of many of the latter material, the amount of Norman Romanesque work which survives in Britain is a tribute to the strength and achievement of Norman construction.

The Cathedrals and Churches

Because of their importance in eleventh- and twelfth-century community life and the consequent care with which they were erected, it is ecclesiastical buildings which have survived in the greatest numbers. Of massive structure and durable material, the great cathedral, abbey, priory and parish churches exist all over the country. Most of them have been altered and enlarged in later years but a great deal of Norman workmanship remains, especially in the cathedrals. A tremendous effort was expended in building these. Many were erected on the sites of Saxon cathedral churches, but generally the Saxon building was demolished and the Norman one started from the foundation upwards.

The *plan* of early Romanesque cathedrals in western Europe was evolved on functional lines. The church was divided into two parts, east and west; the former devoted to use by the clergy, the latter for the lay public. From the tenth century onwards, the worship of saints became a growing custom and more chapels were needed for this in the eastern part of the cathedral. The French contribution to the Medieval church plan was either to build an ambulatory round an apsidal east end and design chapels which radiated from it, or to extend the choir aisles forwards to be almost flush with the apsidal end of the choir and also, sometimes, to build out chapels from the transepts.

The plan of an English cathedral developed from the Normandy design as set by the pattern of such churches as St Étienne in Caen. This has twin western towers, a long nave and short choir, both aisled, transepts and a semi-circular termination to the eastern apse. (At St Étienne, as in many French churches, this was replaced later by the typical French chevet, wherein chapels were built radiating round a larger apse.) Often, in Norman examples, each transept was also finished on the eastern side by an apse, giving a tri-apsidal termination to the building.

The usual pattern in England was a cruciform structure, that is, a plan based on the cross. The western arm, the nave, was generally longer than the other three arms, which were quite short. This is known as the Latin cross plan, in distinction from the Greek cross plan with four equal arms, more common in eastern Europe and later Renaissance work. English cathedrals usually had a longer nave and choir than their Continental counterparts and early examples were not aisled.

After 1100, the English plan began to diverge from the Continental pattern by playing down the importance of the eastern apse or apses. Sometimes the transepts were built forward with chapels also flush with the central apse and, later still, the east ends of the majority of English cathedrals were altered to a square termination. *Ely, Winchester, Peterborough, Lincoln* and *Durham,* for example, have square ends (33). Generally, this was achieved by building on to the eastern arm a Lady Chapel or retro-choir. This provided greater space here, but at the same time it was no longer possible to walk round the ambulatory in the choir, behind the high altar. Among the English cathedrals which still preserve the ambulatory and apsidal east end are *Norwich* (41, 42) and *Canterbury,* while amongst churches, *St Bartholomew-the-Great in Smithfield* (London) is now restored to its original plan on this pattern. Again, in English cathedrals, the crossing was usually covered by a low, square, Norman tower, with or without a stumpy spire. On the Continent, a lantern or cupola was more common. The western towers were also square and these might be capped by low spires, as at Southwell* (46). Often, however, the Norman towers have suffered damage or collapse and have been replaced by slenderer Gothic ones.

Inside, the cathedral was usually designed in three horizontal stages. On the ground floor was the arcade (nave, choir or transept), above this was the triforium arcade and the third storey comprised a row of

---

* These are modern replicas.

38   *Trani Cathedral, Italy, c.1094*

39   *One bay of nave arcade, Durham*
      Cathedral from 1093

NAVE VAULT

CLERESTORY
WINDOWS

TRIFORIUM
ARCADE

TRIFORIUM
PASSAGE

VAULTING SHAFT
WHICH DIVIDES
THE BAYS

NAVE
ARCADE

NAVE
CAPITAL

AISLE
WINDOWS

NAVE
COLUMN

WALL
ARCADING

NAVE
BASE

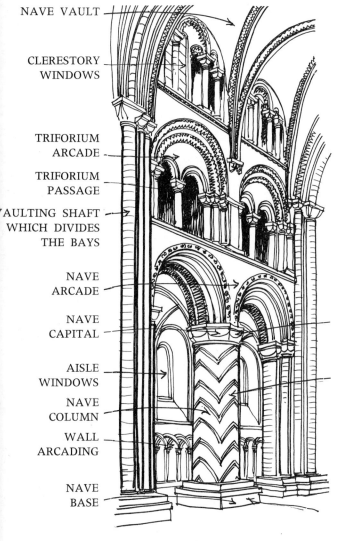

40   *Chapel and Tower of St Rule,*
      St Andrews, Scotland

windows. These are termed clerestory (clearstory) windows, in contrast to the triforium arcade, which is also commonly known as the blind-storey. The clerestory windows light the building while behind the triforium arcade is a passage often extending all round the church. This backs on to the sloping roof which covers the aisles and extends from the lower part of the clerestory to the upper aisle arcade.

Reference has already been made to the Norman innovation of articulating the church into bays by means of a vertical, stone shaft extending from floor to nave or choir timber roof. Where a church was stone vaulted, this shaft, or group of shafts, terminated in a capital which supported the vault arch springing (*Durham*) (39); where the nave roof was timber spanned (*Ely*), the shaft(s) extended to the top of the nave wall on which the roof was supported. In cathedrals where bays were so articulated, the bay usually contained one round arch at nave arcade level, two arches, or two small arches encompassed in a larger one, at triforium level, then one window in the clerestory stage; *Ely* (nave), *Peterborough* (nave and choir), and *Norwich* (transept) Cathedrals are like this. The nave arcade is then supported on piers of grouped shafts alternating with half columns. At *Durham* (nave and choir (39, 52)), the bay articulation is wider permitting two round arches in the nave arcade. Here, then, thick columns with incised decoration, alternate with shafted piers at this level, while in the triforium above, are two arches further subdivided into two.

In the naves of *Gloucester* and *Hereford Cathedrals*, and of *Tewkesbury Abbey Church*, it is the plain, heavy, round columns of the arcade which divide the bays and set the articulation pattern. The triforium arches and clerestory windows are then aligned above the centre of the round, nave arcade arches. A third variation comes in the aqueduct type of design as in *Southwell Minster* nave (48), wherein there are vertical shafts on the walls and each of the three stages is cut into deeply and widely by round-headed arches, one above the other. The stages are divided horizontally by string courses. Between the arches are the round columns at ground floor level, piers at triforium level and solid walling between the clerestory openings. This is an effective spatial design, dramatic, and characteristically Anglo-Norman Romanesque in its contrast of solid wall and column with deeply-shadowed round-arched openings. On similar pattern are many of the Scottish Abbey Churches of this period, for instance the nave at *Dunfermline* (55). Of related design, also, is that at *Worksop Priory*, Nottinghamshire.

Many Norman cathedrals were built with *crypts* under the main floor of the building, and wholly or partly below ground level. These were often used to house the relics of saints and pilgrimages were held to visit them. Two of the finest examples remaining are those at *Canterbury* and *Rochester Cathedrals* (50, 51).

Durham Cathedral. Begun 1093

This is the prime example of Anglo-Norman Romanesque cathedral building in England. Many cathedrals possess extensive Norman workmanship but only at Durham is almost the whole structure in this style. The cathedral is sited magnificently above the River Wear, on a massive rock, appearing to grow out of it. The hill on which it stands is wooded. The differing greens blend superbly with the mellowed warmth of the stone when the rays of the evening sun fall upon the western façade. Although the building from this view is homogeneous, the three towers are not now all of Norman building. The massive central tower, which was originally capped by a low spire, dates from the fifteenth century, while the slenderer, twin western towers partly stem from *c*.1220 (34).

The cathedral was built, like many others at this time, as a monastic centre and as a fortification; in this case against the Scots. It was begun in 1093 on cruciform plan (33) and most of the interior, including the vault, is of Norman style. The cathedral interior, in its massive, powerful proportions and rows of differently incised columns, is superb. One can gain an impression of how Norman cathedrals must have appeared in the twelfth century, since this is one of the rare examples where clerestory windows have not been enlarged at a later date to give greater illumination (39).

Of greatest significance in architectural history are the stone vaults spanning nave and choir at Durham; the east end was vaulted by 1104 (later rebuilt) and the nave by 1135. These are thought to be the earliest rib vaults of Europe and of consequent importance in the development of Medieval architecture. Their ribs decorated with Romanesque ornament, these vaults give life and mystery to the cathedral design which

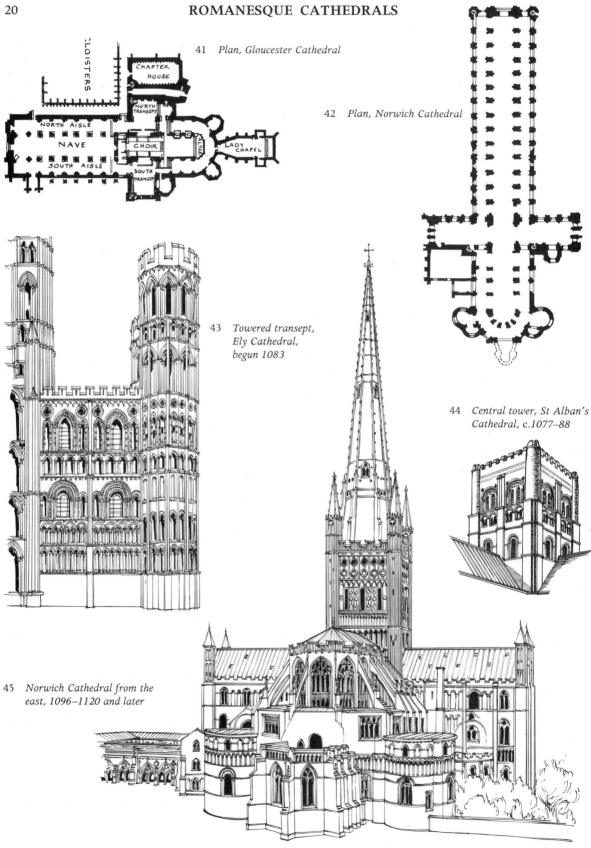

41   *Plan, Gloucester Cathedral*

42   *Plan, Norwich Cathedral*

43   *Towered transept,
Ely Cathedral,
begun 1083*

44   *Central tower, St Alban's
Cathedral, c.1077–88*

45   *Norwich Cathedral from the
east, 1096–1120 and later*

46 *Southwell Minster, c.1130 and later*

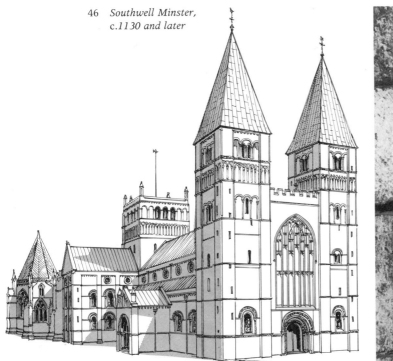

47 *Shaft detail, west doorway, Lincoln Cathedral, c.1150*

48 *Nave, Southwell Minster, c.1130*

50   *Crypt, Canterbury Cathedral, c.1096–1107. Groined vault*

49   *Crypt, Lastingham Church, Yorkshire, 1078–88*

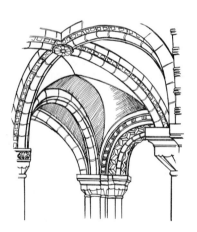

51   *Ribbed vault, monastic building, Canterbury Cathedral, 12th century*

52   *Nave and choir, Durham Cathedral, 1093–1133*

flat, timber roofs, rising on vertical walls, cannot do. They reiterate the rhythm of the vertical bays and round-arched masses, they extend the wall shafts upwards into curved planes, furthering the development of the spatial controlled design begun in the nave arcades. Durham is a powerful, homogeneous interior, dynamic, redolent of its age (52).

Churches

Parish churches were built all over the country at the same time as the cathedrals. Saxon churches were rebuilt as well as new churches on new sites. Similar styles of building and plan were attempted as in the cathedrals, though on a less ambitious scale. While some churches were simple, consisting only of aisleless nave and chancel, others were aisled, or had only one aisle, the other being added at a later date. The cruciform plan was most usual as was also a central tower, with short spire, over the crossing. Many chancels were apsidal, but these were frequently altered to a square termination when the eastern arm was extended in the Gothic period. The majority of Norman churches in England have been altered greatly or totally transformed. Of those which retain much of their character, especially in nave, tower and doorway or porch are *Kirkby Lonsdale Church*, Yorkshire, *Walsoken Church*, Norfolk, *Iffley Church*, Oxfordshire (58, 64), *Old Shoreham*, Sussex (67), *Barfreston*, Kent (81, 82), *Kilpeck*, Herefordshire (75, 76, 77, 78), and *St Bartholomew-the-Great*, Smithfield (72, 73). The last-named, already mentioned, has been considerably restored, mainly to the original design. In areas where stone was not easily available to bond the corners of a square tower, round towers were built. A number of these survive in Norfolk, where the lower courses are often of Saxon construction. Good examples include *Hales Church* and those at *Haddiscoe* and neighbouring *Thorpe-next-Haddiscoe*.

A few churches were built in England on centrally planned lines. They are based on the Early Christian church type like S. Costanza and S. Stefano Rotondo in Rome (fourth and fifth centuries) which, in turn, stemmed from the Ancient Roman mausoleum concept (59, 61). The English ones are Anglo-Norman Romanesque instead of classical like the Rome examples, but they have the same circular plan, with an inner ring of arcaded columns supporting triforium walling and arcade and, above, clerestory windows.

There is usually a conical roof over the central part above the clerestory windows, and a lower roof, at triforium level, over the circular aisle. The *Holy Sepulchre Church* at Cambridge dates from *c*.1130 and, though restored in the 1840s, is patterned on the original design (60). The *Temple Church* in London, dating from 1185, is another example. This was seriously damaged in the Second World War and has been rebuilt and added to.

Arches, columns, piers, arcades

The Romanesque *arch* is round. This can vary in form from the *semi-circular* shape, which is the most usual, and where the centre is on the diameter line, to the *segmental*, with a centre above diameter level, and the *stilted*, where it is below. The horseshoe arch, so common in southern Italy and Spain, is of Saracenic origin. Here, the curve is carried below the semi-circle; it is rarely used in England. Since Norman walling is thick, there is considerable depth between the two faces of the arch, inner and outer. In early work, the arch is not recessed; the edges are square in section and not moulded or ornamented (57, 87). Later work is moulded in deep rolls and rounds and often enriched with chevron (zig-zag), nail-head, billet, lozenge, cable or star decoration (48, 89, 90, 95, 97). Arches are constructed with radiating wedge-shaped blocks of stone, called *voussoirs* (77, 82). The central one at the top is the *keystone* and the horizontal ones at the sides, the *springers*. This is the point at which the arch springs from the capital. The under surface of an arch is termed the *soffit*, the upper surface, the *extrados*. Good examples of Norman arches are in *Durham Cathedral* nave (39, 52) and galilee, *Gloucester Cathedral* nave, *Ely Cathedral* nave.

Both columns and piers were used in Anglo-Norman building. The columns are circular in section (48, 74, 87, 89, 90, 95) and the piers square, often shafted with heavy half-columns and slenderer shafts (52, 73). They are all massive in scale and either plain, or decorated with incised carving in zig-zag, spiral or network patterns. *Durham Cathedral* (39, 52) and *Dunfermline Abbey Church* (55) have incised columns; *Gloucester* and *Tewkesbury*, plain versions.

The purpose of a capital is to give a larger area from which the arch may spring than the column or pier on which it stands. It also ornaments the junction (36). Early Norman examples are very plain and large. The

53   *Doorway, St Botolph's Priory, Colchester*

54   *Porch, Malmesbury Abbey, 12th century*

55   *Nave, Dunfermline Abbey, Scotland, 12th century*

56   *Doorway capital,*
      Leominster Priory Church

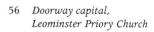

57   *Nave column,*
      Buildwas Abbey

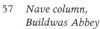

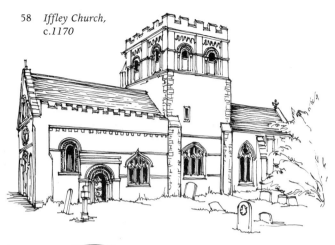

58 *Iffley Church,*
c.1170

60 *Holy Sepulchre Church, Cambridge, c.1130*

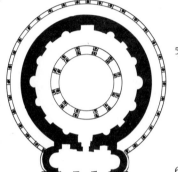

59 *Plan, S. Costanza*

61 *Church of S. Costanza,*
Rome, c.340

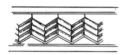

62 *Chevron ornament*　　63 *Star ornament*

64 *South doorway, Iffley Church*

top member, the *abacus*, is a square or round block of stone and, in early work, constitutes the whole capital. Soon mouldings were added below and capitals were circular (*Tewkesbury Abbey*) and octagonal (*Durham Cathedral*) (39, 52). Cushion capitals were most typical (*Peterborough Cathedral* nave and *Kirkwall Cathedral* nave, Orkney); other designs were simply voluted at the corners in a rough imitation of the classical Ionic capital (*St John's Chapel*, Tower of London) (65, 87). From the cushion capital developed the scalloped design (57, 66, 89, 90) (*Holy Sepulchre Church*, Cambridge and *Hereford Cathedral* nave) and late Norman work includes some foliated capitals and others carved in figure and animal motifs (*Canterbury Cathedral* crypt), though these are rarer and never so vigorous and varied as those on the Continent (37, 56, 95).

Early Norman *bases* are plain and insignificant, consisting of an octagonal or square plinth and/or a quarter-round moulding (*Gloucester Cathedral* nave). Later examples have deeper and more complex mouldings, but all are round on a square or octagonal plinth (*St John's Chapel*, Tower of London) (39, 52, 57, 87, 89, 90, 95).

In Medieval architecture the arch is often used in arcading, where a row of columns or piers support arches (39, 52, 87, 89, 90, 95). These arcades may also be of decorative purpose only, standing in front of a plain wall surface. In these cases, the arches frequently interlace one another. They may be seen inside, at triforium level (48, 72) or for any wall decoration as in towers (43) and apses (choir aisle *Durham Cathedral*; south transept, *Ely Cathedral*; façade, *Castle Acre Priory*, Norfolk; façade, *Rochester Cathedral*; central lantern, exterior and interior, *Norwich Cathedral*, 45).

Roofs and Vaults

The exteriors of Norman *roofs* in Britain were covered by tiles or stone slates, wood shingles or thatch. The pitch was fairly steep to throw off water and snow. Later roofs were lead covered and so flatter. Roofs overhung the walls for drainage purposes and were supported by a cornice at the top of the wall. This, in turn, stood upon *corbels*, which are decoratively carved stone blocks. The complete member, cornice and corbels, is called a *corbel table*. A parapet might be built above this. These parapets were generally in the form of an inner and outer wall with lead-lined

passage between. These walls were pierced at intervals to let the water out. In order to project the water away from the wall face, lead spouts were fixed at these intervals and generally set into stone blocks which were carved into *gargoyles*. These were fashioned in many forms: devils, animals, birds, monsters, etc. The usual theory is that they represent the evil spirits which were captured and rendered harmless in stone by the Christian spirit of the building which they decorated. Some gargoyle spouts projected from aisle buttresses also.

The *interior* of the roofing was of timber or stone. Most Norman roofing was in wood, especially over the wider spans of nave or choir in a church or cathedral. In secular building and smaller churches the roof was left open to show the rafters and was of a fairly high pitch. The roof timbers were roughly trimmed heavy baulks, the possible width of span being determined by the length of timber available. Ridge ribs, purlins and wall plates ran horizontally, the latter being supported on stone corbels at the top of the walls. Rafters ran crosswise at right angles to the main beams. A heavy tie beam extended from wall to wall at intervals to counteract the outward thrust of the roof (48, 95).

In larger cathedrals and churches a flat boarded and painted ceiling was constructed underneath the open roof. A number of these buildings still possess such ceiled roofs, but these are usually replacements (the naves of *St Albans' Abbey Church, Rochester Cathedral,* and *Ely Cathedral*). Genuine Norman timber roofing of any kind is a rarity today.

An interior span covered by stone is called a *vault*. The Romans had known how to cover wide spans with stone and concrete and had used such vaults to roof their thermal baths and such domed buildings as the Pantheon in Rome. The art had been almost lost in the west in the years that followed the collapse of the Empire, though it was expanded in areas under Byzantine influence. In southern France and in Italy, where the classical trend persisted, the art of *barrel vaulting* was not abandoned. These barrel, or tunnel, vaults were continuous round arches of stone constructed on centering, that is, by building a wooden frame on the underside to the desired form, then setting stones and mortar in position on top. The framework was moved on to the next section when the mortar had set. Barrel vaults were used in England by Saxon and earlier Norman builders, where the span was fairly narrow. It was a method particularly suited to aisles. A good example survives in *St John's Chapel* in the Tower of London (87).

More common in England was the further development of the vault. Anglo-Norman builders were pace-setters in this field. At a time when barrel vaults were in general use in France and Italy, England had moved on to the *groined* and then the *rib vault*. The latter is generally regarded as a characteristic of Gothic architecture, but it was used with the round arch in England in Norman times. The groined vault is an intersecting barrel vault, where the two tunnels meet at right angles, giving four arches with different direction faces. Massive piers or columns are set at the intersections to support the vault. This was a common means of vaulting large crypts in Norman times. Those at *Canterbury* and *Rochester Cathedrals* are good examples (49, 50).

By the twelfth century builders were urgently seeking methods to cover the wider spans of cathedral naves with stone roofing, partly to enhance the interior design and partly to reduce the risk of fire damage. This problem was first solved at *Durham Cathedral* where the *ribbed vault* was built. In this system a skeleton of stone ribs for six arches is thrown over the span, supported on the pillars below. Two of the arches cross the square vaulting compartment diagonally, the others transverse from side to side from the span making four compartments in between. The arches are all built separately on centering. Infilling in stone was completed later between the ribs. The whole structure is lighter in weight than the barrel vault and, as at Durham, gives height and chiaroscuro to the interior of the building (39, 51, 52).

An essential complement to the subject of stone vaulting is that of *abutment*, though this did not fully develop till the Gothic period of building. A buttress is a reinforcement and projection to a wall. Its use makes the immensely thick wall less necessary. It enhances the design of the structure and economises on building materials. Norman builders constructed massive walls and used little abutment. Their buttresses were flat, of low projection and adhered to the exterior wall (70).

The chief need for abutment comes from the thrust and pressure set up from roofs and towers. With timber roofing and low towers, little abutment is needed, but as the Normans developed stone vaulting the matter of abutment increased in importance. In a timber roof the tie beam structure largely counteracts the outward thrust on walling. Barrel vaults create a uniform thrust along the whole wall so that the massive Norman wall with flat buttresses was adequate. With groined and ribbed vaulting, the maximum thrust is exerted via the diagonal ribs or groins, producing maximum force at points on the wall just above the arch springing. It is here that the buttress must provide the counterthrust needed. In between, the wall can safely be weakened by windows. The Normans, therefore, used a simple flying buttress system, but these are not visible on the exterior of the building (as in later Gothic architecture) but are internal, only to be seen in the triforia passages.

Doorways, porches, window openings

The *doorway* was the most richly ornamented feature in Anglo-Norman architecture; this was especially so in twelfth-century workmanship. It was deeply recessed and heavily moulded in concentric semi-circular arches. In order to concentrate the principal decoration on the exterior face, the door was set nearer to the inside wall surface. The mouldings were then continued down from the arch and impost moulding to the ground; they were often set with shafts, each of which possessed a decorative capital and base.

The actual door was of wood and was square-headed; few have survived. The space between the doorhead and the inner arch was filled by a stone slab called the *tympanum*. This acted as the focal centre of the doorway ornament, being carved in high relief in floral or animal sculpture or, in some cases, in a figure composition representing a scene from the bible. Since Norman doorways were large, it was not necessary to enlarge them greatly in later years (53, 97), so many fine examples are extant. Among the best of these are the façade entrance doorways at *Lincoln* (47) and *Rochester Cathedrals* (37), at *Malmesbury Abbey Church* (54) and at the churches of *Iffley* (64), *Barfreston* (81) and *Kilpeck* (75).

Norman *porches* are in similar style, the side often being arcaded. A very fine example survives from the monastic buildings at *Canterbury Cathedral* (74).

In contrast to the doorways, Norman *windows* are small and narrow. Early examples are little more than round-headed slits a few inches wide. The opening

65   *Capital, c.1080*

66   *Capital, c.1080*

67   *Old Shoreham Church, Sussex*

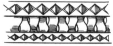

68   *Billet and lozenge ornament*

69   *Window, Castle Rising Church, c.1160*

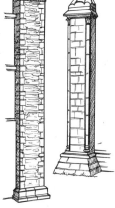

70   *Buttresses*

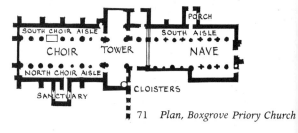

SOUTH CHOIR AISLE   PORCH   SOUTH AISLE

CHOIR   TOWER   NAVE

NORTH CHOIR AISLE

SANCTUARY   CLOISTERS

71   *Plan, Boxgrove Priory Church*

72   *Nave triforium, St Bartholomew-the-Great, London*

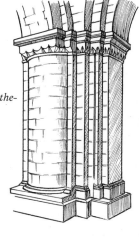

73   *Pier, St Bartholomew-the-Great*

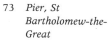

74   *Porch and staircase, Canterbury Cathedral, c.1150–65*

is set near to the outer wall face and is deeply splayed from the inside. They were made so narrow partly because of the lack of glass but chiefly for reasons of defence. These early window openings are usually undecorated (91, 92). Later examples are, like the doorways, round-headed, with carved mouldings in concentric semi-circles and with shafts set at the sides. *Iffley* and *Castle Rising Churches* (69) have windows like this. Not many examples survive as they were mostly enlarged in later Medieval times. A few openings were divided into two lights by a central shaft but tracery had not yet begun to develop. Small windows are also to be seen.

Towers and Steeples

Norman towers are wide and low. Later examples are richly ornamented on all four faces with arcading, which incorporates narrow, slit window and belfry openings. Round the top edge is an embattled parapet, set with gargoyle spouts and, at each corner, a decorative turret (44). Originally, most of these towers, which are set over the crossing and flanking the western façade or transepts of ecclesiastical buildings, had low pyramidal spires of wood. These have generally disappeared. The replacements at Southwell Minster are of this type of design. Many excellent examples of Norman towers exist all over the country. Among the finest are the transeptal towers at *Exeter Cathedral* (79), the central towers at *Tewkesbury Abbey Church, Norwich Cathedral* (45), *Winchester Cathedral* and *Southwell Minster* (46) and much of the western towers at Southwell, and also *Durham Cathedral* (34); *Canterbury Cathedral* has one early Norman tower on the south side.

Sculptural decoration is not common on Anglo-Norman ornamental work. Usually this is abstract or geometrical in form and applied to mouldings, capitals and columns. An exception to this can be seen in the one or two surviving tympana such as the Christ on the *Prior's doorway* at *Ely Cathedral* and the porch sculptures of the Apostles at *Malmesbury Abbey*. The Herefordshire school of sculpture is, therefore, of unusual interest in England, since it produced on a small scale sculptural carvings of vigour and imagination comparable to the richness and variety of French Burgundian work. *Kilpeck Church* is the chief example of this carving, especially on the south doorway (75, 76, 77, 78), while the font at *Eardisley Church* shows

the lion enmeshed in magic plaitwork like the German examples of this time (80). In a different part of the country, *Barfreston Church* in Kent is also notable for its doorway carving (81, 82).

Monastic Building

The Church was the most important factor in the life of Medieval man. The Christian religion, as evidenced in the Church, touched his life in all its aspects, all the time. The Church was the moving spirit behind the tremendous building drive which created the great cathedrals, and the largest contribution in this field was in the monasteries. This is, above all, a religious architecture, though the buildings are practical, both in their arrangement and design, so as to enable the monks to live and work efficiently and harmoniously to the greater glory of God. During the Middle Ages the monastic communities provided education, shelter and guidance and the monks were themselves chief among the learned and educated members of society.

Many Orders built their monasteries in Britain. The mother houses of most of these were on the Continent, primarily in France. The building pattern varied in architectural design and detail but, in general, the layout was similar, so that a monk from one Order could easily find his way about the monastery of another. This was the result of years of developing the best and most convenient way of laying out a large, complex group of buildings.

The important structures of a monastery were first of all built in wood in a temporary manner then, over the years, rebuilt in stone. The church was always transferred first into permanent materials and other buildings followed later. Often large sections of the monastery were left in timber, with thatch roofing, for many years, rendering them liable to periodic, devastating fires. Thus, although the eleventh and twelfth centuries were the most energetic years of building, most monasteries today are the remains of later, Gothic styles of workmanship, replacing Norman building destroyed by fires.

The church was generally on cruciform plan with a central tower over the crossing.* This is, in most

---

* The Cistercian Abbey Churches were, in accordance with the dictates of their Order, very plain and simple. Early examples were aisleless and had no tower over the crossing. Later Norman Cistercian building, like *Fountains*

75   *South doorway, c.1140*

76   *Doorway voussoirs*

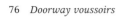

77   *Doorway detail*

78   *Doorway detail*

80 *Font, Eardisley Church*

81 *Doorway, Barfreston Church*

79 *North transeptal tower, Exeter Cathedral,
c.1112–40*

82 *Doorway voussoirs, Barfreston*

instances, the only building surviving intact from many monasteries because, after the Dissolution in the time of Henry VIII, the church was converted into use as a parish church or cathedral for the lay community of the neighbouring town or village. Only those in remote areas, such as the Cistercian monasteries of Yorkshire – *Fountains, Rievaulx, Jervaulx, Kirkstall* – and those in Scotland, such as *Melrose*, or in the west country – *Tintern* – were left to ruin. But for the repair work of the nineteenth and twentieth centuries these monuments would probably have disappeared by now. Among the abbey churches later converted to cathedral and parish use may be listed such famous buildings as *Canterbury, Winchester, Ely, Rochester* and *Norwich Cathedrals; Westminster* and *Sherborne Abbeys*.

The domestic buildings of the monastery were usually arranged round a quadrangle, one side of which was formed by the nave of the church, while its transept provided one right angle corner of the court. In the centre of this was generally a lawn – the *cloister garth*. On all four sides was a stone-flagged walk with an open, stone screen and lean-to roof covering it. This was called the *cloister* and has survived intact in many cathedrals and abbey churches. The cloister was often built on the south side of the church nave, to face the sun and to give protection from the north-east wind. Around it were then constructed the dormitory, refectory, chapter house, infirmary, almonry, library, calefactory and abbot's lodging. The dormitory was usually built next to the church transept. The monks could then enter the church undercover during the night, for services, by way of the night stairs. These still exist in a number of churches.

The Castle

Life was turbulent and insecure. Protection was equally important to the lord of the manor and his meanest servants. Security was provided by the grouping together of the community in a fortified centre. This varied in size according to the wealth and lands owned by the nobleman, but the manner of living was similar, whatever the size of his estate. If this was important, a large castle was built, if small, then a modest house, but in each case fortified defences were essential.

Before 1100 most castles and houses were built of wood, with thatch roofing, on the *motte-and-bailey* principle. The *motte* was a large natural or artificially made hill or mound (94). A deep ditch was dug round its base. Round this was the *bailey*, an area of land enclosed by a wooden stockade which, in turn, was encircled by an earth rampart and a further, outer ditch. On top of the motte was built the house or castle, enclosed by a wooden fence. In this lived the lord, his family and servants. Inside the bailey were erected wooden buildings for storehouses and granaries, barns, smithy, kitchens, soldiers' quarters, villagers' cottages and stables. When under attack, everyone retreated to the castle, which could withstand a long siege. The only access route was via fortified bridges over the ditches and these were kept full of water.

In the twelfth century the wooden structures in important centres were replaced by stone ones. The hill castles were built in the form of keeps or strongpoints. These were of two types; the rectangular ones and the shell keeps. Both were built in large numbers but the latter were less strong and fewer have survived. The rectangular *keep* was an almost impregnable structure, large and heavy, too heavy to be constructed on an artificial mound, so it had to be sited on a natural eminence. The keep, up to 150 feet in height, was usually square in plan, with immensely thick walls, up to 20 feet thick at base, and with flat buttresses at the corners and in the centre of the four faces. These buttresses die away into the splayed base. Passages, bedrooms and garderobes were built into the thicknesses of these massive walls. Turrets were constructed at each corner of the keep, containing spiral stone staircases, with a central newel which extended through all the four or five floors. These staircases were designed so that one man could defend them against many ascending attackers as his right, sword hand would be free while those of the attackers were restricted by the newel.

The main entrance to the keep was on the first

Abbey Church, has a central tower and the nave has aisles. It is noteworthy, though, that the nave arcade (as is frequent in Cistercian Norman building) has pointed arches and a plain wall where the triforium stage is usually built. Cistercian churches almost invariably have square eastern terminations. The large numbers of churches built in this way by the Order was undoubtedly an influential factor in developing this characteristic in other ecclesiastical building in England.

83 *The White Tower, keep of the Tower of London, 1078–90*

87 *St John's Chapel, Tower of London, c.1080*

84 *The keep, Goodrich Castle, c.1160*

85 *Plan, Dover Castle keep*

86 *Plan, third floor of keep, Tower of London*

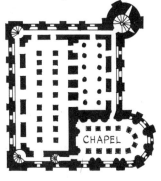

88   *Plan of second floor
       of keep*

89   *Second floor of keep
       as it is now*

90   *Impression of how 89 would have looked in the 12th century*

91 Guildford Castle
keep, 12th century

92 Malling Castle
keep, c.1070

93 The Jew's House, Lincoln, c.1160

94 Keep and mound, Cardiff Castle,
11th century

95 Great Hall, Oakham Castle,
c.1190

96 Carved moulding

97 Doorway, Jew's House

floor; below this was an undercroft, used for storage, and this had a stone vaulted roof and solid, unpierced walls. The first floor was occupied by the garrison and servants and had only slit windows. The chief room in the castle was the great hall, which generally occupied the whole of the second floor. In larger keeps, this would be about 45 feet square and 30 feet high: a span too wide for timber baulks, so a stone dividing wall was built across the centre, pierced with open arches so that the room could still be used as one chamber. Ceiling timbers then spanned each half with great baulks slotted into holes in the stonework and smaller rafters crossing them at right-angles. This gave a flat roof to one storey and floor to the one above. *Fireplaces* were set into the outer walls with flues extending upwards at an angle to the exterior face. *Sanitation* was provided by the garderobes built into the wall thicknesses. These had stone seats and a vent gave exit to the wall outside or a cesspool below.

The *great hall* was where everyone ate, lived and slept. Its stone walls were hung with woven fabrics, its floor strewn with rushes. There was no privacy. Small *bedchambers* were built into the thicknesses of the walls for the lord and his family but, even for these, the only access was through the arched doorways in the hall. There were no doors. The windows in the outer walls corresponded with these openings, thus giving light to the hall. There was no glass, only wooden shutters which could shut out the cold air but only at the expense of cutting out the light as well. Bedsteads, in these bedchambers, were wood platforms piled with bedding – sheets, pillows, quilts and fur rugs. Curtains hung round to keep out the draughts were suspended from poles projecting from the walls on either side of the bed.

In the hall, there was little *furniture*. Oak chests, often only hollowed-out tree trunks, banded with iron, were used for storage of linen and silver as well as being seats. These are the oldest type of furniture. Trestle tables* and benches were set up at meal times. The lord and his guest sat at one end of the hall, their table often raised on a daïs. A wooden gallery for the musicians was usually built opposite to this, for music was an essential accompaniment to meals. At night guests and servants slept on the floor near the fireplaces. Artificial lighting was provided by sputtering torches, dipped in fat, and stuck in iron holders, lamps holding burning oil, home-made rushlights and, very costly, candles. The latter were set in iron candleholders, suspended from the ceiling beams. The hall was the centre of castle life for everyone from all social classes (89, 90, 95).

A number of the larger rectangular Norman keeps survive in Britain, as well as a few shell ones. The best preserved is the *White Tower*, keep of the Tower of London, built by William I c.1080 (83, 86). The *chapel* was an important chamber in larger keeps and *St John's Chapel* here is a magnificent example of its type (87). Other keeps of considerable interest include *Rochester Castle* (88, 89, 90), *Castle Hedingham*, Essex and *Dover* (85), *Porchester*, *Goodrich* (84) and *Colchester Castles*.

Little exists of domestic Norman building apart from the great castles. Most *houses* were of wood. The stone ones were fortified like the castles and the hall was the living and bedroom for everyone. It usually had a central hearth, logs piled against iron firedogs on a brick hearth. The smoke escaped through a louvre in the roof timbers. The *Jew's House* in Lincoln, c.1160, is a rare survivor, in much altered form (93, 97).

---

* The expression 'bed and board' had a literal meaning in Medieval times, signifying the two essentials for a traveller or guest.

CHAPTER THREE

The Gothic Style:
Ecclesiastical Architecture
1150–1550

The Gothic form of architecture emerged from the Romanesque in a gradual transition. For some decades in the twelfth century, both in Britain and in France (where the new form was established first), characteristics of both types of building were present, side by side, in one structure. In Britain we refer to such work as 'transitional', where pointed arches are supported on heavy, round columns, as in Cistercian monastic churches, and ribbed stone vaults are carried on a Romanesque arcade, as at Durham, the flying buttresses being hidden from view behind the triforium arcade.

Gothic architecture is readily definable and recognised wherever it is to be found. Its characteristics are well known – the pointed arch, the stone ribbed vault and flying buttress. But none of these was previously unknown. The style is a fusion of these factors into a new concept, which evolved and grew to maturity over four whole centuries, adapting to the aesthetic ideals and needs of the people. In Britain, where the style developed early and was abandoned late, there are four distinct interpretations of the form. Each developed from the preceding one and made steady progress away from the solidity of the Romanesque towards the seeming ethereal fragility of the soaring spires and panelled stone and glass of the later fifteenth century.

Although Gothic architecture evolved gradually from the Romanesque, and it is not easy to ascribe a specific date to its emergence, it represents a completely new artistic and structural expression which was a reflection of the different spirit of the time in which it was born. The term 'Gothic' was coined in a later age as one of disapprobation and contempt. It was the sixteenth-century Italian artist and historian, Giorgio Vasari, who used the term and, in doing so, was merely expressing the thinking of his time, equating Medieval architecture with barbarism. To a post-Renaissance scholar, the Middle Ages had advanced only a small way beyond the sixth-century Goths; it was the Renaissance which brought greatness to architecture. The Romanesque style of building had been based upon the (Roman) classical tradition and, though no doubt regarded as a crude version by sixteenth-century Italy, it followed the basic, stable pattern.

The term 'Middle Ages' was similarly coined, in this case by a seventeenth-century German scholar, who likened it to an intermediate era between the collapse of the Roman Empire and the re-birth of classicism in the Renaissance ideals of the fifteenth century. To him also it represented a period of barbarism and decline.

Today, seen from a more distant perspective, we appreciate that Gothic architecture (for the term is now synonymous with Medieval building), was a great art form in its own right and one which had its birth and dominance in northern Europe not, as in the case of classicism, south of the Alps.

The all-pervasive influence during the Middle Ages was Christianity. The Church and its buildings were not only concerned with Sunday worship but formed an integral part of people's daily life. Everyone put tremendous effort into building the House of God, whether this was a great cathedral, a monastic structure or a simple, village church. This was the most important building of the community; it was in a durable material, and upon it was lavished the wealth, time and skill of the whole district. In return, the buildings and the men of God gave to the population security in times of danger, advice, interest and assistance in their daily lives, and they represented the chief source of education and knowledge for the community. To an illiterate population the decoration of the church gave a visible reality to their beliefs. On exterior and interior could be seen a pictorial record of the Bible story and teaching. The great sculptured portals of France, the wall and ceiling mosaics of Italy, the wall paintings and carved capitals and jambs of Britain, together with the beautiful coloured glass everywhere, all depict the theme so that the word of God could be passed from generation to generation and the intensity of faith kept alive.

It is difficult to pinpoint the exact time and place of the birth of a new movement. It is accepted that the earliest buildings completed in the Gothic style were in the Île de France, that small area in the vicinity of Paris, and that the classic pattern of the northern Gothic cathedral was established there in such examples as Notre Dame in Paris and at Amiens, Reims and Laon. It cannot be argued so categorically that this was the sole source of the style in the twelfth century or that it would not soon have developed in a similar manner elsewhere if the Île de France had not then produced it.

Great movements in all subjects – arts, sciences, medicine – begin and establish themselves because the climate is ready to receive them. The need is there and so is the ability to create the new development. The pointed arch was evolved because it became the key to constructing buildings which were then desirable. It was of vital importance that the House of God and its accompanying monastic buildings should be saved from the ravages of fire which were taking such toll of the timber-roofed Romanesque churches. Only a handful of these, for example Durham Cathedral, had stone vaults. It was the need for the development of the stone vault, to cover all ranges of height and width, which led to the evolution of Gothic architecture with its characteristic pointed arch. For the round Norman arch presents great problems in vaulting a church.

The pointed arch was not new. It had long been used in the Middle East and, in Europe, had been employed in areas subject to Moorish influence, such as Spain and Sicily. It was being developed in such regions in the twelfth century, but northern France was, at this time, a more stable area, less troubled economically and by warfare. The stability of the Île de France region led to the creation of schools of artists and craftsmen, who travelled widely to execute commissions in different parts of Europe. Soon southern England too was creating its own schools of craftsmen.

The pointed arch is particularly suited to the stone vaulting of a church because of its flexibility of design. The problems arising from the use of the semi-circular arch stem from the fact that the nave and choir and their aisles often have different widths and heights. Vaulting is constructed in bays and the semi-circular arch lends itself to the square bay. The form of the bay is decided by the positioning of the supporting piers or columns. In Romanesque cathedrals the bay was transversed at roof level by two ribs which curved in diagonal line from nave pier to nave pier. As the diagonal ribs were longer than the four ribs connecting the four sides or faces of the bay, it was impossible for all those ribs to be semi-circular in section unless the vaults were dome-shaped and so making an uneven ridge line; alternatively, the side arches had to be stilted, not semi-circular or, more commonly, two bays were handled as one, making a longer, rectangular, not square, bay. Further problems arose because aisles were narrower and lower than nave and choir and this was even more difficult to reconcile with the rigid concept of the semi-circular arch. In consequence, few Romanesque buildings were stone vaulted. The pointed arch was more flexible for this purpose since it can be varied in proportion of width to height in order to accommodate differing spans and levels. The French aptly term this arch the *arc brisé*, the broken arch, which gives a clear picture of its function.

As the Gothic period advanced, churches became larger and higher: window and doorway openings increased in size so that the buildings were flooded with light. This was in contrast to the lower Romanesque churches, lit only by small, narrow windows. The knowledge of structure in masonry was extending quickly and, with this advance in technique, came the means to erect buildings which were mere shells of stone ribs and pillars. The area of solid wall shrank and the design became correspondingly more complex. Each individual member of the structure became more attenuated. Heavy columns and piers gave place to slender, lofty piers, encircled with clustered shafts, terminating in small moulded or foliated capitals. Towers became slenderer, many completed with equally elegant spires. The exterior of the church became a forest of vertical stone pinnacles stretching upwards into the vaults of heaven; the interior a mystic chiaroscuro in stone, gently illuminated by shafts of sunlight, gloriously coloured by their transition through the window glass.

This miracle of immense stone cathedrals pierced by great openings and carved into tracery was made structurally possible by the engineering development of the stone vault and its associated abutment. Both of these stem from the original adoption of the pointed arch. The basis of structures employing this form of arch, supported on piers, led, over many years, to great variety in vault design. In Britain especially many types of vault were designed, each evolving a stage further in delicacy and complexity, from the simple, ribbed, quadripartite vault, with four ribs and four compartments, of the thirteenth century, to the lierne and star designs of the fourteenth and the fan vault of the final phase. The Gothic buttress is the complement to the vault. As the latter progresses and becomes higher, wider and more complex, so must the abutment. The structure of a Gothic church, its arches, piers and vault, exerts an outward and downward pressure on the walls. In order to avoid thickening the whole wall area, as Romanesque builders had done, the Gothic mason provided reinforcement in the form of a stone buttress at the point on the wall where it was most needed. This point is just below the springing line of the vault. The abutment system moved, step by step, with that of vault design, from simple, wall buttresses to the forest of flying buttress pinnacles seen in fifteenth-century structures. Like all component parts of Gothic architecture, such abutment acquired an aesthetic and spiritual quality – an art form in itself – which stemmed from the original structural need.

The Cathedrals and Abbeys

The affinity between the fellow craftsmen grew closer during the Gothic period. The rapport among masons, glaziers, painters and metalworkers was complete and satisfying. No craftsman was of more vital importance than the sculptor. Carvers and modellers enjoyed freedom of expression and were presented with an immense architectural canvas on which to experiment and design. The Gothic cathedral façade was a supreme vehicle for such expression. The pattern was established in France in the early thirteenth century of a twin-towered façade with triple portico at base, spreading across the width of the elevation. The whole of this façade was decorated with symbolic sculpture, but it was the portals which were the focus of the design. On French cathedrals jamb and trumeau figures, tympanum scenes, archivolt groups, gargoyles and cresting, all played a part in relating the Bible story from Old and New Testaments. French sculptors were supreme and travelled widely in Europe, showing other nations how to enrich their cathedral façades.

In Britain there was much less sculpture. Carved decoration was largely restricted to capitals (foliated and with animals and birds), tympana and wall designs. The triple portal with its richly sculptured ornament is rare in Britain. At *Peterborough Cathedral*, for example, the west front has an immense triple portico, but the decoration is architectural, not sculptural. The great exception to this, in the thirteenth century, is *Wells Cathedral*, where in the niches of the west façade were over 300 statues and reliefs, of which about half remain (103). The general theme, representing the Fall and Redemption of Man, depicts this story from the Creation to the Enthronement of Christ. The sculptures still retain traces of the colour with which they were once vividly painted. There are a number of later Gothic porches and portals which are richly sculptured as, for instance, the south porch at Gloucester Cathedral (141).

The prototype of the Gothic cathedral is the Île de France pattern. Buildings like *Amiens Cathedral* represent, in Gothic form, a similar contribution to the architecture of their time as that made by the Parthenon to Hellenic Greece. One of the very first experiments in the Gothic style, using the pointed arch and vaulting system supported on slender columns, was the *Abbey Church of St Denis*, built between 1135 and 1145. Now in a Paris suburb, most of the church has been restored or rebuilt, but part of the original choir exists and the reconstructed west front still shows the early mixture of round and pointed arch heads.

In Britain it was not perceived for some time, in the twelfth century, that buildings such as St Denis and the *Cathedral of Paris*, begun in 1163, were creations of an entirely new structure and style in architecture. The British were using the pointed arch, but did not appreciate its structural possibilities. The Cistercians, for instance, preferred the pointed arch for its austere, aesthetic qualities and it can be seen in the nave arcades of such monastic churches as Fountains and Rievaulx Abbeys, set in a plain arcade upon massive Norman piers and columns. The pointed arch was also employed decoratively as a wall arcade.

The prototype equivalent in England to St Denis in France is the choir of *Canterbury Cathedral*. This, the first Gothic structure in Britain, was largely the work of a Frenchman, *William of Sens*. So called after the town of his birth, William had watched the *Cathedral of Sens* being built in Gothic design and when, in 1174, Canterbury Cathedral choir was severely damaged by fire and William was given the task of rebuilding, he constructed it in Gothic style. A revolutionary English structure for the time, William directed operations from 1175 until, five years later, he was crippled by a fall from some scaffolding and returned to France. The choir was completed by another William, known for distinctive reasons as the Englishman. The choir of Canterbury Cathedral is not only the first Gothic structure to be built in Britain, but it is entirely Gothic and owes nothing to Romanesque ancestry. Elegant columns and clustered piers, with foliated capitals, support the moulded, pointed-arched arcade. Above is the arcaded triforium and lancet clerestory windows, while the vaulting shafts, which carry the quadripartite vault, stand on the same nave capitals. The eastern termination of the choir is also of French design in that it is apsidal, with ambulatory behind the altar, while the circular eastern chapel is appropriately named Becket's crown (110).

It was *Thomas Rickman*, writer and ecclesiastical archaeologist, who, in 1817, classified the English styles of Gothic architecture under names which are still popularly used. He considered that Gothic architecture extended from 1066 until the middle of the sixteenth century and divided this long period into sections which replaced the previous divisions into centuries. His terms were Norman, Early English, Decorated and Perpendicular.

Since the time of Rickman many writers, both Victorian and twentieth-century, have given different classification, names and dates to Gothic architecture, but Rickman's description and nomenclature has

survived. By later study we have learnt that it is inaccurate to be too dogmatic in applying specific dates to these subdivisions because one style merged gradually into another. Each period evolved into the next during a transitional time, when some features of one style were used together with the newer one on a single structure. In different parts of Britain the onward progress was attained at different speeds and in different stages. One style of Gothic architecture did not prevail over the whole country at a given date. Gothic architecture is now thought to extend from the simple Lancet (or, as Rickman called it Early English) style, beginning with Canterbury Cathedral choir of 1175–84, until Elizabethan Mannerism took over from the Tudor version of Gothic about 1550.

The differing phases of the Gothic style are mirrored most richly and informatively in our cathedrals. These were the most important structures of their age and were therefore in the van of new ideas and art forms. Many of these cathedrals were built originally as the abbey churches of the monastery. After the Dissolution by Henry VIII, a large number of them survived as parish churches and later became cathedral churches. Some of the most famous of our cathedrals come into this category. None of the cathedrals in Britain is now in one style of Gothic architecture, though nearly all of them were built between 1066 and 1550. Most of them have some Norman workmanship, and some have vestiges of Saxon remains. The majority were added to and altered during the whole Medieval period, each retaining a larger proportion of one style in particular.

The *Lancet* or Early English type of Gothic architecture, often referred to as the springtime of the style, was fully developed between 1200 and 1275. It was a form of simplicity and grace. In Britain, where there was less sculptural decoration than on the Continent at this time, there is a certain austerity of form, but also a singular beauty of proportion, a freshness and unclutteredness. The characteristics of the architecture of these years are the plain, quadripartite ribbed vault, slender towers, with spires, replacing the square, squat Norman ones and thinner walls, now buttressed more strongly to offset a larger window area and the thrust of the stone vault. The windows are typically lancets, that is, narrow, pointed-arched lights, arranged singly or in groups of two, three or five. The vertical emphasis of the Gothic style is making itself felt (in contrast to the horizontal theme of both classical and Romanesque design). This can be seen in the higher vaults supported on taller nave and choir piers, which are slender and grouped in clustered shafts with delicate capitals and tall bases (100, 128).

As Durham Cathedral is the supreme example of Romanesque ecclesiastical architecture in Britain, so *Salisbury Cathedral* represents the early Gothic theme. It is the only British Gothic cathedral to be built largely in a single operation and, therefore, single style. On a new site, it was begun in 1220 and, by 1258, was mainly complete; the tower and spire are a little later. Salisbury is also unusual in that it is now surrounded by a green-swarded cathedral close and can be viewed from all angles. Medieval cathedrals were built where they were needed, that is, in the heart of the city, and were closely hemmed in by timber houses. In many instances these Medieval houses have been replaced by later brick and stone buildings, often now of a commercial nature. At Salisbury, the whole exterior of the cathedral can be seen and enjoyed at leisure; the views of it, across the meadows, have barely changed since Constable painted it from there (99, 142).

Apart from its situation and unity of style, Salisbury is also remarkable for its high standard of design and craftsmanship. It is built on the traditional English cruciform plan, with a central tower and spire* over the crossing. The plan itself is typically English in its widely projecting transepts and square east end, completed by a square Lady Chapel. This is in contrast to the French pattern where, by this time, the apsidal end had developed its chevet of radiating chapels, as at Le Mans Cathedral. This is only one instance of the fundamental divergence of the English Gothic from the Continental version. The narrow strip of sea between Britain and the Continent of Europe was sufficient to impede the easy passage of ideas. Britain was isolated from Continental thought and was evolving national characteristics in architecture, as in other fields. The lofty tower and spire over the crossing was another example of this national independence, seen most clearly at Salisbury. French nave and choir vaults were much higher than the English. They built their twin towers at the west end

and sometimes one over the crossing, but these are only seldom capped by spires. Partly this is because the money ran out at this stage and they were not built (or only one was completed, as at Strasbourg), but, more importantly, it was found that the high, wide vault would not take the strain of a tall crossing tower and spire.

At Salisbury, the nave and choir vault, much lower, is finely designed and there is the customary three-storeyed division of the wall structure into nave and triforium arcade with clerestory above. The windows of the latter are now much larger than their Norman predecessors though, sadly, at Salisbury little of the original coloured window glass survives. This gives to the interior here the cold, clinical appearance so at variance with its original thirteenth-century look. Colour was an integral part of Gothic architecture and the difference that this makes can be judged by the warmth given by the superb glass at Chartres Cathedral in France or León in Spain, both contemporary with Salisbury.

A quantity of early Gothic work in lancet style survives in other English *cathedrals*. The west façades of *Peterborough* and *Wells* have already been referred to (103); beautiful workmanship can also be seen in the nave at *Wells* (100). *Ripon Minster* has a thirteenth-century façade, with grouped lancet windows across the whole width of the gable and flanking towers (98, 143). At *Lincoln* the Norman cathedral on the summit of Lincoln Hill was largely rebuilt between 1185 and 1280, after a collapse following upon an earth tremor. The façade is unusual in that an immense stone screen was built, incorporating the earlier Norman front. Inside, the nave, transepts and choir are much of one style with ribbed vaults, moulded, pointed arches and foliated capitals arising from Purbeck marble shafts (144, 145). It is a homogeneous, impressive interior. At *Lichfield*, the cathedral nave, transepts and façade are largely in early Gothic style. The west front screen is enriched across the lower part by sculptured statues in niches. In reddish stone, this is a richly decorated example for English design.

One of the largest contributions to Medieval architecture was made by the *monastic orders*. Norman workmanship here has been discussed (page 29). During the whole Gothic period, until the Dissolution of Monasteries in the sixteenth century, building work proceeded in the founding of new monasteries and the rebuilding and enlarging of older

---

* This is the tallest in the country, 404 feet high.

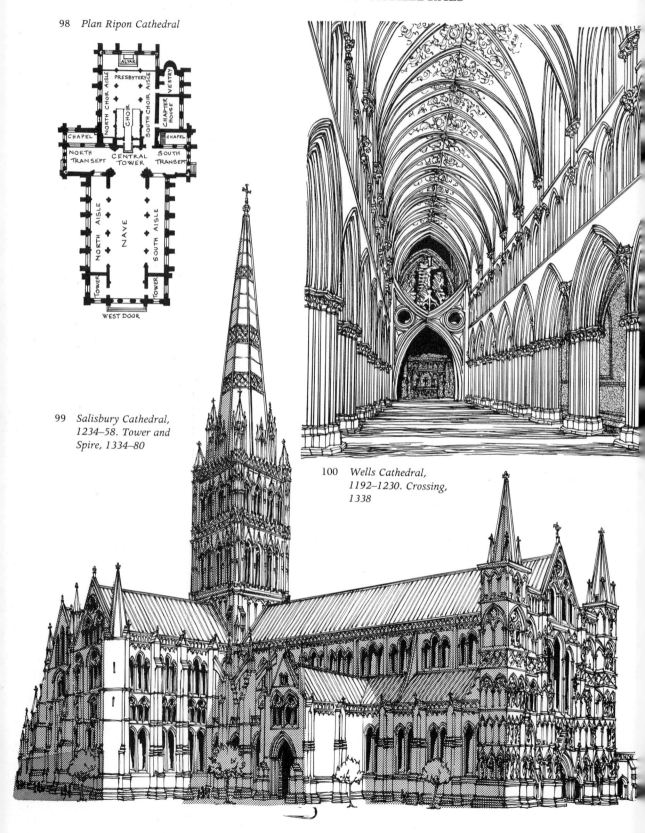

98   *Plan Ripon Cathedral*

99   *Salisbury Cathedral,
1234–58. Tower and
Spire, 1334–80*

100   *Wells Cathedral,
1192–1230. Crossing,
1338*

ones. Between 1000 and 1300 AD, 500 abbeys and priories were founded or re-established in Britain, under the jurisdiction of different orders; the chief of these were the Benedictine, Cistercian, Cluniac, Carthusian and Premonstratensian.

The Cistercian monasteries were probably the greatest loss as a result of the Dissolution because, by the nature of the order, they were set in remote sites and their churches could not, by reason of this remoteness, be used subsequently as cathedral or parish churches, as were those of so many other orders which had been built nearer to towns and villages. This circumstance has had the advantage, however, that the churches and coventual buildings, though in ruin, have not been partly rebuilt in later styles, as have their Continental counterparts, which are now frequently Baroque designs on a Gothic structure. During the sixteenth, seventeenth and eighteenth centuries such British monasteries fell into ruin, the stone being taken for local building and time and weather completing the decay. Since the mid-nineteenth century this process has been halted and repair work has saved the total loss of such superb structures as *Glastonbury Abbey*, Somerset, *Tintern Abbey*, Monmouthshire and *Fountains* and *Rievaulx*, Yorkshire in England and *Jedburgh* (167), *Dryburgh* and *Melrose Abbeys* (166) in Scotland.

Typical of Cistercian Abbeys was *Fountains*. The Norman workmanship here has been mentioned (page 29). In the thirteenth century the choir was extended and the transept known as the 'Chapel of the Nine Altars' was built. The remains of these give us some impression of the high quality of Early English workmanship in such abbeys. The fifteenth-century tower still dominates the Skell valley and many conventual buildings remain in part, such as the undercroft with its early ribbed vaulted roof (120).

Among the abbey churches still in use is *Hexham* in Northumberland, formerly an Augustinian Priory. The interior of the transepts, in particular, have retained their Early English characteristics in ground arcade, triforium and clerestory, and the façades are lit by six beautiful lancets. This church, earlier mentioned for its crypt (page 6), has also retained its midnight stair, a rare example and probably the finest in Britain. The Canons used to descend this stairway every night on the stroke of midnight for Matins. It is still used by the Abbey Choir.

The most famous of the abbey churches remaining

to us is *Westminster* which, because of its importance, shows the imprint of every architectural style from Saxon to nineteenth century. A greater part of the abbey church was rebuilt under the direction of Henry III between 1245 and 1269, leaving us a heritage of pure early Gothic workmanship. Remaining of this work are much of the eastern arm, transepts and part of the nave. These show a strong French influence, since Henry had succeeded in attracting some of the finest artists from France, as well as from England, to work in his service. Westminster Abbey is the most French of our churches; this can be seen clearly in the great height of the vaults, the tall clerestory and lofty nave arcade with its high pointed arches. Especially French also is the north transept façade with its deep porches and rose window. The sculpture here also is French in its life and quality of movement.

The second stage in the steady development of Gothic architecture was called, by Rickman, 'Decorated'. It is thought of as the high summer of the style, a further stage in its evolution from the spring-like simplicity of lancet work. This second phase became established in the last quarter of the thirteenth century and lasted for about 100 years, until 1375. When we compare a fourteenth-century cathedral to a thirteenth-century one we note immediately three distinct changes: firstly, the larger window openings containing rich coloured glass and complex stone tracery in the head; secondly, the contracting area of plain wall, increasingly broken by more extensive abutment, and, thirdly, a greater variety and complexity in the design of stone vaulting.

These differences are the visible effects rather than the cause. Throughout the development of Gothic architecture, the aim of designers and builders was to create exteriors and interiors which would be more exciting, more three-dimensional, and to use their expanding knowledge to the full in order to obtain more varied effects. It was due to increased experience that builders were able safely to construct higher, wider and more delicate stone vaults. They supported these by an extended system of flying buttresses, which transferred the thrust to the aisle roofs and then down the wall buttress to the ground. At the same time, and for the same reasons, they were able to risk weakening the wall by larger window openings.

Designers experimented with new spatial forms

101   *Exeter Cathedral choir, 1328–90*

103   *Wells Cathedral, west front, c.1230–60*

102   *Exeter Cathedral, west front, 1328–75*

and lighting. The work at *Ely Cathedral* (1323–30) is an example of this. Here, the old central tower over the crossing was replaced by the unique octagon and lantern. From the interior, in particular, the effect is three-dimensional and remarkable; the tall crossing piers, with their alternating arch openings and windows, support the ribbed vault, which extends upwards on all eight sides to the panelled lantern. From directly underneath the view is of a star pattern in the centre of a radiating web of ribs, which culminates in the glowing coloured glass and curvilinear tracery of the windows (114).

Window tracery, though designed in many variations, is in one of two distinct types of pattern. The earlier style is termed *Geometric* and here the tracery of the window head incorporates motifs based upon the circle and its component parts. Later fourteenth-century work is termed *Curvilinear*, or flamboyant, and in this the window head tracery follows designs of complicated pattern in which the ogee curve is predominant.

Vaults also, though many variations are to be seen, fall into two distinct types. The earlier designs stem from the quadripartite vault. Here, intervening ribs are inserted, extending all the way from pier to ridge rib, between the structural quadripartite ribs. A fine example of this type of vault is to be seen in *Exeter Cathedral* (101). The other type of vault evolved from the proliferation of *lierne* ribs. These are ribs which do not extend from pier to ridge-piece, but run in any direction, crossing from one rib to another and making star patterns. Such ribs are not constructional but merely decorative. The term derives from the French *lier* – to bind or to tie. Beautiful examples of this type of vault are displayed in *York Minster* (104) and the choir of *Gloucester Cathedral*.

In the fourteenth century building work of all kinds was halted by the terrible visitation of plague, usually called the Black Death, of 1348–9. This was one of the recurring waves of infection which swept Britain and Europe in the Middle Ages. On this occasion it was so severe that about a third of the population died. Because of this, it is common to find in cathedrals and churches work of the two styles of Decorated architecture, side by side. A window head of pre-1348, often in Geometric design, will flank one of post-1349 – generally 1360 or later – in Curvilinear style. Characteristic of this later period also is the greater richness apparent in coloured glass and sculptural decoration.

Exeter Cathedral is the finest example of Decorated Gothic workmanship in Britain. The west façade is outstanding, with a richly sculptured entrance screen and, above it, the superb, traceried west window (137). The façade is flanked by the unusual (in Britain) two, earlier, transeptal towers (102). This is a construction more favoured in German work as in St Stephen's Cathedral in Vienna. Inside, Exeter Cathedral is also mainly in fourteenth-century style. Both nave and choir are covered uniformly by an impressive ribbed vault with carved bosses set at each intersection along the ridge rib. There are large traceried clerestory windows which beautifully illuminate the interior. The dignified piers, their clustered shafts of Purbeck marble, support deeply moulded arches on the small, moulded capitals. The triforium stage is shallow and delicately arcaded (101).

The west front of *York Minster* is also a first-class specimen of work of this period. Here, the wealth of decoration is in the form of tracery and window glass rather than sculpture, as exampled by the curvilinear centrepiece. This façade (apart from its fifteenth-century towers) dates from 1291–1345; the nave stems from the same time. Its impressively high vault is of lierne structure in distinction to that at Exeter, which has radiating ribs (104, 105, 106, 135).

Apart from these two superb specimens, extensive workmanship of the years 1275–1375 can be seen in a number of cathedrals. There is the spectacular Angel Choir (138) as well as the central tower (131) and Judgement Portal (140) at *Lincoln*, the curvilinear east window at *Carlisle* (134), much of *Bristol*, the choir of *Gloucester*, the façade of *Winchester* and *Salisbury's* chapter house and central tower and spire (99). At *Wells*, the central tower, the choir high vault (115) and the chapter house date from these years, as do *Hereford's* and *Worcester's* central towers and *St Albans'* Lady Chapel and nave.

The *final phase of Gothic architecture* in Britain evolved in the second half of the fourteenth century and lasted a long time, changing slowly but not greatly. It was not abandoned until after the middle of the sixteenth century, when Renaissance and Mannerist designs at last filtered through from the Continent. In this extended period, from about 1360 until 1550, the development of British architecture was in marked contrast to that of Continental countries. In previous stages of the Gothic evolution,

104   *Interior, 1291–1341*

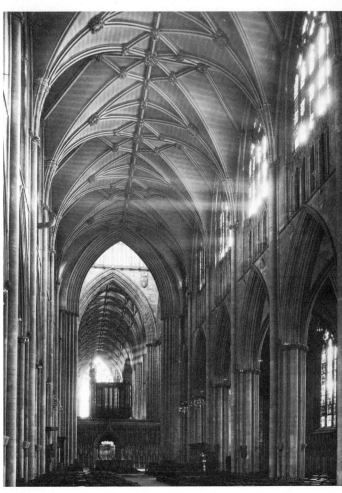

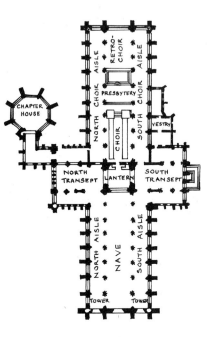

105   *Plan*

106   *The Minster from the south-east*

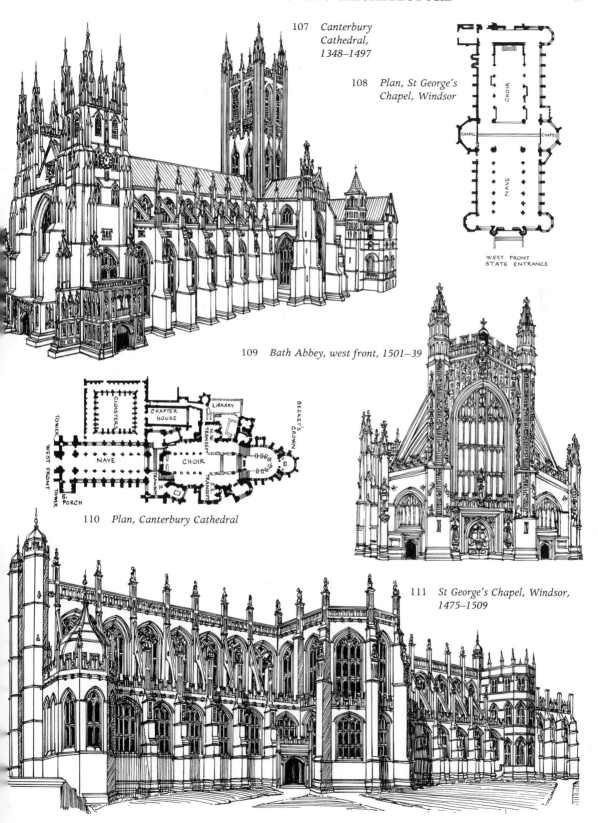

107 *Canterbury Cathedral, 1348–1497*

108 *Plan, St George's Chapel, Windsor*

109 *Bath Abbey, west front, 1501–39*

110 *Plan, Canterbury Cathedral*

111 *St George's Chapel, Windsor, 1475–1509*

through Romanesque, Lancet and Decorated periods, there had been a parallel development in the different countries in Europe, although national characteristics had produced variations on the theme. From about 1360 onwards a separation occurred. Italy, the mainspring of the Renaissance, had no late Gothic development at all; France was also early affected by Renaissance ideas; Germany, Spain and Portugal continued Gothic building, but it was a further expression of fourteenth-century conceptions, becoming richer and richer in decoration which, in Spain, was carried to extremes in plateresque all-over ornament.

The English development is characterised by a restrained richness. *Perpendicular Gothic architecture* is, as its name indicates, an exercise in vertical lines, but there is also a new emphasis on the horizontal. The three principal features of this style are panelled decoration all over the building on windows, walls and vault alike; an increasing area of window space, and consequently of flying buttresses, in proportion to wall area and roofing by means of the fan vault. The best Perpendicular examples are not only cathedrals, as hitherto, but parish churches, chapels and houses. Of edifices which display in their entirety the new style, the royal and college chapels are supreme. These are mainly of later fifteenth-century construction. *Eton College Chapel* was begun in 1441, *King's College Chapel, Cambridge* (112) was built 1446–1515 and *St George's Chapel, Windsor* (108, 111, 136) in 1475–1509. These chapels all display the main features of Perpendicular Gothic: the plan is roughly rectangular and very simple (108); there are many windows along the side elevations and a gigantic multi-light one at each end. All have Perpendicular tracery and are separated by finialled flying buttresses, leaving only a small area of plain wall. Inside is a delicate but rich and complicated fan-vaulted roof and walls which are similarly stone panelled all over. These chapels are masterpieces of their time, supremely English, and represent the climax of craftsmanship and design in the Gothic style, achieving a harmonious balance of mass and space.

There is a quantity of work of this period in the *cathedrals*, but it is chiefly in the replacement of towers and vaults as well as in the enlargement of clerestory windows to increase the natural illumination. This, of course, is interesting as it affects the individual part replaced, but does not alter the concept or appearance of the building as a whole. As clerestory windows were enlarged, this had to be at the expense of the triforium, so, in cathedrals where such alterations to the fenestration were carried out, the windows became separated from the nave arcade by merely a band of carved decoration in sunk or pierced panelling. In the new Perpendicular windows not only was vertical panelled tracery substituted for the curves of Decorated work but the equilateral arch head was replaced by the flatter four-centred arch. This is especially typical of the years 1480–1540.

The principal examples of such work in cathedrals are at Canterbury, Winchester and Gloucester. The rebuilding of the nave at *Canterbury* was begun in 1378 and continued into the fifteenth century. Typically the clerestory was enlarged at the expense of the triforium and a lierne vault was constructed to roof the nave. The crowning glory of Canterbury is the central tower (its Angel Steeple), which rises over the crossing to 235 feet. This was completed in 1503 (107, 110). At *Winchester* the rebuilt nave is the finest work, completed in 1450. At *Gloucester* a very early instance of fan vaulting is to be seen in the reconstructed choir and cloisters, carried out in the mid-fourteenth century. It is on the exterior that the superb central tower, *c.*1450–7, shows the best Perpendicular work; it is dignified, solid, yet delicate and graceful. The great west window dates from 1437, the Lady Chapel 1499 and the richly sculptured porch *c.*1420 (141).

These years also saw the final phase in the building of and additions to the monastic structures. *Sherborne Abbey Church*, Dorset presents a complete example in Perpendicular style. The church was largely rebuilt in the fifteenth century in two stages between 1415 and 1504, introducing the large Perpendicular windows and fine flying buttresses and ornament (113). In 1539 the monastery was suppressed and the Abbey purchased by the parishioners of Sherborne from Sir John Horsey for £230, since which time it has served as the parish church. Other fifteenth-century monastic work includes the tower of *Fountains Abbey*, Yorkshire and that of *Christchurch Priory*, Hampshire, as well as the impressive flint and stone gateway to *St Osyth's Priory*, Essex.

In the *sixteenth century*, whilst France was imbibing Renaissance ideas from Italy and Francis I was gathering around him Italian artists and craftsmen, his contemporary English monarch, Henry VIII, tried to do the same. Britain was less attractive to Italians than

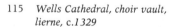

113   *Sherborne Abbey, nave fan vault,*
      c.1475–1500

112   *King's College Chapel, Cambridge,*
      1446–1515 (organ omitted)

115   *Wells Cathedral, choir vault,*
      lierne, c.1329

114   *Ely Cathedral, lantern and octagon, 1330*

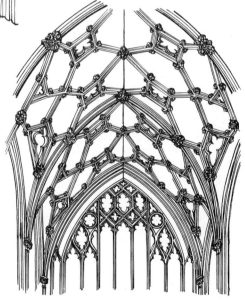

France, being further away and having a more intemperate climate, so Henry's success was limited. He succeeded in persuading *Pietro Torrigiano*, the Florentine sculptor, to come to design the tomb of the king's father, the late Henry VII, with consort, in the new chapel at *Westminster Abbey*. The tomb was completed in 1518, but it remains an isolated example for, after Henry VIII's break with Rome, England's tenuous links with Renaissance Italy were broken and the English retreated into isolationism. The English Renaissance was postponed and its form was also altered. Torrigiano's monument is Italian classical, the Elizabethan Renaissance forms are Mannerist, from Flanders and Germany.

The *Henry VII Chapel* at Westminster Abbey, which houses the tomb, is a masterpiece of panelled, fan-vaulted Perpendicular Gothic art (116, 121) and the outstanding instance in Britain of sixteenth-century chapel building.* Its counterpart in *abbey churches* is at *Bath*. Here, the essence of Perpendicular Gothic design is carried to its ultimate conclusion. The exterior is finely decorated with central tower, flying buttresses and ornamented turrets (109, 129). The whole interior is delicately fan vaulted; the perpendicular lines of the slender piers soar majestically towards these vaults (118).

Scotland

It was King David I who, in the twelfth century, laid the foundations of a stable Church and State in Scotland, which lasted through the Middle Ages. Monasticism, closely linked to the mother houses in France as well as to England, flourished and by the end of the thirteenth century a large number of foundations had been established, especially in the south and east of the country. The thirteenth century was Scotland's 'golden age' of *monastic building* and many abbeys survive in partial ruin from this time. The work was of fine quality which compared favourably with French and English contemporary building, but losses have been greater. Partly these were due to war, especially in the border monasteries which lay in the path of English armies, partly the buildings suffered from actual destruction in times of religious controversy, while neglect and use as convenient

---

* A later, excellent specimen was built at Trinity College, Cambridge.

stone quarries completed the sad tale. The abbey churches survive in part, walls, window openings, columns and fragments of vault, but little trace remains of their once rich carving, painting, ceramic and metalwork.

Although building continued during the fourteenth and fifteenth centuries in Scotland, the outstanding workmanship dates from the years 1150–1300. Earlier examples show fine quality transitional work with round and pointed arches used together in one building, such as the nave of the Augustinian *Abbey Church* at *Holyrood* in Edinburgh, which was founded by David I, also the remains of the Cistercian *Abbey Church* at *Dundrennan* in Galloway. Excellent specimens of the thirteenth-century Lancet style survive in quantity at *Jedburgh Abbey* in Roxburghshire (167) (though the fine west façade is of Transitional late twelfth-century design) and at *Dryburgh Abbey* in Berwickshire. One of the most famous Scottish *Abbey Churches* is *Melrose* in Roxburghshire (166). Founded by David I in 1136, this Cistercian Abbey endured a turbulent history. It was colonised from Rievaulx in Yorkshire and became one of the largest foundations in Britain, but suffered repeatedly in border wars. The finest remains date from the years 1380–1520 and these are fairly extensive.

Apart from the ruined abbeys, Scotland's Medieval heritage is not extensive. Again, the greatest building activity was in the thirteenth century, from which time some quality work survives at the *cathedrals* of Glasgow, Elgin and Dunblane (169). *Glasgow Cathedral* was begun, on the site of more than one earlier church, towards the middle of the thirteenth century. Despite the loss of its western towers in the nineteenth century, and other alterations, it remains the largest and best preserved Gothic building in Scotland. It is an interesting construction in that, although the thirteenth-century building was begun virtually from scratch, the original layout of the previous church was retained. This, like the early Christian basilicas in Rome, has an eastern arm on two levels, the upper one raised high to accommodate a large and splendid crypt or lower church, which houses the shrine of St Mungo, the patron saint (170). This type of structure is made possible by the uneven site on which the cathedral is built. Like most Gothic structures in Scotland, the east end is square, but the Scottish equivalent of the French chevet is obtained at Glasgow by extending the choir aisles round the eastern end behind the altar to form an ambulatory, then beyond this extend four chapels. The ambulatory plan is repeated in the lower church where, with the building of double staircases, the pilgrims visiting the shrine are able to circumnavigate it.

Glasgow Cathedral, despite the quality of its building, displays a solemn, dour appearance which characterises so much Scottish architecture. This is not so at *Elgin Cathedral*, possibly because it is partly ruined and, being roofless, permits the sunshine to enter. Also it did not survive as a cathedral, so did not suffer the heavy hands of nineteenth-century improvers. Elgin was a magnificent cathedral church (168), which suffered damage more than once by fire and attack and was repaired on each occasion. The structure was finally abandoned at the Reformation and, after the collapse of the central tower in 1711, suffered still further damage. The remains, which are still most impressive, date mainly from the thirteenth century.

After 1300 Scottish ecclesiastical architecture diverged from both Continental and English design and developed along its own individual lines, which were mainly backward glancing. There was a reversion to the Romanesque semi-circular arch and the solid column or clustered pier as well as a reintroduction of earlier styles of ornament. Ecclesiastical work on these lines is interesting for its individual and local character but, unlike the twelfth- and thirteenth-century work, is not of outstanding merit. The final Gothic phase in Scotland in the later fifteenth and early sixteenth centuries is marked by a florid, heavy decorative style with window tracery of curvilinear or flamboyant design and towers surmounted by crocketed and crowned open steeples.

Parish Churches in Britain

After the tremendous surge of building activity under the Normans, few new churches were constructed in the thirteenth century and much of this work was altered in the later Middle Ages. These early Medieval churches were built either on cruciform or simple rectangular plans. The Norman crossing tower was now often replaced by a single or twin western tower design. As in the case of Norman cathedral and abbey churches, the eastern apse was generally re-designed to give a square termination and the chancel lengthened to provide more space for chapels; grouped

lancet windows lit this eastern façade. Aisles were added to some naves and when these were roofed it became necessary to raise the nave wall to greater height and insert clerestory windows to illuminate the interior. Interesting thirteenth-century churches include *West Walton*, Norfolk, *St Denys, Sleaford*, Lincolnshire, *Uffington Church*, Berkshire and *Stoke Golding Church*, Leicestershire (124).

Through the fourteenth century, the process of enlarging parish churches, adding aisles and inserting larger windows continued. Most of these retained their timber roofs, covered by tiles, lead, wood shingles or thatch. Among the fine specimens of the time are *St Wulfram*, Grantham, *Heckington*, Lincolnshire, *Patrington*, Yorkshire (126), and *Holy Trinity*, Hull.

There exists a superb heritage in Britain of churches built or enlarged between 1375 and 1550 in Perpendicular Gothic style. Some are magnificent, almost of cathedral dimensions, a reflection of the new wealth and increased population in certain areas. Due largely to the cloth and wool trades, England was in the fifteenth century becoming a prosperous country and these churches are a symbol of this wealth. Most of them were crowned, usually at the west end, by tall towers and, in many instances, spires. A famous example is *St Botolph's Church*, at *Boston* in Lincolnshire, popularly called the 'Boston Stump' because its top storey was added so much later than the rest of the church and for many years the tower had a decapitated appearance (125). This tower is 295 feet high, while the spire of *Louth*, Lincolnshire, another fine parish church of the period, is 300 feet. Other beautiful spired churches are *St Mary Redcliffe*, Bristol and *Thaxted Church*, Essex (123), while *St Michael's*, Coventry, later the Cathedral, which was damaged in the Second World War and is now preserved as a memorial tower adjacent to the new cathedral, was one of the best of such churches (130).

There are also many towered churches (without spires) which exhibit the characteristics of the period, such as panelled walls, large, Perpendicular traceried windows, flying buttresses and lengthened chancels. In these years aisles were being added to existing nave, choir and transepts to give greater space, so the plan of such fifteenth-century churches is often rectangular, the cross being obscured by the increased width of the arms. These buildings are also noteworthy for their ornamentally carved, panelled

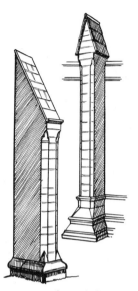

117   *Early English buttresses*

116   *Henry VII Chapel, Westminster Abbey, flying buttresses*

118   *Bath Abbey, 1501–39*

119   *St Mary's Church, Woolpit. Double hammerbeam roof, 1439–51*

120 *Fountains Abbey,*
undercroft, 12th century

122 *13th-century angle*
and flying buttress

121 *Henry VII Chapel, fan vault, 1503–19*

123 *Thaxted Church,
15th century*

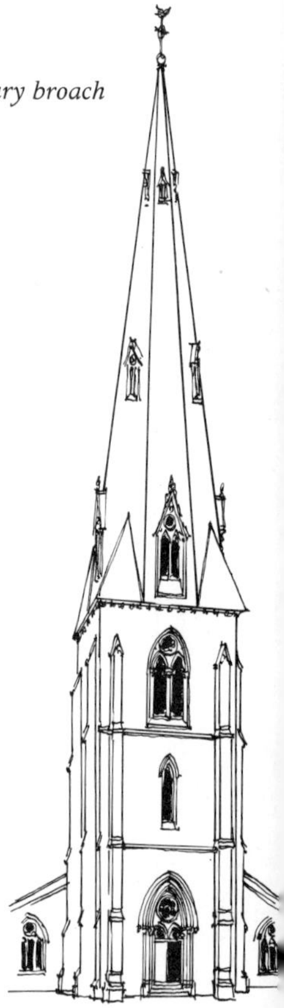

124 *13th-century broach
spire*

125 *St Botolph's Church,
Boston, 1425–1520*

126 *St Patrick's Church,
Patrington, 14th century*

127 *Church of St John the
Baptist, Cirencester,
c.1400–1500*

128 *Ely Cathedral, west tower, 1150–75*

129 *Bath Abbey, central tower, 1501–39*

130 *Old Coventry Cathedral steeple, 1373–1433*

131 *Lincoln Cathedral, central tower, 1240–1311*

132 *York Minster, south-west tower, 1432–74*

parapets and enriched porches while, in a number of instances, timber roofing was being replaced by stone vaults. Examples include *Lavenham Church*, Suffolk, *St Mary's, Taunton, St John's, Glastonbury, St John's, Cirencester* (127) and *St Peter's, Tiverton*.

Building materials for churches varied greatly from region to region. Stone and granite were used where available. Flint was extensively employed and the flints were now more carefully selected and graded for size. Flush-work was introduced into East Anglian building; stone blocks were cut into thin slabs for economy of the imported material and the flints were arranged round them to produce patterns between the panels, but they were set flush with the stone not raised above it. Elaborate designs were produced, especially on porches and towers as at the Suffolk churches like Eye and Woolpit. The method spread to other counties – Essex, Sussex, Wiltshire and Berkshire. Brick was used less than other materials, as yet, but it is particularly to be seen in the counties just mentioned because of lack of stone. For the same reason, timber was widely used in these regions.

Windows

During the Middle Ages window designs followed one predominant trend: they became larger. In the same period, the pattern of stonework which held the glass in place underwent many changes, with a general tendency to become more intricate and decorative. It is probably easier to date or identify the style of a Medieval building by its window openings than by any other single factor. This is because the designs changed frequently; the development was steady and in one coherent movement. Thus each period is known for its characteristic pattern and construction. This is not to say that window design all over the country at any given date would be identical; it was, naturally, in the large and important buildings that new trends first appeared.

Romanesque windows had been small, partly for defensive reasons and partly so as not to weaken the wall structurally. With the introduction of the pointed arch and the development of skill in masonry and engineering, window openings in the *thirteenth century* became larger and more numerous. The lancet style takes its name from the window pattern of the time, when *lancets*, or narrow windows, whether singly or in groups, were evolved. Such lights had

narrow, pointed heads (133). Many famous grouped lancet windows survive; even better known than those from *Hereford Cathedral* (1220) are the beautiful north transept windows in *York Minster*, the 'Five Sisters', each of which is 50 feet high and 5 feet wide, (*c.*1250). These also represent the finest example of grisaille glass which was developed at this time. This glass gives more light to the interior than the earlier, richer glass work. In grisaille, the plain glass is painted delicately with a floral pattern in grey monochrome. At York, red and blue glass strips are incorporated.

It was in the lancet period that *tracery* – the carved stone mouldings containing the glass – was developed. The idea evolved from the grouping of two or more lights under one arch. This created a space above – the spandrel – which presented an awkward feature of design. This was overcome by carving it into quatrefoil or trefoil shapes. These were pierced and thus the earliest form of tracery, called *plate tracery*, was created. In this type of work the stonework is comparatively solid and the circular, cusped holes are pierced in it. A superb example is at *Lincoln Cathedral, c.*1220 (139).

By the Decorated Gothic period, *bar tracery*, where the stonework is much narrower and in 'bars' while the volume of glass is larger, became fully developed. The window area was now much larger and wider and was encompassed by an equilateral arch. The window was divided vertically by stone mullions, giving five, seven or even nine lights; the head was then decoratively designed. Such designs varied according to date, at first generally *geometric*, based on circles, trefoils and quatrefoils and later *curvilinear*, wherein the bar tracery divided the window head into flowing, flame-like shapes based on the ogee form. Many magnificent windows of both types survive, for instance, at *Lincoln* and *Carlisle Cathedrals* (134), *Melrose Abbey* in Scotland (166), *Exeter Cathedral* (137), *York Minster* and the chapter house at *Salisbury Cathedral*. The tracery of this time is especially suited to the circular, rose window, usually to be seen on the transept façades. One of the most beautiful of these is the 'Bishop's Eye' at *Lincoln Cathedral, c.*1325 (138).

The last phase of tracery design comes with Perpendicular Gothic work. Here the window is divided vertically by mullions and horizontally by transoms into panels (135). The proportions of the window are wider and the head may be enclosed by an obtuse arch or by the flatter, four-centred arch.

134 *Carlisle Cathedral, east window, c.1350*

133 *Oundle Church, lancet window, c.1200*

136 *St George's Chapel, Windsor, west window, c.1485–1509*

135 *York Minster, east window, 15th century*

137 *Exeter Cathedral, west front, 1328–75*

138 *Lincoln Cathedral, rose window, c.1325*

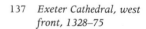

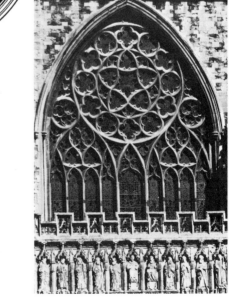

139 *Lincoln Cathedral, plate tracery, c.1220*

The number of lights is greatly increased as, for example, at *St George's Chapel, Windsor,* where there are 75 lights in the main window area (136). A particularly fine early instance is at *Westminster Hall* in London. The same theme continued into Tudor Gothic buildings, where sometimes the arch was replaced, or was enclosed by, a rectangular panelled window area as at *Bath Abbey.*

Doorways and Porches

The shape and proportion of *doorways* developed in a similar way to window design and this makes the doorway another suitable feature on which to base recognition of a period or style. Slowly, openings became larger and the arch mouldings surmounting them passed from narrow pointed form to equilateral, to obtuse, to four-centred. The more important early Gothic doorways were encompassed by an equilateral arch head. This was deeply recessed and richly moulded, with splayed sides. The shafts are often of contrasting material – Purbeck grey marble being the most common – to the capitals and bases. Some doorways have foiled heads, carved in cinquefoil or trefoil forms. Beautiful examples include *Ripon Minster* (143), *Salisbury* and *Chichester Cathedrals* (142) and *Bolton Priory Church.*

Fourteenth-century doorways are generally wider, covered by an obtuse arch, and can be very rich in carved ornament and quantity of mouldings (140). More actual *doors* survive from this time, made of wood with elaborate scrolled ironwork furniture. *Perpendicular Gothic* doorways often possess a square hood-mould over the obtuse or four-centred arch. The space between the square and the arch – the spandrel – is filled with carved stone decoration in the form of tracery, heraldic motifs or foliage. Doors are panelled rather than decorated with iron. In the late fifteenth century and Tudor times such panelling was usually in carved linenfold pattern. *Tudor* doorways have four-centred arches and decorative arch mouldings but plain jambs, often without shafts. Outstanding examples of fifteenth- and sixteenth-century doorways include *King's College Chapel, Cambridge, Magdalen College Chapel, Oxford* and *Chester Cathedral.*

Most large churches and cathedrals have *porches.* On the west front these are frequently in triple form, with the central doorway larger than its flanking companions. From the fourteenth century onwards, such buildings also have porches on the south and north transept façades – in single form but canopied and projecting. The most elaborate porches date from the fifteenth century, when they were often added to an existing building. They are profusely ornamented with sculpture, panelling, tracery and pinnacles. In architectural detail these porches display the characteristics of their time as at *Salisbury* (142) and *Lincoln Cathedrals* (Early English), *Gloucester* (141), *Canterbury* and *Chester Cathedrals, Lavenham Church* and *St John the Baptist, Cirencester* (127) (Perpendicular Gothic).

Towers and Spires

The tall graceful spire set upon an elegant tower is typical of the Early English period. This architectural feature is essentially Gothic in inspiration and spans the whole Medieval era. A spire has no constructional purpose; indeed, it presents structural and aesthetic problems, without performing any function save looking beautiful and acting as a landmark. To Gothic builders, the need to create churches of elegance and grandeur dedicated to the glory of God and to draw attention to these creations was so profound that hundreds of churches, from small parishes to great cathedral dioceses, boasted their spires and many still do. In general, the taller spires are to be found in the flatter, eastern part of the country, where they are visible for miles, and the smaller, sturdier towers in the hills and mountains of the west.

The chief structural problem of a spire is to accommodate its octagonal form on top of a four-sided tower. The union, especially in early examples, is often awkward; both visually and structurally unsound. Some steeples collapsed soon after building. Two common designs were the parapet and the broach. In the former instance, the parapet acted as support and also covered the junction; in the second type, squinches across the corners of the tower supported the other four sides of the spire and from these squinches pyramidal buttresses, called *broaches,* were built up the spire sides (124). An impressive early example of this is *St Denys' Church* at *Sleaford* in Lincolnshire, where the spire of 1220 is set upon the earlier tower of 1180.

In the fourteenth and fifteenth centuries the parapet design was more common. By this time the

140 *Lincoln Cathedral, the Judgement Portal*

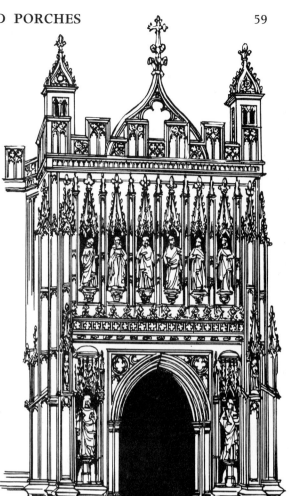

142 *Salisbury Cathedral, west front portal, c.1258–66*

141 *Gloucester Cathedral, south porch, c.1420*

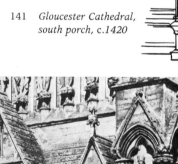

143
Ripon Minster, west front, c.1220–50

tower was extended upwards at the four corners by crocketed stone pinnacles which then buttressed the spire by means of arches in flying buttress manner. *St Patrick's Church* at *Patrington*, Yorkshire (126) and *St Wulfram, Grantham* are fourteenth-century churches of this type and *St James' Church, Louth*, Lincolnshire is an excellent fifteenth-century specimen.

England is rich in Gothic towers. Especially fine are the early example at *Ely Cathedral* (128), the fourteenth-century ones at *Salisbury* (99), *Lincoln* (131), *Hereford* and *Wells Cathedral* and the Perpendicular Gothic designs at *Gloucester Canterbury* and *York Cathedrals* (132), *St Botolph's Church, Boston* (125), *St Mary's, Taunton* and *St John's, Glastonbury.*

Abutment, Vaults and Roofs

These parts of a Medieval structure are essential and interdependent factors in the whole scheme. Abutment is the necessary corollary to secure the stability of a building which is roofed by a stone vault; with timber roofing its presence is less vital. The Gothic architectural form evolved because it became essential, due to fire hazard, to roof large churches with stone instead of timber. Such vaults required the flexibility inherent in the pointed arch (see page 38); the resulting vaults became ribbed structures, rising higher and covering wider spans, and these in turn demanded more extensive, carefully engineered abutment.

The *barrel vault* had been used by the Romans and, throughout Europe, in Romanesque architecture. Satisfactory for narrow spans, such as church aisles, the barrel vault, exerting the immense thrust which it does along its whole length, was dangerously unsuitable for the wider spans of the high vaults of nave or choir. It was for these spans (of which Durham Cathedral is an early example, see page 19) that the *ribbed vault* was evolved. In general, the ribbed vault and the pointed arch were developed at roughly the same period and both are typical of Gothic, rather than Norman, architecture. In a ribbed vault a framework of stone ribs is supported during construction upon wood centering until the spaces in between are filled with stone panels. The whole construction is lighter than the barrel vault and more flexible in design.

The resulting outwards and downwards thrust was counteracted by the development of the *abutment system*, which provided strengthening of the wall from the exterior face at the point where the greatest thrust was to be expected. Trial and error established this to be just below the springing line of the vault on the interior wall face. The *flying buttress* system was evolved to produce this strengthening at the specific point. It serves a dual purpose: the counter thrust at a given place on the exterior wall surface conveys the vault pressure away from the building and down to the ground and also, by means of a heavy pinnacle above, helps to offset the vault thrust (116).

The earliest Gothic vaults were ribbed designs in quadripartite pattern, with four ribs crossing diagonally to make four compartments. In the fourteenth century more complex vaults were designed by introducing intermediate ribs called *tiercerons*, which extended from the vault springing to the ridge rib, as at *Exeter Cathedral* (100, 101, 120). This style is typical of the earlier fourteenth century, but soon the *lierne vault* was developed. In this the lierne ribs extended in any direction from the structural ribs and might join any other rib. Lierne vaults became very complex as, for example, at *Wells* (115), *York* (104), *Gloucester* or *Winchester* Cathedrals; some patterns are described as star or stellar vaults.

In Perpendicular Gothic work the *fan vault* – a peculiarly British design – was evolved from the desire for a vault which would accommodate ribs of different curves as they sprang from the capital. The radiating ribs of the fan are of equal length and the bounding line is in the shape of a semi-circle. The whole group of ribs is made into an inverted concave cone. The radiating ribs are crossed by lierne ribs so that the complete surface is then, like the windows and walls of the time, panelled and cusped. Superb fan vaults can still be seen at *Henry VII's Chapel* in *Westminster Abbey* (121), *St George's Chapel, Windsor, King's College Chapel, Cambridge* (112) and *Bath Abbey* (118). Typical of Perpendicular architecture is the smallest possible wall area with large windows and extensive vaults; the necessary complement to this is an equally extensive flying buttress structure. A pinnacled flying buttress is set between each window. The characteristic forest of decorative, vertical stone pinnacles blending with the lines of delicate stone arches all diminishing in perspective along the façades is characteristic of such fan-vaulted structures (109, 111, 116).

Of equal interest in Medieval architecture is the contemporary evolution of the open *timber roof*, which provided the alternative method of interior roofing. Because of the fire risk, stone vaults were built where possible, but timber roofs had to suffice in areas where stone was not readily available and for smaller buildings. Most cathedral and abbey churches had timber roofs originally, but these were gradually replaced by vaults during the Middle Ages. The cathedrals which today retain timber roofing have had this renewed more than once and original timber ceilings are rare in such structures. The existing wooden covering is generally of boarded, ceiled type, often painted in coloured designs. *Ely Cathedral* nave is still roofed in this manner.

The decorative, open timber roofs are to be seen in parish churches and in secular architecture. Like the vaults, early designs in the thirteenth century were simple, generally of collar-beam type. These evolved slowly via tie-beam structures to the beautiful, complex hammerbeam roofs of the fifteenth century, of which many superb examples survive. The structure and development of such roofs is discussed more fully in Chapter 4 on Secular Medieval Architecture (page 76). By the fifteenth century the craft of the woodworker had reached a high standard. In East Anglia and neighbouring areas, where stone was not easily available, the hammerbeam roof was especially used for parish churches, where it was more suitable than the tie beam since it provided less visual interruption for the congregation. Among the many surviving examples of high standard are *South Creake Church* and *Trunch Church* in Norfolk, *Woolpit* (119) and *Needham Market* in Suffolk and *March Church* in Cambridgeshire. Tie-beam roofs can be seen at *Addlethorpe* in Lincolnshire and *Walpole St Peter* in Norfolk, while the arch-braced design is used at *Sparham* in Norfolk.

Capitals, Piers and Bases

These, together with ornament and mouldings, provide a useful means of identifying a period in Gothic architecture. The designs changed quickly and characteristically. The general trend between 1150 and 1550 was towards slenderer piers, grouped capitals and tall bases. Early English piers are clustered with shafts which are often of contrasting colour and material; dark Purbeck marble was frequently used for this on important buildings, as at *Salisbury Cathedral*. Capitals are moulded or foliated and are surmounted by a round abacus, unlike the Norman square one. Foliated capitals are carved stiffly, the stalks standing out from the capital bell and, later, falling in heavy clusters. These designs are vibrant and three-dimensional; beautiful examples can be seen in the chapter house and transept of *Southwell Minster* (147, 150) and in *Lincoln Cathedral* (144, 145).

Fourteenth-century piers are often designed on a diamond-shaped plan, with a central shaft surrounded by slenderer ones (148). Foliated capitals are carved naturalistically, with shorter stalks and a profusion of flowers and fruit; *York Minster* nave has some typical examples (149). Perpendicular piers are slenderer still and the vaulting shafts continue up the front and back of the piers in an unbroken line from ground to vault. Many capitals are plainly moulded; in larger buildings they are carved, but these are more stylised than before, lower in relief and include figures and foliage. Bases are tall and slender and often bell-shaped with an octagonal plinth below. *Winchester Cathedral* nave illustrates these (146).

Mouldings and Ornament

Early English mouldings are deeply cut, giving strong shadows. Ornament is restrained and only a few mouldings are decoratively carved, unlike the richly ornamented Romanesque arch mouldings. The most typical Early English ornamental motif is the *dogtooth*. This is a small pyramidal form cut into four leaves and repeated (165). Diaper decoration (161) and crockets (157) are also typical (164). The most usual motif of the Decorated period is the *ball flower*. This is a globular form with the flower partly opened to show a small sphere (160). Crockets are richly carved in vine motifs (155). Mouldings most often used are the ogee and the roll. Perpendicular design is distinguished by its panelled forms on all surfaces. Finials and crockets are finely carved, using animal and human figure designs as well as plants (151, 152, 153, 154, 157, 158). Mouldings are shallow and broad.

144 *Lincoln Cathedral, choir capital, from 1256*

145 *Lincoln Cathedral, choir capital, mid-13th century*

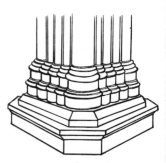

146 *Perpendicular pier base*

147 *Southwell Minster, transept capital, 13th century*

148 *Exeter Cathedral, pier base, c.1335*

149 *York Minster, nave capital, c.1310–20*

150 *Southwell Minster, chapter house, 13th century*

151 St Peter's Church, Tiverton, 15th century

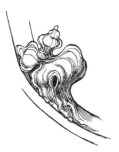

152 Lavenham Church, Suffolk, crocket, 15th century

153 Stone ornament, 15th century

156 Exeter Cathedral, west front screen, c.1350

154 Thaxted Church, gargoyle, 15th century

155 Winchester Cathedral, crocket, 14th century

158 Thaxted Church, gargoyle, 15th century

157 Early English crocket

159 Stone finial, 15th century

160 Ball-flower ornament, 14th century

163 Dripstone, 14th century

162 Exeter Cathedral, west front screen

164 13th-century ornament

161 Diaper decoration, 14th century

165 Dog-tooth ornament, 13th century

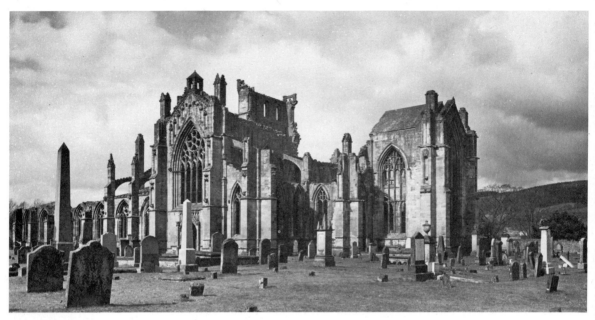

166   *Melrose Abbey, Roxburghshire, c.1390–1540*

167   *Jedburgh Abbey, Roxburghshire, 12th and 13th centuries*

168 *Elgin Cathedral, Morayshire, from 1224*

169 *Dunblane Cathedral, Perthshire, 13th century* 170 *Glasgow Cathedral crypt, 13th century*

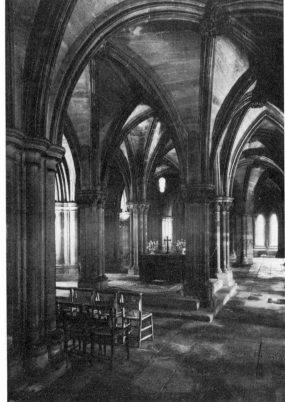

CHAPTER FOUR

The Gothic Style:
Secular Architecture
1150–1550

Not many secular buildings have survived intact from the early Middle Ages. The great majority were constructed of wood and plaster, wattle or thatch and were rebuilt over and over again during the centuries, when either they were destroyed by fire or replaced by a larger, more modern structure. The survivors are mainly stone castles or fortified large houses. The later Middle Ages, from about 1400 onwards, present a different picture. Increasingly, throughout the fifteenth century and under the early Tudors, reflecting the growing wealth of the country, elaborate buildings were designed in more permanent materials. We have inherited a range of these, constructed for a variety of purposes. There are inns, guildhalls, university and school buildings, town and country palaces and houses, castles, bridges and tithe barns.

Such secular work was built from a variety of materials, depending upon the availability in the region concerned. The chief are stone, brick, timber with plaster and/or brick and flint. Stylistically the buildings show the same characteristics at any given period as those described in Chapter 3 on Ecclesiastical Architecture. Elaborate decoration and carving as well as stone vaults and rich, timber roofs can be found in secular work just as in ecclesiastical, but, in the smaller, simpler structures such as the average town or country house, ornamentation was at a minimum, coloured glass uncommon and tracery limited.

The Medieval Town

London was the Medieval capital as it had been in Roman times. It was the only large city in the country but, even here there were gardens and orchards within the walls. A contemporary account, written about 1160,* describes the impressiveness of the Tower of London, its walls and bailey rising from deep foundations, the 'mortar being mixed with the blood of beasts', and of two other strong castles on the west side, linked by a continuous high great wall round the city, containing seven double gates and towers at intervals. The writer also refers to the river Thames as 'teeming with fish' and describes the expanding 'populous suburbs'.

Other towns in Britain were small by modern standards. There were only a few of any size; these included *York, Bristol, Norwich, Southampton* and *Lincoln.* An average town would only have 3000 to 4000 inhabitants who were thus able to enjoy the advantages of both town and country. Houses had gardens, orchards and paddocks, so town dwellers supplied their own food while their pigs and poultry wandered at will as in a rural area. The surrounding country was easy of access and citizens often owned cattle and held arable tenements outside the walls.

On the debit side the streets were narrow, poorly paved or cobbled and sloped towards the centre, where flowed the open drain. Horses, carts and people shared the same roadway. The streets were unlit, dirty and insanitary and all the prevailing smells from slaughter houses, tanneries and breweries may have been different from but were more powerful than the

---

* Preface to the biography of Thomas Becket, by William fitz Stephen.

diesel fumes we complain of today. Steep Hill in Lincoln gives a good impression of a Medieval street since it is reserved for pedestrians, being too narrow and precipitous for wheeled traffic (though, of course, it is not dirty or insanitary). The Jew's House here (93) has already been mentioned. It is suggested that the Jews were among the first to build stone houses in our towns in order to give themselves fireproof protection against their debtors.

The greatest hazard to Medieval towns was always the danger of fire. After the passing of the law of 1189, making it compulsory to build at least the lower party walls of stone, conflagrations were reduced and there was less danger of fire spreading. Defence was also a vital question for towns, which were all surrounded by city walls and, in larger instances, by a moat also. These walls were studded at intervals by watch towers and fortified gateways (171, 206). Sites for important towns were carefully chosen, partly for defensive purposes and partly for fresh water supplies and easy transport facilities. The latter were generally by river or sea. The town was also planned so that the streets, with their open sewers, drained off into a water course. *London* had been chosen by both Romans and Saxons as well as the Normans as a suitable capital site on the river Thames. *Edinburgh* was selected for its easily defensible natural site on a narrow ridge above the plain with precipitous rock sides as fortification. It also has convenient access to the Forth Estuary and so to direct sea routes. *Stirling* likewise is a natural acropolis.*

The layout of towns in different parts of the country varied according to geographical factors. Some were sited adjacent to a river, to a harbour, on a defensive rock or ridge, in the shadow of a protecting castle, abbey or cathedral. Town planning was also affected according to the foundation date of the settlement. Those which originated in Roman times, such as Colchester or Chester, were on a rectangular plan, built with city walls which had an entrance gate on each face. Those of Norman origin generally grew up more haphazardly round the great castle or cathedral as a focal centre. Medieval foundations of thirteenth- and fourteenth-century origin were often more

symmetrical, with wider main streets, intersecting at right angles. Many such towns exist on the Continent but few have survived unaltered in England. *Winchelsea* is one of these, planned as a seaport by Edward I, on a new site, as the sea had encroached on the old town; three of the town gates still exist. Another town founded by Edward is *Kingston-upon-Hull*, where a harbour was made at the point where the river Hull flows into the Humber estuary. The harbour was completed in 1299 and roads were built across the low-lying marshes to the present-day suburbs (then villages) of Hessle, Anlaby, Holderness and Cottingham. The *Church of the Holy Trinity* survives from the fourteenth-century Medieval city, as do also gatehouses and part of the town walls. Good examples of such gatehouses can also be seen at *Canterbury* (172) and *Rye*.

In the fifteenth century increased wealth flowing from the prosperity of the cloth and wool trades caused expansion of old towns and the founding of new ones. The *Cotswolds* and *Essex* were two such areas of expansion where some beautiful stone and timber houses of this time survive. Newer towns, such as *Wakefield* and *Halifax*, were flourishing while rising villages destined to become great cities were developing fast; Manchester and Birmingham were two of these.

The *market* was an important function in the life of all towns, large and small. The bigger population centres had a square laid out in the middle of the town, on which the chief streets converged. The church was usually set at one corner of the market place. In less pretentious towns the hub of life was the High Street, where were to be found the principal buildings – guildhalls, church, large houses. Halfway along such High Streets the road was widened for a short stretch and here was held the market. Several towns still possess such characteristic Medieval streets. *Edinburgh* is one example, with its Grassmarket and Lawnmarket; *Elgin* is another. *Market crosses* survive in a number of towns, generally today a bone of contention between traffic engineers and conservationists. Beautiful late Medieval stone examples include those at *Chichester* (176), *Salisbury* and *Winchester*.

* The Greek word meaning literally the city upon a hill. A defensive concept used by many earlier civilisations from the Ancient Greeks to the Medieval and Renaissance Apennine cities of Italy.

Castles

The years 1275–1350 were notable for the building of

172   Christ Church, Canterbury, gateway, 1517

171   York city walls and Minster

173   The Shambles, York

174   The Guildhall, Lavenham. Half-timber, c.1529

175   The George and Pilgrims Inn, Glastonbury, c.1475

176   Chichester market cross

many castles which are termed 'Edwardian', after Edward I, who was responsible for the erection of a number of them in order to consolidate his domination of Wales and Scotland. Earlier castles had consisted of a central keep surrounded by an enclosed area of land, which was defended by a fence, a moat and a gatehouse. Edwardian castles were concentric, that is, there is no reliance upon a central strongpoint or keep, but the castle consisted of rings of walls, one built inside the other, defended along their whole lengths by fortified towers. These mural towers were designed to provide covering fire against the attacker from every point of the compass. No part of the structure was then weaker than another and there were usually three defensive walls, each thinner than the Norman ones.

The concentric system was being used in England before Edward became King, but it was developed under Edward and his name is associated primarily with such Welsh and border examples as Caernarvon, Conway, Beaumaris and Harlech (179).

Such castles, which were new structures, needed no keep. The central space was an open courtyard where was constructed domestic accommodation comprising the separate buildings of the great hall, the chapel and those for living space. Between the inner and second ring of walls were built other necessary structures and in the outer bailey was room for garrison buildings, stables, cattle and villagers. Beyond the outer wall was a moat, defended by a strong gatehouse or barbican. Typical is Beaumaris Castle on the Island of Anglesey, where the moat is still water-filled and the mural towers are in good condition (177). Caerphilly, in South Wales, remains one of the finest of the concentric castles in Britain, though partially ruined. It has a rectangular inner ward of 70 by 53 yards, with a drum tower at each corner and a gatehouse in the centre of each end wall. The hall, 72 by 33 feet, is flanked by a chapel and private apartments. The second ward is 106 by 90 yards, its walls descend some 20 feet into the water; use has been made here of the lake, supplemented by a man-made moat. A third ward is defended by gatehouses, towers and portcullis and was connected to the second by bridges (184).

In a number of cases Norman castles were converted into concentric designs. Here, the central keep was retained for accommodation and as a final strongpoint and the curtain walls with their mural towers, gatehouses and moat were built around the exterior of the original castle. The Tower of London is one such example, where the White Tower, the original keep (83), is now surrounded by many other towers and walls. On the borders of England and Wales are Goodrich Castle, Herefordshire and Chepstow Castle, Monmouthshire. At Goodrich Castle (183), the original Norman keep (84) can be seen inside the later walling on the right side of the bailey. Fig. 178 shows a view of Chepstow Castle from the bridge over the river Wye. The strategic defensive character of the site can be judged; built as it is, the castle occupies a ridge whose cliffs drop sheer into the valley of the fast flowing river. The Norman keep, called the great tower, is marked 'A'. It has been added to later, as can be seen by the presence of Norman and Gothic fenestration. The great gatehouse (B), the main entrance to the castle, was built 1225–45 and the great tower (Marten's Tower) (C) in the years 1270–1300. In Scotland there was a similar development at Bothwell, Lanarkshire and Kildrummy, Aberdeenshire. Such castles had the best of both worlds, a spaciousness of living accommodation unknown to the Normans; yet, if the concentric system failed, the keep or donjon remained as a last line of retreat.

Fourteenth-century castles which were built as part of a town's defences, as opposed to the single unit out in the country, were designed in a rather different form. In North Wales there are two famous instances of this type: Caernarvon and Conway. These are roughly rectangular in plan and have strong mural towers set round one chief ring of walls. It is necessary for such castles to be built on commanding and, if possible, impregnable sites. Caernarvon, with polygonal towers, is almost encircled by the river estuary (182); Conway, with circular towers, rises steeply above the harbour's edge.

By 1375–80 the quadrangular plan began to supersede the Edwardian concentric arrangements. Bodiam Castle in Sussex is an excellent example of such castle building. It is approached over an oak bridge, which spans the moat, to the octagon. During the approach, the intruder would be under fire from the towers and would then have to pass the barbican, cross a ten-foot moat over which a drawbridge could be dropped as required, and storm the main gatehouse. This was fitted with three portcullises with their individual doors and chambers (181). Bodiam still presents the

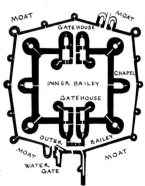

177 *View and plan, Beaumaris Castle, Anglesey, 1295–1325*

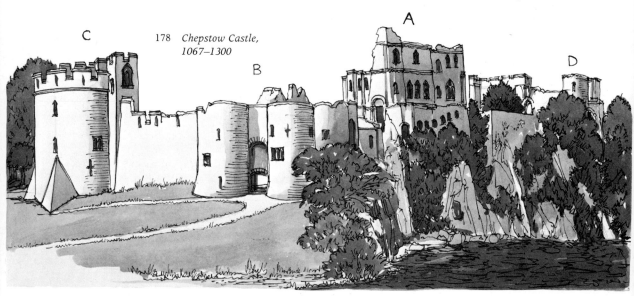

178 *Chepstow Castle, 1067–1300*

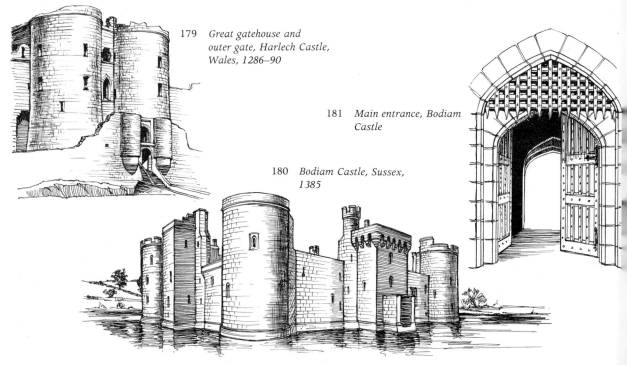

179 *Great gatehouse and outer gate, Harlech Castle, Wales, 1286–90*

181 *Main entrance, Bodiam Castle*

180 *Bodiam Castle, Sussex, 1385*

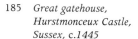

184　Caerphilly Castle,
Glamorganshire, late 13th
century

185　Great gatehouse,
Hurstmonceux Castle,
Sussex, c.1445

183　Goodrich Castle, Herefordshire,
12th century to 1300

182　Caernarvon Castle, North
Wales, 1283–c.1330

shell of a great castle. Its outer walls, lapped by the moat, are in good condition (180). The barbican is in ruins but the main gatehouse is well preserved. On entering one steps into a quadrangular court surrounded by buildings and towers and containing the great hall, chapel, private chambers and kitchen. Other fifteenth-century castles include *Hever, Warwick* and *Hurstmonceux*. This last named is a fine example of brickwork and the gatehouse is especially well preserved (185).

Gatehouses were important centres of defence in the fourteenth and fifteenth centuries. A large castle or city wall system might have several, but generally there was one principal gatehouse, larger and stronger than the others. Outside this, across the moat, was a further gatehouse, the barbican, which was the outer point of protection from attack and which could be abandoned if necessary. Gatehouses were generally built on rectangular plan and were flanked by drum towers which might contain staircases. At ground level the gatehouse was defended by one or more portcullises and beyond this was an oak double door. The portcullis was of iron or oak with iron spikes. It was suspended by ropes or chains, fitted into side grooves. The chains were worked by a winch or were fastened to a counterpoise. The portcullis chamber, from where it was worked, was above. Gatehouses were built to defend city, castle, university and domestic house entrances (172, 179, 185, 186, 192, 206, 213).

Palaces

Medieval palaces survive only fragmentarily; until 1500 precedence was given to ecclesiastical structures and important palaces have mainly been rebuilt or replaced. Of the *Royal Palace of Westminster*, the Medieval hall adjoins what is now the Houses of Parliament. *Westminster Hall* was built in 1097–9 and from about 1178 was used primarily as Courts of Justice and for royal and parliamentary occasions. It was also the scene of state political trials such as that of King Charles I in 1649. The hammerbeam roof was erected during the reconstruction of the hall under Richard II in the years 1394–1401. It is a tremendous span for an open timber roof – 69 feet; the structure, design and carving are all magnificent.* Of *Eltham Palace*, Kent, the great hall survives. This is also roofed by a fine hammerbeam structure, though the

span is only half that of Westminster Hall. It dates from 1475–80 and is lit by Perpendicular traceried windows on all sides (188).

It was in the sixteenth century, under Henry VIII, that the secular age of building began to replace the ecclesiastical. After the Dissolution, many monastic properties, their lands and wealth, accrued to the State and Henry apportioned them to his supporters. The most famous palace of these years is *Hampton Court*, of which the Tudor part still remains, adjacent to and blended skilfully with Sir Christopher Wren's seventeenth-century additions. Hampton Court was begun by Cardinal Wolsey in 1514. It was not intended as a palace but as a large house to be lived in by a wealthy churchman. It was consequently laid out on a domestic and university quadrangular-court plan. After Henry VIII took over Hampton Court from Wolsey in 1525, he made it into a palace, but the collegiate scheme was retained, only on a more splendid scale. The style is Tudor Gothic, and the structure largely in brick with stone facings and tracery.

Wolsey had made, as was the custom of the time, a rough design himself, then contracted artisans for each trade to carry out the work. It was entirely executed by Englishmen except for some of the ornamental work, which was done by Italians. An example of this is in the terracotta portrait roundels on the gateway (186) by Giovanni da Maiano and the plasterwork ceiling and frieze in the small linenfold-panelled room known as Wolsey's Closet. This suite of rooms survives much as Wolsey left it. Henry VIII's chief contribution to the palace is the great hall of 1531–6 with its notable hammerbeam roof (187) which was the creation of James Nedham. This roof is in direct line of descent from Westminster Hall, but at Hampton Court the decoration is richer, and the emphasis on the four-centred arch and on horizontals and verticals is stronger. Hampton Court is also famous for its beautiful river façade (186, 189, 190) and Tudor kitchens.

Of Henry's other palaces, *Whitehall* in London was largely destroyed in the seventeenth century. Here also Wolsey had begun work and Henry took it over. *St James's Palace* in London was built 1532–40 and the gatehouse survives. *Nonsuch*, in Surrey, was

---

* Some of the timbers have been replaced over the years owing to decay and insect attack on the originals, but the form is unaltered.

186 (above left) The great west gatehouse, Hampton Court Palace, 1515–25

187 (above) The great hall hammerbeam roof, Hampton Court Palace, 1531–6

188 Great Hall, Eltham Palace, 1475–80

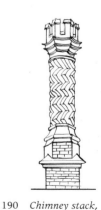

189 Finial, Hampton Court

190 Chimney stack, Hampton Court

Henry's most extravagant and fantastic palace. Our knowledge of it is confined to drawings and descriptions for it was demolished about 1670. Begun in 1537, it represented a stage in Henry's continuous rivalry with Francis I of France and the French influence on its design was strong. Both French and Italian craftsmen worked in it and there was extensive Renaissance detail on a fundamentally English structure.

In *Scotland*, although in the fifteenth and sixteenth centuries there was the same general tendency towards building palaces which were more domestic and less military than earlier in the Middle Ages, the pace of change was slower than further south. Paradoxically, in the royal palaces at *Falkland* and *Stirling* the façades display some of the earliest attempts in Britain to design on Renaissance lines, not just decoratively, but as a coherent structure. This lead was not taken up and it was the seventeenth century before the concept was generally followed. Only slowly was the Medieval castle, with its great hall, chapel, kitchens and living rooms incorporated into a single palace instead of remaining separate buildings inside the castle bailey. The great hall at *Linlithgow Palace* is an example of the newer trend, though that at *Stirling*, before its eighteenth-century mutilation a magnificent late Gothic hall comparable to Westminster, was built originally as a separate structure.

Houses

The majority of Medieval houses were built of wood and most have perished. This is particularly true of houses in *towns* where space was more limited and constant rebuilding on the same site took place over the years. Also the congestion of narrow streets and overhanging upper storeys caused the loss of many hundreds of Medieval timber houses by fire. Most of the Medieval houses which survive are of timber and plaster, or timber and brick structures in the country, or houses of brick, stone or flint. As it was the wealthier citizens who could afford to build in more permanent materials, extant Medieval houses are mostly of manor house design or are smaller fortified houses.

In the early Middle Ages the main concern of the larger house owner or builder was protection against the marauder and so houses were fortified. They were defended by outer walls, a moat – which was spanned by a drawbridge – and protected by a portcullis and one or more gatehouses. The walls were battlemented with a parapet behind and were also machicolated. Such houses, built before 1400, were planned round an open courtyard, generally in two or three storeys. The windows were small for defensive reasons, and on the lower floor were often only slits. This semi-basement floor, the undercroft, was used for storage of food and household necessities which would be needed in times of siege, while the living area was above, reached through a front door or porch via a flight of stone steps. This door generally led into the hall, the most important room in the house.

The *hall* was two storeys high and had an open timber roof; the wood, brick or stone floor was covered in rushes and the walls painted or partly covered by wool hangings or tapestry. Bright colours were used. It was a large room, up to 40–50 feet long and, as in Norman times, was used as a general living room by everyone in the house. There was little privacy: everyone needed somewhere to keep warm, to enjoy recreation, to eat and to sleep. Most often there was a central hearth where massive logs burned, supported on iron fire dogs. The smoke escaped through a hole in the roof which was covered by a louvre. Some halls had wall fireplaces with stone hoods which directed the smoke upwards and outwards through the wall. There were no chimneys at this stage.

At one end of the hall was a raised platform called a daïs, on which was set the lord's table and canopied bench. Also at this end there was usually an oriel or bay window, which gave more light to this end of the hall and provided a decorative feature with its vaulted ceiling and coloured glass. At the other end of the hall were the 'screens'. These were in the form of a passageway divided from the main hall by a wood panelled partition in which door openings were made. From the other side of the screens, openings led into the buttery, pantry and kitchen. The wooden kitchen* was, at this time, often in a separate building due to fear of fire and the screens provided a covered way through which to bring the food into the hall. They

---

* An interesting stone kitchen survives at *Glastonbury Abbey*, Somerset. The Abbot's kitchen here is square with an octagonal roof and louvre above for the escape of smoke and steam. It had several large fireplaces and ovens.

191 *Great Hall with screen and gallery. Based on Haddon Hall, Derbyshire*

192 *Gatehouse entrance, Oxburgh Hall, Norfolk, from 1482*

193 *Manor House, Lower Brockhampton, Herefordshire, c.1400*

194 *Manor House, Boothby Pagnell, Lincolnshire, c.1180*

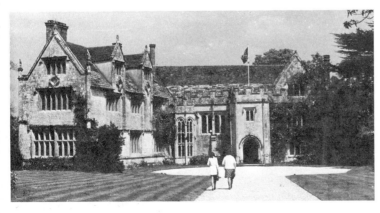

195 *Athelhampton, Dorset, from c.1485*

also prevented draughts from the front porch reaching the hall itself. Above the screens was often a gallery where minstrels played (191, 203).

Staircases to provide access from the hall to other parts of the house were either stone spiral ones, as in castles, when they were constructed in a turret or tower, or wood ladders. Very common were exterior staircases of stone steps built up the side walls of the house (194).

Good, typical examples of *manor houses* of the years 1180–1400 include the stone one at *Boothby Pagnell*, Lincolnshire, c.1180 (194), the early brick example of *Little Wenham Hall*, Suffolk, 1270–80 (196, 199), *Old Soar* at Plaxtol, Kent, c.1290, *Markenfield Hall*, Yorkshire, c.1310 and *Penshurst Place*, Kent, c.1340, all in stone. At Penshurst, there have been several later additions and alterations to the house, but the superb fourteenth-century hall survives, with its central hearth, daïs and open timber roof. Fig. 203 represents the hall as it would have looked in 1340.

The half-timber little manor house at *Lower Brockhampton*, Herefordshire, c.1400 (193) is particularly interesting for the survival of the separate gatehouse still spanning the moat. There is a fine timber-roofed hall and minstrel's gallery in the house itself. An unusual stone, tiny manor house is in the main street at *Tintagel* in Cornwall. This fourteenth-century building is long and low, covered by a slate roof. Inside, there is a parlour, a bedroom above it and a galleried hall.

The open *timber roofs*, used to cover both church naves and great halls, were the wooden counterparts of the stone vault. As time passed and the timber roofs of large churches were replaced with vaults, the domestic roof remained of wood, but the construction became more complex and ornamental. The British developed these designs as did no other nation; they extended from the tie-beam structures of the twelfth century to the final phase of the gilded, painted and angel-sculptured hammerbeam roof.

The Medieval roof (see Glossary) was gabled at each end with a fairly steep pitch. A long beam – the ridge purlin – extended horizontally along the ridge from one end of the hall to the other and further beams (purlins) were set at intervals parallel to it, down the pitch from apex to wall. Rafters were inserted across these at right angles, supported on the wall plate (the horizontal beam at wall level) at the bottom and attached to the ridge purlin at the top. The wall plate itself was secured by stone corbels.

The earliest and simplest design was the tie-beam roof. Here, a massive beam was thrown across the hall from wall plate to wall plate to counteract the outward thrust on the walls. It was pinned to the wall plates and usually curved slightly upwards in the centre. A central *king post* (or two queen posts) and side struts were often supported on the tie beam to strengthen the structure (191, 203, 207). Developing from this came the *trussed rafter roof* and *collar-braced* design. These obviated the tie beam and gave better visibility and more height to the room. In these, curved collar beams or straight struts braced and strengthened the rafters and purlins (198, 203).

The *hammerbeam roof* was evolved at the end of the fourteenth century. It consists of a series of horizontal hammerbeams which are extensions inwards, like abbreviated tie beams, and vertical hammer posts. The hammerbeams are supported on braced corbels and are usually decoratively carved with angels, animals or birds. The hammer posts support the appropriate purlins. The whole roof was originally brightly painted and gilded. The complete, rigid system of timbers was tenoned and pinned to provide a stable structure against the outward thrust of the rafters. External abutment was used as necessary (187, 188). In a double hammerbeam roof there are two sets of hammerbeams and posts, one above the other (119).

On the first floor of a house was generally to be found a smaller chamber, the withdrawing room or *solar*, which was a retreat for the lord and his family from the noise and bustle of the hall. Often there was a tiny rectangular window, called a squint, where the lord could look through from the solar to the hall below to see what was happening there. Several houses retain these as, for example, Penshurst and Great Dixter manor house in Sussex. A typical solar is illustrated in Fig. 198.

By the fifteenth century there was less need for fortification, so the extra available space provided more privacy in the form of bedrooms and reception rooms. The hall was still the principal room of the house, but was used less than formerly by the family themselves. The central hearth gave way to wall fireplaces with roof chimneys (191). The moat was still often retained, but the drawbridge and portcullis were replaced by a bridge leading to an elegant gate-

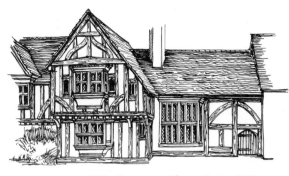

197   *Stoneacre, Otham, Kent, c.1480*

199   *Plan, Little Wenham Hall*

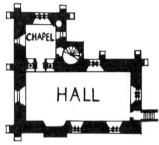

196   *Little Wenham Hall, Suffolk, c.1270–80*

198   *Manor House solar, c.1475–85*

200   *Chimney stack, Hengrave Hall, Suffolk, 1525–38*

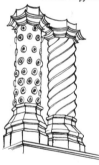

201   *Linenfold panel, c.1510*

202
Oriel window, Compton Wynyates, Warwickshire, c.1530

203   *14th-century hall based on Penshurst Place, Kent*   204   *Tudor parlour, c. 1530, based upon the Abbot's room, Thame Park, Oxfordshire*

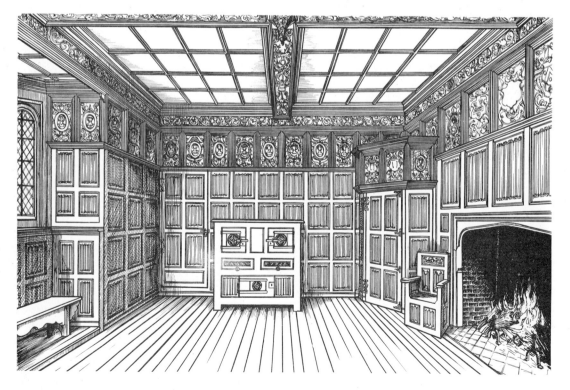

house, which accommodated a chapel in an upper room (192). Such fifteenth-century houses were spaciously laid out round a courtyard and have rooflines of various levels broken by tall chimney stacks and gabled ends. There are stone, brick and half-timber examples. The stone and brick ones have Perpendicular Gothic window openings and projecting porches. Timber houses have carved corner posts, barge boards and corbels. Of the many existing houses, interesting stone ones are *Compton Castle*, Devon, fourteenth and fifteenth centuries, *Cotehele Manor House*, Cornwall, 1485–1539, *Lytes Carey Manor House*, Somerset, 1343–1450, *Great Chalfield Manor House*, Wiltshire, *c.*1480, *Athelhampton*, Dorset, fifteenth and sixteenth centuries (195) and *South Wraxall Manor House*, Wiltshire, fifteenth century. *Oxburgh Hall*, Norfolk is a fine moated, brick house (192) and *Ockwells Manor House*, Berkshire, 1466, is built from timber and brick. There exist a variety of half-timber houses, large and small. Of particular interest are *Stoneacre, Otham*, Kent, 1480 (197), *Rufford Old Hall*, Lancashire, 1463–1505, and *Great Dixter Manor House*, Sussex, mainly fifteenth century.

The houses of the first half of the sixteenth century represent a transitional stage between the Medieval pattern and the Elizabethan great house. The years 1530–50 were a time of energetic house building, from large mansions to small homes. As Henry VIII re-allocated the monastic property, wealthy landowners built fine houses on their newly acquired estates. The need for defence continued to decline and these houses were more spacious, with larger windows (202), better staircases and with chimneys (200), gables and cresting finally replacing Medieval crenellation. Timber was becoming more costly as a result of centuries of felling without replanting. On the other hand, brickwork skills were developing and brick houses, decorated with terracotta, were typical of Tudor building. Inside, the flat, wood and plaster ceiling replaced the open timber roof, and walls were covered by a wood and decorative plaster frieze and, below this, oak panelling where the linenfold panel was most often seen (201, 204). Imposing houses of this time include *Sutton Place*, Surrey, 1523–5, *Barrington Court*, Somerset, *c.*1530, *Coughton Court*, Warwickshire, *Hengrave Hall*, Suffolk, 1525 (200), *Horham Hall*, Essex, 1502–20, *Stoke-by-Nayland*, Suffolk and *Compton Wynyates*, Warwickshire (202). Many structures of different kinds survive from the energetic building activities of the later Middle Ages. These comprise buildings in towns such as guildhalls and inns and, in the country, farming structures such as barns and dovecotes, also bridges, and buildings for education at the universities and schools.

The *Guildhalls* of *London* and *York* were superb examples of their kind, but both have been altered over the years and largely rebuilt after devastation in the Second World War. From a rural area, the half-timber Guildhall survives at Lavenham, Suffolk (174). In *York*, the *Merchant Adventurers' Hall* retains its timber roofed hall and undercroft (207). Several fifteenth-century inns exist and are still functioning as hotels and public houses. The *George Inn* at Glastonbury is a stone example of 1475 (175), as is also the *Angel Inn* at Grantham. In half-timber work there is the *Mermaid Inn* at Rye and the richly ornamented *Feathers Inn* at Ludlow (205).

Several fine Medieval *barns* exist. These were built in stone or wood and had open timber roofs like the houses. Larger examples were divided into nave and aisles as in a church and were strongly buttressed on the exterior. Of especial interest are the tithe barn at *Bradford-on-Avon* and the abbey barn at *Glastonbury*, both of the fourteenth century (210). From the fifteenth century we have those at *West Pennard, Abbotsbury* and *Ashleworth*, all in the west country.

There are many Medieval *bridges* still spanning rivers in different parts of the country. Surviving examples are of stone or brick and have one or more round or pointed arches. The roadway rises to the centre, unlike Roman ones which were flat. Medieval bridges were constructed on timber piles, which were reinforced with iron and driven into the river bed. A starling of piles was built round each main pile and filled in solid. The starling tops were boarded and a stone platform was laid to support the actual bridge, which was constructed of ashlar blocks laid with mortar. Excellent examples can be seen at *Aylesford* (209) and *East Farleigh* over the Medway, *Radcot* and *Newbridge* over the Thames, *Bakewell* over the Wye, the *Clopton Bridge* at *Stratford-upon-Avon* and the beautiful round-arched 'Old Brig' of the fifteenth century at *Stirling*. Many bridges were built with a chapel on them, where a priest would bless travellers, hold services and collect alms. One of these bridges survives at *Bradford-on-Avon* (211). In troubled areas, military bridges were common, where a forti-

205   *The Feathers Inn, Ludlow, c.1520–30*

206   *The city walls and Micklegate Bar, York, 1198–1230*

207   *The Merchant Adventurers' Hall, York, 1357–69*

208 Monnow Bridge with military gateway, Monmouth, late 13th century

209 Aylesford Bridge, river Medway, 14th century

210 The Abbey Barn, Glastonbury, c.1330

211 Chapel Bridge, Bradford-on-Avon, 14th century

212   *Corpus Christi College,*
Oxford, early Tudor

213   *Trinity College, Cambridge,*
the Great Gate, 1518

215   *Magdalen College, Oxford,*
c.1490–1509

214   *Christ Church, Oxford,*
Tom Quad, early Tudor

216   *Gateway decoration, St John's College, Cambridge, early Tudor*

fied gatehouse controlled the passageway at the centre of the bridge. The *Monnow Bridge* at *Monmouth* is one of these (208).

At *Oxford* and *Cambridge Universities* the Medieval halls of residence give a clear impression of the house plan of the Middle Ages as they contain a great hall, chapel and rooms grouped round one or more quadrangles with gateways set at the entrance and exit of each. Remains of Medieval work is considerable and some is of finest quality Gothic architecture, such as *Magdalen College* façade and tower (215), *Merton College* chapel and *New College* chapel, all at Oxford. In the sixteenth century, under the early Tudors, *Trinity College* was founded in 1546 at Cam-

bridge when much of the Great Court was built, including the hall and chapel as well as the Great Gate (213). The decorative gateway to the outer court at *St John's College* also belongs to this time (216). At Oxford, Cardinal Wolsey founded his 'Cardinal College', now *Christ Church*. As at Hampton Court, Wolsey began building and Henry VIII took over. He moved the see to Oxford and called the college 'The House of Christ's Cathedral in Oxford'. It is still known as 'The House'. The Tom quad, with Tom Tower, was largely built at this time, but Wren completed the work in the seventeenth century (214). Front quad at *Corpus Christi College* is typical early sixteenth-century workmanship (212).

PART TWO

CLASSICAL DOMINANCE

CHAPTER FIVE

Elizabethan and Jacobean
1550–1625

Shakespeare's England was a 'golden age' for the country. By 1565 the struggles, both religious and economic, of the mid-century had abated, if they were not fully resolved. Medieval restriction was over and industrialisation had not yet begun. Most people lived in villages and small towns and, though not all were wealthy, extreme poverty was much rarer. Apart from the intermittent rumblings from Spain, the country was at peace and a middle class was establishing itself. The yeoman farmers were evidence of this change, as were also the houses built by middle class people in town and country. This was a phenomenon unknown in feudal Europe. The English had forged for themselves an individual freedom not, even now, available to many nations of the world.

At this time also the United Kingdom was taking a shaky step nearer towards its future foundation. Wales, long the land of conflict between Marcher Lords and the Celtic Welsh, was now peacefully amalgamated with England under the Crown. The monarchy itself was of Welsh (Tudor) line and the union of the two countries, effected militarily under Edward I, became a reality under Elizabeth.

In the north, in the borders and in Scotland, it was a different story. The region was poor, feudality persisted and there was a religious problem. Many years had to pass before the Union was achieved.

Elizabethan England, while enjoying its 'golden age' at home, encouraged the exploration overseas of the mariners who travelled the oceans of the world, extending English influence and bringing back fruitful contacts, trade and merchandise. In turn, this led to increased prosperity at home.

Elizabethan Towns

The population of England and Wales was growing. By the end of the sixteenth century it is thought to have passed four millions, as opposed to the two to two-and-a-half millions of Medieval times. Most people lived in rural areas, cultivating the land or tending sheep; cottage industries supplied the local needs. Even town dwellers spent part of their time in agricultural pursuits. Towns were still small but were larger than their Medieval counterparts. The average town now had about 5000 inhabitants, most of whom had ample living space, including gardens, orchards and farmsteads. About 20,000 people lived in each of the important towns of the country – York, Norwich and Bristol – other than London.

London was much the largest of these towns, becoming more important all the time and one of the greatest in Europe; by 1600 it had about 200,000 inhabitants. It was a microcosm of the nation, reflecting the changes which had taken place. This could be seen in the disappearance of the great monasteries and the importance of secular building and activity in contrast to the Medieval ecclesiastical. The City of London was now an essentially merchant community of great power and wealth, while the buildings of the monarchy and aristocracy were outside the city boundaries, in Whitehall, Westminster and beyond.

London was said by travellers to be the cleanest city in Europe, but by twentieth-century standards it would be considered filthy. The refuse littering the streets and the stench from the open drains and slaughterhouses had not improved since Medieval days. The city was still walled and with its famous gates – now just districts to us – Aldersgate, Cripplegate, Bishopsgate, Oldgate, Moorgate, Newgate, Billingsgate, all clearly named from their locality. London Bridge, the only one across the Thames until the eighteenth century, had been built in stone between 1176 and 1209, replacing the earlier, timber ones. It was a remarkable structure for its period, supported upon 18 stone piers, which were built on to oak planks and bedded in pitch. The bridge, with the starlings which protected these piers from the scour of the strong tide, acted as a dam, holding back the ebb tide. It was this, together with the lack of embankmentation, which caused the river to freeze over in cold winters. The roadway was supported on the piers, which were connected by pointed arches of differing size to accommodate vessels of varied tonnage. On the road were constructed houses and shops whose rent paid for the upkeep of the bridge. They suffered destruction by fire from time to time and were rebuilt, generally larger than before. In Elizabethan times, though the bridge roadway was 20 feet wide, only 10–12 feet of passageway remained and the houses jutted outwards over the river. On iron spikes, at the Tower end of the bridge, the decapitated heads of traitors were left to dehydrate slowly as a warning to others (217).

Stone houses were slowly replacing timber ones, but the great majority were still of half-timber with the upper storeys projecting to nearly meet across the narrow streets. Fire continued to be a great hazard in towns. Houses were often extended vertically instead of laterally as the population grew larger. This was especially so in London and in the north of the country. In Scotland the tradition of the tower house led to easy acceptance of such building. Edinburgh, in particular, was noted until the late eighteenth century for the tall tenement houses, many of which survive in the Old Town (219).

The market was still an important feature of town life, taking place in a market square or a widened section of the High Street. Shops were few, the needs of the community being served by the craftsman working in his house, travelling fairs and the market. The tolbooth, especially in Scotland, survives in several instances as a picturesque feature of the town High Street. As the name implies, this was the place where taxes and tolls were collected: it was the customs house. Medieval and Elizabethan ones were

tall buildings with a belfry and a clock and containing a court room, toll room and cells below for debtors. The buildings later developed into the town hall. The Canongate tolbooth of 1591 is an existing example in Edinburgh (218).

The Architectural Style in Britain 1550–1625

This was a time of energetic building activity, not of cathedrals and chapels, but of great country houses. From the aristocracy to the merchant and yeoman there was a deep desire to create a new, more spacious home, in keeping with the new spirit of the age, displaying the affluence of the owner. Throughout Europe the Renaissance ideals in philosophy, literature and the visual arts were now established. Britain came late to the field; Medievalism had lingered long here. In literature the English were a leading force, but in architecture they were backward. The aristocracy travelled abroad, particularly to France and Flanders, saw the new classical forms replacing the old Medieval ones, and returned to build their own new architecture. But the British interpretation was not pure classicism. In England, the established tradition for asymmetry, the gabled manor house, the mullioned window, the disinterest in sculpture was still strong. Protestant England still had little contact with Catholic Italy and few of the Italian artists who came westward to France extended their travels to England. The English architecture of these years is a blend of three sources: the Italian Renaissance, the French châteaux of the Loire valley and the Flemish decorative style, and all this is grafted upon an essentially English foundation of the Medieval manor house. The results are vital and plastic, a new English art form, national and different from that of much of Europe.

Classical Architecture: Origins, Greece and Rome

In Britain, as in Western Europe, there have been only two basic styles of architecture until the modern building of the twentieth century: Gothic and classical. Each has been subject to development and variation on its main theme, each enjoyed a period of some hundreds of years in which the development took place, and each was the subject of nineteenth-century revivals. Gothic architecture flourished

217   *View of London from the south bank of the Thames, early 17th century (after Hollar)*
A   *Old St Paul's Cathedral*   E   *Guildhall*
B   *St Laurence Poultney*   F   *St Dunstan-in-the-East*
C   *St Andrew's, Holborn*   G   *London Bridge*
D   *St Michael*

during the Middle Ages – some 400 years in Britain – and the Renaissance re-initiated classical design. In Britain, coming late to this new classical form, the sixteenth century was a time of tentative experiment. Classical tenets were only established in the seventeenth century when they became the accepted mode of building.

An important distinction between Gothic and classical building is that the former is indigenous to north-west Europe, including Britain, and grew up steadily and nationally in each area, while the latter was an importation, first from Rome, then Greece. Because the climate of these countries is different from that of Britain, adaptations had to be made, but the style remained basically the same. In beginning a study of the architecture of Renaissance Britain, it is helpful to look at the origins of the classical forms. Historically, Greek architecture is the prototype upon which Roman work was based, but the rediscovery and importation of these styles into Renaissance Europe worked in reverse. Greece was under the subjugation of the Turkish Empire; it remained unknown to and unvisited by the West for another two centuries. The architecture of Ancient Rome was studied by the Italians in the fifteenth century and by England much later. For some time it was believed

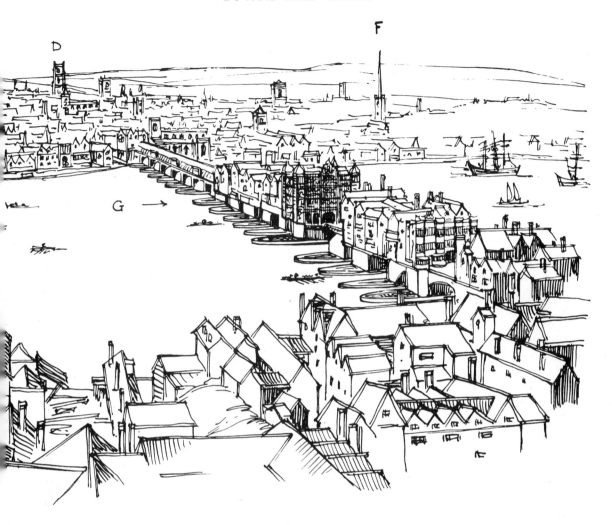

throughout Western Europe that Rome was the originator of the style; the Italians were jealously proud of this supposed fact.

What is commonly described as the *architecture of Ancient Greece*, the Hellenic building style, emerged from archaic beginnings about 700 BC and reached its zenith, in beauty and quality, in the mid-fifth century BC. The Ancient Greek civilisation continued until 146 BC, when Greece became a subject state of Rome. Many fine buildings date from the later years, but the later fifth-century work was never surpassed. The Greek style of building was simple in line and form and of limited design, whatever the purpose of the structure. It is a *trabeated* type of architecture and this is fundamentally different from the Gothic *arcuated* style. Medieval construction was based upon the arch, at first round then pointed, then from this

developed the vault supported on piers. In classical architecture, based upon the trabeated form (from Latin *trabes* = a beam), the construction is of a post-and-lintel type, consisting of vertical supports (the columns) and horizontal beams or blocks of stone or marble. From the early discovery that a lintel stone supported on two columns could form an opening, the colonnade evolved, in which a row of columns would carry a long, extended lintel and this became the exterior elevation of a building. In the Greek climate, an outdoor life was usual and colonnaded buildings provided shade from the sun as well as fresh air.

The beauty of Greek architecture derives, not from its variety of forms, but from its subtle and detailed attention to proportion and line. The Greeks developed a system of *orders* wherein the proportions of

219   *John Knox's house, High Street, Edinburgh, 1490 and later*

218   *Canongate Tolbooth, Edinburgh, 1592*

221   *Gate of Honour (upper part), Gonville and Caius, Cambridge, 1573–5*

220   *Queens' College, Cambridge, mid-16th century*

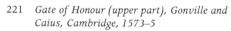

the individual parts were studied and crystallised. Each order consists of a column, sometimes a base, a capital and an entablature. The entablature is the group of horizontal mouldings which is supported, as was the original lintel, on top of the columns. It, in turn, is subdivided into three basic parts: the *architrave*, above this the *frieze* and, at the top, the projecting *cornice*. In each order the types, proportions and decoration of the mouldings, the proportion of the column, the relationship of width to height and to the base, the capital and the entablature, all are regulated. The quality of Greek building varies, from the ordinary to the magnificent, according to the architect's subtle interpretation of these rules.

There are three Greek orders: *Doric, Ionic* and *Corinthian*. The Greeks preferred the Doric which, especially on the mainland, features in the majority of the best Greek buildings (222). The most famous of all, the *Parthenon*, is in this order. Built in the finest period, 447-432 BC, it is today partly ruined; in Fig. 224 it is shown restored. Much of the sculpture from the pediments and the interior frieze is in the British Museum in London. The Parthenon shows the chief features of the *Doric Order* (222, 224): a sturdy column, fluted but without base, a plain architrave and a deeply projecting cornice, with the intervening frieze enriched by alternate triglyphs and metopes. The former are vertical bands of stone and the latter alternating panels in which are set decorative sculptural groups. At either end of a Greek temple there is a triangular *pediment* which has similar mouldings to the cornice and is decorated in the tympanum with sculpture. The timber roof was covered with marble tiles. The Doric capital is simple; it has a square top member, the *abacus*, and below this the *echinus* with narrow rings cut in rows beneath (222).

The *Ionic Order* (226) has a narrower column shaft and a moulded base, a capital with curved side scrolls, called *volutes*, and a frieze which is usually decorated along its whole length by relief sculpture; the cornice projects less strongly. Near the Parthenon, on the Athenian Acropolis, is a beautiful example of the Ionic Order – the Erechtheion – also built of the local, white marble (227). The third order, the *Corinthian* (228) was rarely used by the Greeks. It is similar to the Ionic except that the capital is bell-shaped, with small volutes at the four top outer corners, and the bell is clothed in two rows of acanthus leaves curling over and outwards.

The *Roman civilisation* lasted several hundred years, overlapping the Greek one by a long time, but achieving its best architectural work between the first century BC and the third century AD. The Romans also built in the trabeated style and used the orders, adapting the Greek Doric, Ionic and Corinthian (226, 228) and adding two more, the *Tuscan* and the *Composite*. The first of these was similar to the Doric; the Composite has a capital which possesses some Ionic and some Corinthian features (225). The chief differences between Greek and Roman architecture are:

1. The Greeks used one order per façade. The Romans often used several, one above the other, as in the Colosseum (230).
2. The Greeks built primarily in the trabeated manner. The Romans also used arcuated methods and combined both forms in one building. This too can be seen in the Colosseum (230), where arches are structural and the orders decorative.
3. Roman orders and ornament are generally coarser and heavier than the Greek. The Romans preferred to use the Composite and Corinthian Orders (223, 225, 226, 229).
4. The Romans were great builders and engineers, famous for their concrete vaults, public baths, bridges and aqueducts, as well as temples. The Greeks were perfectionists of the subtleties of the simple classical temple form.

The Sources of the English Classical Style of 1550-1625

Of the three classical sources which formed the English style of these years, the influence of the purer classicism of the Italian Renaissance was weakest. The knowledge of the English builders came from books of drawings and designs, the impressions of the aristocratic travellers who returned to commission their homes and the craftsmen who came to work in England from the Continent. Though the purer Italian classical model was available in the publications of Vitruvius, Palladio, Alberti and others, the English were more drawn towards the French and Flemish interpretations. Great landowners visited France and Flanders more widely and they could see from the châteaux of de l'Orme and Bullant, Lescot's work on the Louvre and, in Flanders, Floris' Town Hall at Antwerp and de Key's at Leiden, what the finished

223   *Roman entablature (Ostia)*

222   *The Greek Doric Order*
      (Parthenon)

228   *The Roman Corinthian*
      Order (Ostia)

225   *The Roman*
      Composite Order
      (Arch of Titus)

226   *The Roman Ionic Order*
      (Temple, Rome)

224 *The Parthenon, Athens (restored), 447–432 BC*

227 *Greek ornament (Erechtheion, Athens)*

229
Roman ornament (Trajan Forum, Rome)

230 *The Colosseum, Rome, AD 70–82*

structure should look like. Few of them, at this stage, reached Rome or Florence. It was seventeenth-century England which returned to Palladio and Vitruvius through Inigo Jones.

Elizabethan England absorbed all the decorative possibilities of the new style from French and Flemish sources and interpreted them from the pattern books. Builders took their designs from Serlio's treatise, from de Bry and de Vries and from the German Dietterlin. In 1563 the Englishman John Shute published his *Chief Groundes of Architecture*, showing the five classical orders, based on Serlio's work. The Flemish pattern books on ornament were riotously ornate and the Elizabethans absorbed with enthusiasm the strapwork and cartouche designs, the ornamented orders, the decorative cresting and gabling. They incorporated these into their buildings, caring little and understanding less if their orders were wrongly proportioned and, from a classical viewpoint, wrongly employed, since they were added to a fundamentally Medieval building as decoration, not construction.

There were no architects yet in the modern understanding of the term. Surveyors and builders made 'platts' and 'uprights' (plans and elevations) but, in general, a building was designed as it progressed, with the prospective aristocratic owner explaining what he wanted, instructing his master mason on these lines and giving him some books on classical orders and decorative design to work from. Thus, at *Burghley House*, built largely in the 1580s, it was William Cecil, Lord Burghley who was largely responsible for the form of the house. He supplied his master mason with French architectural books and employed Flemish craftsmen.* He was the first of many aristocratic architectural dilettanti.

---

* Such craftsmen, masons, carpenters, glaziers, plaster-workers etc., were directed by a master of their trade, with the whole building operation supervised by a master mason or surveyor. The names of most of these are not known. Records are not generally available and Queen Elizabeth, unlike her father, inaugurated little building work herself, so royal records are few. The exceptions include *John Thorpe* and *Robert Smythson*. Thorpe was employed for some time at the Office of Works and, while there, made many drawings of the houses being built at the time and these are now in the Soane Museum. Smythson is thought to have been connected with the direction of three of the great Elizabethan mansions: Longleat (231), Wollaton and Hardwick. He was buried at Wollaton (235).

The Great Houses

The wealth of the Elizabethan and Jacobean era, architecturally, was funnelled into domestic construction. Few churches were erected and there was little civic or university building. It is the great houses which represent the architectural expression of the age. The aristocracy, who commissioned and partly designed them, vied with one another to create palaces suitable for the monarch, accompanied by her court retinue, to visit on her annual summer progress. For such a purpose and such a monarch a house had to be great indeed, both impressive and capacious. Each subject tried to outdo his predecessors when building a new house, in style, ornamentation, splendour and scale.

The House Exterior

The *plan* of these mansions varied, but there was a growing acceptance of a greater symmetry (the influence of the Renaissance), also a preference for a more compact house built round an open, rather than a closed, four-sided court. Early in the 1560s, the *E-plan* house was developed. In this, wings were extended forwards at each end of a rectangular house, while in the centre the short stroke of the E was provided by a projecting entrance porch. The house was then symmetrical, with the hall, solar and other reception rooms on one side of the porch and the screens passage and offices on the other. Often the latter would be given an oriel or bay window, extending much of the height of the house, to balance that of the hall. *Cobham Hall* in Kent has this type of plan. The *H-plan* then evolved from the E-plan design. Here, the side wings were extended as far to the rear as to the front. In the later decades of the century, a greater perfection of symmetry was achieved; bay window matched bay window, gable matched gable, chimneystack matched chimneystack. *Montacute House* is a classic example (238) as also is *Longleat* (231).

Window area increased in proportion to the wall rather as it had, a century earlier, in ecclesiastical building. Now the country was at peace, defence and fortification were unnecessary and advances were being made in the production of window glass. The notable change that this brought about prompted the contemporary jingle that at *Hardwick Hall* (Derbyshire), there was 'more glass than wall'. The skylines

231 *Longleat House,*
Wiltshire,
1550–80, stone

232 *Speke Hall, Lancashire, 1598, half-timber*

233 *Trerice Manor House,*
Cornwall, c.1573, stone

234 *Crathes Castle,*
Kincardineshire, c.1590

235   *Wollaton Hall, Nottinghamshire,*
      1580–8, stone

236   *Craigievar Castle, Aberdeenshire, c.1620*

237 *Little Moreton Hall,
Cheshire, 1559–80,
half-timber*

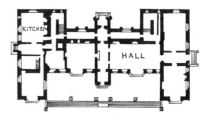

238 *Plan, Montacute House,
Somerset, 1588–1601*

239 *Elizabethan main
chamber, c.1575–80*

of these houses are one of their most attractive and characteristic features. They are varied and lively in silhouette, illustrating more the traditional English Medieval manor house than the new Renaissance concepts, which tended to horizontal rooflines, broken only by few classical stacks. The skylines of Elizabethan and Jacobean great houses were a riot of cresting, projecting, curving gables and decorative chimneystacks of the greatest variety in design. Often grouped in two, three or four columns, these stacks were ornamented in differing patterns and shared the same base and cresting. They represent the outrageous English adaptation of the classical coupled columns stripped of their classical characteristics.

The *entrance porch* or frontispiece was an Elizabethan development from the early Tudor gatehouse. As the main entrance to the building it was the focal centre for the employment of new Renaissance forms and ornament. Here the designers interpreted the classical orders and used them, not as structural elements, but in ornamental manner. The entrance porch generally had two or three storeys, each usually with single or coupled columns or pilasters. There was little attempt to study the correct classical proportions or forms, but the Elizabethan application of the classical tenets shows great vitality and richness of ornament inspired by Flemish sources. Two or more orders were used unrelatedly in one porch. Interesting *Elizabethan* examples include those at *Cobham Hall*, Kent (242), *Keevil Manor House*, Wiltshire and *Studley Priory*, Oxfordshire. *Jacobean porches* were even richer and more impressive, as at *Hatfield House*, Hertfordshire (246); *Bramshill House*, Hampshire (244), *Charlton House*, Greenwich (245) and *Audley End*, Essex (243).

The House Interior

At the same time as the need for defence declined, there was evinced a greater desire for privacy. The purposes of different rooms in a house altered and more and smaller rooms were included in the plan. The use of the *hall* as a living and sleeping room was abandoned. Elizabethan halls are smaller and of one storey only. They have flat ceilings decorated all over with plaster panels and strapwork, enriched with floral, animal and heraldic motifs. Some are in high relief and many are pendant designs (239, 247, 248, 249). The walls are panelled in wood, but here the linenfold panelling of early Tudor times has been replaced by simple moulded and beaded panels, plain or inlaid with coloured woods and ivory (239, 241). There is a deep frieze of plaster, decorated and often painted, like the ceiling.

In Jacobean houses the whole room was beginning to be designed as one unit in classical form, with pilasters and columns dividing the sections and with windows, doorways and chimneypieces as focal centres (249). The classical details were still inaccurate by Italian Renaissance standards but the format was being accepted and interiors, like exteriors, were being planned as a whole to include all architectural motifs and details as part of the scheme. The hall screen was, in these years, still of wood but now very richly carved. Some examples, like those at *Audley End* and *Knole*, are most ornate and extend from floor almost to ceiling in a riot of Flemish mannerist treatment (241). Among the fine examples of hall plaster ceilings are the ribbed designs at *Knole House*, Kent, *Levens Hall*, Cumbria, the strapwork ceiling at *Hatfield House*, Hertfordshire and the pendant form at *Dunster Castle*, Somerset and *Trerice Manor House*, Cornwall (247). The hall floor was of stone, brick, wood or tiled. There were one or more wall fireplaces, generally two-tiered and an integral part of the architectural scheme of the room; they too were ornately carved in Flemish mannerist pattern (241, 266).

The Medieval solar had now been replaced by several reception rooms of which the main chamber (great drawing room) was the largest. Generally on the first floor, this had an architectural and decorative scheme second only in richness and quality to the hall. It was not so lofty and there was no carved screen, but the ornamentation and treatment of windows, ceiling and walls was similar. The floor was of wood (239, 249). Good examples include *Athelhampton House*, Dorset (248), *Montacute House*, Somerset, *Speke Hall*, Lancashire, *Hatfield House*, Hertfordshire and *Levens Hall*, Cumbria (253). Small parlours were in use by different members of the family and for dining privately.

Bedchambers were now more common, though they were still passage rooms; as there were few corridors, the bedrooms were actually a wide passage divided up and having a door at each end, which led into the adjoining rooms. The Tudor wing at Hampton Court Palace is of this design. As this system was draughty,

240   *Castle Ashby, Northamptonshire, c.1624, brick and stone*

241   *Jacobean hall, Audley End, Essex, 1603–16*

242   *(far left) Cobham Hall,
       Kent, c.1594*

243   *(left) Audley End,
       Essex, 1603–16*

244   *(below left) Bramshill House,
       Hampshire, 1605–12*

245   *(below centre) Charlton House,
       Greenwich, 1607–12*

246   *(below) Hatfield House,
       Hertfordshire, 1611*

247 *Ceiling, Trerice House, Cornwall*

248 *Ceiling, Athelhampton, Dorset*

249 *Jacobean drawing room, c.1615–20*

the vast four-post bedstead, with its ornately carved headboard, posts and canopy frame and enveloping curtains and frill, provided a cosy room within a room. Many examples of such bedsteads survive in museums, such as the Victoria and Albert Museum in London, and in a number of houses in different parts of the country, for example, *Rufford Old Hall*, Lancashire and *Oxburgh Hall*, Norfolk. These bedsteads were so costly and so important that they were willed from father to son over several generations as one of the most precious of family possessions.

A new type of room which originated in the sixteenth century was made fashionable by the Elizabethans: this was the *long gallery*. It was located on the first or second floor of the house and extended along the whole of one long façade. Some galleries are as long as 170 feet but are quite narrow, about 20 feet wide and only 15 feet high. This long, narrow room had windows on three sides, on the two short ones and on the outer, long side, while on the fourth, inner side were two or more fireplaces. The purpose of the gallery was to provide plenty of space in which children could play and adults sit and talk, listen to music, stroll about or play games, in the winter months, without getting in one another's way or on their nerves. Modern multi-purpose, open-plan living rooms have a similar theme; the drawback to these is that they are not 170 feet long and the occupants, while not as numerous as in an Elizabethan long gallery, often get in one another's way. Long galleries survive in many great Elizabethan and Jacobean houses though some, as at Syon House, have been redesigned in a later age to alter the appearance of the proportions. Among the beautiful galleries are those at *Knole House*, Kent, *Hatfield House*, Hertfordshire, *Ham House*, Surrey, *Little Moreton Hall*, Cheshire, *Montacute House*, Somerset, *Hardwick Hall* and *Haddon Hall*, both in Derbyshire.

The third characteristic feature of these houses, together with the porch and the long gallery, was the *staircase*. It was not until the second half of the sixteenth century that this became a distinctive feature in the aesthetic design of a house as well as a means of access from one floor to another. Elizabethan staircases were of oak, solidly built and designed in generous proportions to accommodate the farthingale skirts of the ladies of the family. They were constructed in short flights of six to ten stairs and were called *dog-legged* because each flight returned back

alongside the one immediately above and below it. At the top and bottom of each flight was a massive newel post, decoratively carved in panels and surmounted by a finial. Each newel was joined to the next by a heavy, moulded handrail and an equivalent baulk of timber, the string, ran parallel, joining the treads. Ornamented balusters connected the two (251).

By the Jacobean period the staircase had evolved into a magnificent feature and a number of these survive, at *Hatfield House* and *Knole* for example (250, 252). Though still of oak and solidly built, these staircases were constructed round an open well, taking up much more space than the Elizabethan dog-legged type. The treads are broad, the flights short and the ascents easy. Some of the newels, especially the finials, are beautifully and interestingly carved (250, 252, 264).

Examples

There are a number of great houses of Elizabethan and Jacobean times in different parts of Britain which have survived with only marginal alterations since they were first built. Changes in furnishing, furniture, heating and lighting have been made to all those which are still lived in and restoration has taken place, but most give a clear picture of what such houses would have been like. The large mansions were generally built of stone or, at least, of brick and stone. Of particular interest among these are *Hardwick Hall*, Derbyshire, 1591-7, *Cobham Hall*, Kent, 1594-9 (242, 260), *Longleat House*, Wiltshire, 1550-80 (231, 263), *Montacute House*, Somerset, 1588-1601 (238), *Wollaton Hall*, Nottinghamshire, 1580-8 (235, 261), *Hatfield House*, Hertfordshire, 1607-12 (246, 252, 254), *Castle Ashby*, Northamptonshire, c.1624 (240, 256), *Burghley House*, Northamptonshire, c. 1585, *Bramshill House*, Hampshire, 1605-12 (244), and *Knole House*, Kent, c.1605 (250). Other large houses retain certain features of note from this time, such as the hall at *Audley End*, Essex, 1603-16 (241) and the long gallery at *Haddon Hall*, Derbyshire, 1585.

Of the smaller houses in stone and brick should be noted *Keevil Manor House*, Wiltshire, *Cothelstone Manor House*, Somerset (257), *Brereton Hall*, Cheshire, c.1586, *Fritwell Manor House* (258) and *Studley Priory*, both in Oxfordshire and all Elizabethan. From

250 *Jacobean staircase, Knole, Kent, c.1605*

251 *Elizabethan dog-legged staircase*

252 *Carved oak staircase, Hatfield House, 1607–12*

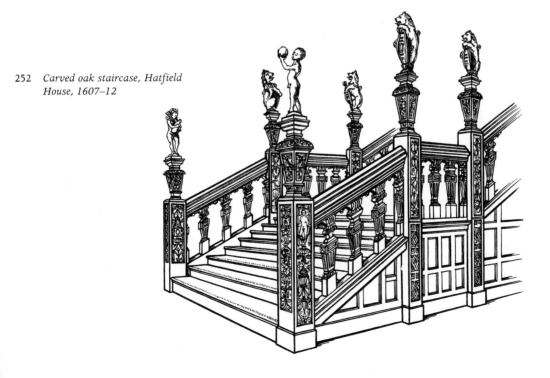

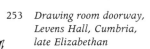

253   *Drawing room doorway,*
      Levens Hall, Cumbria,
      late Elizabethan

254   *Entrance doorway,*
      Hatfield House,
      Hertfordshire, c.1607–12

255   *Half-timber gable and*
      window, Little Moreton
      Hall, c.1580

256   *Bay window, Castle Ashby,*
      Northamptonshire, c.1624

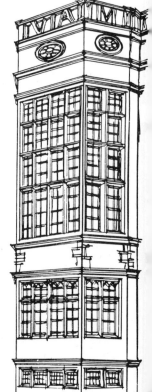

257
Stone gable and window,
Cothelstone Manor House,
Somerset

258   *Window, Fritwell Manor*
      House, Oxfordshire, stone

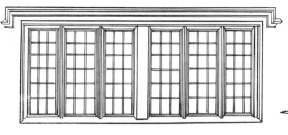

261 *Timber roof of hall, Wollaton Hall, 1580–8*

259 *Carved oak pilaster and panelling, c.1600*

260 *Porch detail, Ionic Order, Cobham Hall, 1594*

264 *Jacobean carved oak staircase finial*

262 *Elizabethan carved panelling*

263 *Doric pilaster capital, Longleat House, c.1575*

265 *Brick chimneystack, Penshurst Place, Elizabethan*

266 *Carved stone fireplace with carved oak mantel, c.1600*

267 *Wood panelling, Chastleton House, c.1610*

268 *Detail, hall screen, Knole House, Jacobean*

269 *Carved wood corbel bracket, Queens' College, Cambridge*

the Jacobean period are *Charlton House*, Greenwich, 1607–12 (245) and *Chastleton House*, Oxfordshire, 1603–12 (267). There are many beautiful half-timber houses dating from this time. These are to be found chiefly in the areas with little stone available, in Cheshire, Lancashire, East Anglia and Kent. Of particular interest are *Little Moreton Hall*, Cheshire, *c*.1559–80 (237, 255), *Rumwood Court, Langley*, Kent, Elizabethan, and *Speke Hall*, Lancashire, *c*.1598 (232).

The development of the plan of the great house in *Scotland* was different from England. Whereas south of the border the house plan was being opened up from the restricted courtyard and defensive features were being abandoned, the more troubled conditions and economic weakness of Scotland caused landowners, large and small, to cling to the *tower house design* until well into the seventeenth century. The tower house had been the most characteristic type of domestic building for the upper classes in Scotland since the twelfth century. It was a compact, easily defensible residence with small land area and small windows yet, with its height, it provided adequate domestic comfort. Similar in outward form to the Norman keep, it attracts no special attention in early Medieval times but, by the end of the sixteenth century, it presents a contrast to the Elizabethan mansion. These years represent the Indian summer of the Scottish baronial style, when a number of fine houses were built in this manner of which several survive in the north-east around Aberdeen. Of particular interest are *Crathes Castle* (234) and *Craigievar Castle* (236), which both exhibit the characteristic corbelled turrets with pointed roofs, small windows and a tall, graceful silhouette.

The seventeenth century brought several attempts to follow the new fashions in Renaissance mansions. One example is the reconstruction of the *Palace of Pinkie* in Midlothian by the Earl of Dunfermline, begun in 1613. The ambitious plans for a grand courtyard house were not completed but, in the two ranges which were built, there was included a long gallery. Renaissance decoration and fenestration have been employed and earlier Scottish characteristic forms blend with these in a not unattractive manner. Another interesting courtyard building was the *Earl's Palace* at *Kirkwall* in Orkney, which dates from about 1600–5. This included some palatial apartments on the first floor, one of which was a large hall. It was a characteristically Scottish building despite clear influence from both France and England.

CHAPTER SIX

Inigo Jones and Wren
1620–1700

Inigo Jones 1573–1652

In Britain, architectural style had developed steadily and logically from Romanesque, through the various stages of Gothic to Elizabethan and Jacobean Renaissance forms, based upon Flemish mannerism but imposed upon a Medieval base. In the 1620s it was Inigo Jones who brought the Italian Renaissance to Britain and, in so doing, created a stylistic revolution. This was almost 100 years after the French architects Lescot, Bullant and de l'Orme had been experimenting with Italian Renaissance forms in their châteaux in France. Being so long delayed, the movement in England burst forth, fully mature, in Jones' *Queen's House* at Greenwich, clearly following the Italian villa pattern developed by Palladio at Vicenza. The Queen's House is the English interpretation of the Palazzo Chiericati; this is no copy, though, but an original design, restrained and characteristically national. The French architects had absorbed the Italian Renaissance form slowly, moving step by step from the purely decorative approach to the fully comprehended constructional one, treating the building as a whole, a considered classical scheme. Inigo Jones, coming much later on the scene, took the complete step in one stage, alone, the first English architect in the Italian Renaissance meaning of the term.

Inigo Jones was born in London, the son of a cloth maker. His father was poor and the young Inigo's education was scanty; he was largely self-taught. He became known first as a painter and designer of costumes and décor for Court masques. It was in 1611

that he was appointed Surveyor to Prince Henry of Wales. After the prince's premature death, Inigo Jones took the opportunity offered to him by Lord Arundel to tour Italy and France in search of works of art. He took full advantage of this chance to see for himself works of the Renaissance of which he had read. He spent one-and-a-half years travelling, studying, making drawings and measurements of both the antique Roman buildings and the Italian and French examples based upon them. For Englishmen this was a completely new idea; up to that time Renaissance styles and forms had been taken from the books published on the Continent and the results of these third- and fourth-hand studies were to be seen in Jacobean building.

One of the chief sources of information in Italy for the earliest Renaissance buildings, such as Brunelleschi's and Alberti's designs in Florence, were the works of *Marcus Vitruvius Pollo*, the Roman architect and engineer who wrote on the designs, proportions and basic principles of classical architecture in the first century BC. His manuscripts were discovered in AD 1414 and, from that time, provided invaluable material for Italian and other Continental architects on the Roman architectural style of the late Republican period. Drawings and descriptions were given by Vitruvius of the orders, ornament, building methods and materials used by the Romans at his time.

By the early seventeenth century Italian architects did not all follow closely the precepts laid down by Vitruvius, but one of them based his work closely upon Vitruvius' books. This architect was *Andrea Palladio* (1508–80) who, in turn, published in 1570 his drawings and designs. Inigo Jones was much impressed by Palladio's books '*I Quattro Libri dell' Architettura*' and '*L'Antiquità di Roma*' and took copies* with him to Italy where he checked, *in situ*, the measurements and drawings against the actual remains and buildings. When he returned to Britain he showed in his own work that, despite the strong influence of Palladio and Vitruvius, he was no mere copyist. Inigo Jones was a highly original architect, always intent upon studying for himself at source, then evolving his personal designs.

Although few buildings designed by Inigo Jones survive and much of his work on great schemes,† such as Whitehall Palace, was never carried out or has been destroyed, his importance in the history of English architecture cannot be too strongly stressed. He was the first English architect to work in the wider manner on the pattern set by the Italians, from Brunelleschi and Alberti onwards, and later by the French, led by such men as de l'Orme, Bullant and Lescot. These Renaissance architects were rarely masters of only one profession, most were either painters, sculptors, mathematicians, for example, as well as architects. They did not design only a part, or even the whole, of a building as the Medieval men had done, leading from their position as master masons, but envisaged an extensive scheme and controlled the operation of all the artisans employed on the project, responsible only to the client.

Inigo Jones' fame as the first Englishman to practise architecture in this manner is assured, even though the *Banqueting Hall* is all that survives from the ambitious Whitehall Palace scheme. However, the *Queen's House* (270) was begun a little earlier, in 1616, and so is the prototype in Britain for a pure classical building. Designed on Palladian villa lines for Queen Anne of Denmark, James I's consort, work was held up when she died. The building was completed later, in 1635, for the next Queen, Henrietta Maria and this

little masterpiece owes its survival to the intervention of a third Queen, Mary II, who insisted on its retention in the Greenwich Hospital scheme of the later seventeenth century.

Both the Queen's House and the Banqueting Hall (1619–22) are based directly upon Italian Renaissance forms and owe nothing to the mannerism of Flanders and Germany. They were a revelation to both patrons and architects in Britain at this time and though Flemish design, in domestic architecture in particular, continued until the mid-seventeenth century, Inigo Jones' structures set a pattern which provided a basis for the work of Wren, the Baroque school and the golden age of eighteenth-century British classicism. Both buildings have simple exteriors, the orders on the façades being used in designs which are symmetrical and compact. The *Banqueting Hall* (273) uses two orders, one above the other in Roman manner, Ionic below and Composite above, the only other decoration being in the classical window openings with their alternate triangular and rounded pediments and the balustraded parapet. The *Queen's House* (270) is plainer still with a rusticated lower storey and the Ionic Order confined to the central block. Inside, the chief room is the hall, a forty foot cube, which is surrounded by a gallery giving access to the queen's apartments.

Inigo Jones was involved in two town planning schemes in *London* which, although only fragments survive, illustrate his early acceptance of the concept of designing classical architecture as a scheme for streets and squares, not just a single building. In this he was developing the theme put forward by Italian architects in cities such as Rome and Pienza. The scheme for laying out *Covent Garden* was sponsored by the Earl of Bedford and the King and Council in 1630. It is thought that Inigo Jones designed the *piazza* lined with houses of classical design and with St Paul's Church built on the west side. Nothing of the original work remains, but the church was later rebuilt in the original style. Lindsey House in *Lincoln's Inn Fields* shows his ideas for the terrace form of architecture, developed on a large scale in the eighteenth century. Here is a giant Ionic Order* spanning two floors with parapet above. The whole order is of low projection and is purely decorative;

---

* Inigo Jones' annotated copy of Palladio has been preserved.

† Inigo Jones held the post of Surveyor-General from 1615 to 1642. It is a great loss to English architecture that so little of his work survives from this long period of office. This is chiefly due to the fact that Parliament permitted so little to be spent on civic and official building and there was even less ecclesiastical construction. From these years of office, only some 20 buildings are known to have been designed by him and of these only half-a-dozen survive.

---

* A concept first used by Michelangelo in his palaces on the Capitol Hill in Rome.

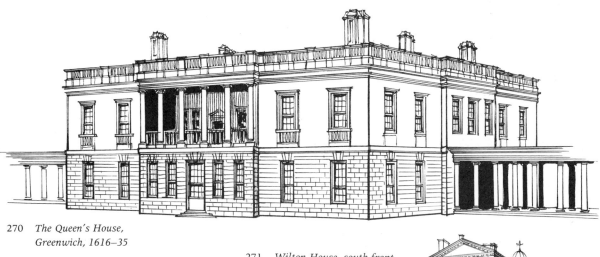

270 *The Queen's House,*
     Greenwich, 1616–35

271 *Wilton House, south front,*
     1647–53

272 *The Double Cube*
     Room, Wilton
     House, Wiltshire

the elevation is completely symmetrical.

Towards the end of his life Inigo Jones rebuilt part of the great house at *Wilton*, assisting the Earl of Pembroke. His court life and his office of Surveyor-General had ended with the advent of the Civil War and at Wilton his south façade (271) and the two superb cube rooms, part of the seven apartments, remain as testimony to this fine achievement of his last years. The exterior is simple, without orders, but with a central great window flanked by sculptured figures. Inside, in contrast, are sumptuous apartments.* The Double Cube Room (272) measures $60 \times 30 \times 30$ feet. The walls are white with gold enrichment and hung with Van Dyck portraits. Between these are carved oak decorative drops of fruit and flowers depended from scrolled cartouches. The carved wood doorcase is of the Corinthian Order, the doors panelled with acanthus decoration (277). The painted ceiling is deeply coved and has a central oval panel. The chimneypiece is of white marble carved in scrolls and swags. Here is a classical Renaissance apartment to hold its own with any Continental equivalent.

Domestic Building 1620–1650

Although Inigo Jones had brought the Italian Renaissance to Britain and this had a lasting effect upon architectural development, its influence until 1650 was small. Building in these years was plainer than Elizabethan and Jacobean work; it was nearer to Renaissance forms but it still reflected Flemish gabling and brickwork more than Italian classicism.

Brick was popular for building at this time; it was beginning to replace timber as the most commonly used material, partly due to an incipient shortage of wood and partly for its greater suitability to Renaissance design. Brick is cheap and durable but builders discovered, as Medieval builders in the Baltic coastal regions of Europe had found in the fifteenth century,

---

* This is characteristic of Inigo Jones. He held strong views on the place of ornament in architecture and interior decoration. These are illustrated in his own words 'Ye outward ornaments oft to be sollid, proporsionable according to the rulles, masculine and unaffected.' This was his intention for the treatment of exterior façades. The interior was much richer but still controlled, unfussy and never overdone.

that it is not a material adaptable to rich or precise decoration. So English and Flemish brickworkers developed their own forms of expression in the medium, this time in classical not Gothic idiom. They introduced classical ornament in brick (or in stone sparingly used for decoration only), as well as pilasters, doorways, window frames and pediments (288). The techniques of Flemish brickwork were also established at this time, such as *Flemish bond* construction, where alternate 'headers' and 'stretchers' were used on all courses and *gauged* bricks were employed, that is, bricks cut exactly to the required size instead of the joint fillings being thickened to make up space.

Brick was especially utilised in domestic work and the Flemish influence was paramount here, illustrated in the curving Dutch gabling and decorative chimney stacks. A classic example of this style is the red brick *Kew Palace* (278) in Kew Gardens, with its typical rectangular sash windows and three-storey entrance with orders in brick. Houses which display similar characteristics, either entirely in brick or with stone-faced decoration include *Raynham Hall*, Norfolk, 1635–6 (279), *Swakeleys*, Middlesex, 1629–38, *Broome Park*, 1635–8 and *Quebec House* at *Westerham*, both in Kent.

University Building 1620–1645

Although the work was generally in stone, college building at *Oxford* and *Cambridge* in the first half of the seventeenth century shows many of the same characteristics and Flemish derivations as can be seen in the domestic field. The theme is classical and it is of a purer form than it had been in the sixteenth century, but *Canterbury Quad*, for example, built 1632–6 at *St John's College, Oxford*, is typical in its Flemish strapwork and other ornament. The colonnades on the west and east sides are each centred by an elaborate frontispiece incorporating respectively the statues of Charles I and his queen (301). Another Oxford structure typical of the time is the *Bodleian Library* tower. This was part of a major project for the Oxford Schools inaugurated by Sir Thomas Bodley in 1613. The tower is its most outstanding part. It is called the Tower of the Five Orders, as each of these is incorporated into the design; the tower is part of a quad surrounded by three-storey buildings (332).

The use of the classical idiom for constructional as well as decorative purpose and comprehension of the

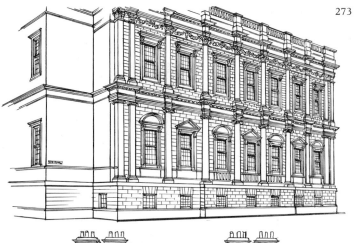

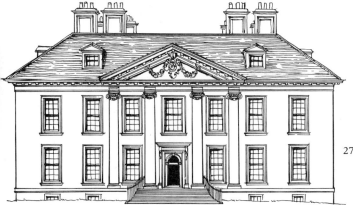

273 *The Banqueting Hall, Whitehall, London, 1619–22, Inigo Jones*

274 *Plan, Coleshill House, Berkshire, 1650–2, Roger Pratt*

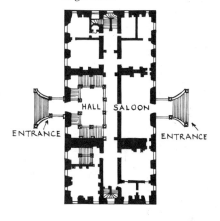

HALL SALOON

ENTRANCE ← → ENTRANCE

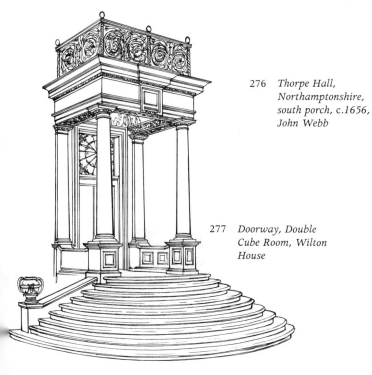

275 *Eltham Lodge, Kent, 1664, Hugh May*

276 *Thorpe Hall, Northamptonshire, south porch, c.1656, John Webb*

277 *Doorway, Double Cube Room, Wilton House*

278　*Kew Palace, 1631*

279　*Raynham Hall, Norfolk, c.1635–6*

280　*Dining Room based upon Thorpe Hall,*
Northamptonshire, c.1655–65

classical concept of a complete entity was clearly not yet understood, except by Inigo Jones. The front quad at *Oriel College, Oxford*, for example, as well as *Brasenose College Chapel*, also the chapel at *Peterhouse, Cambridge* show a blend of Gothic fenestration and detail with Flemish gabling and classical columns. A quieter, more serious approach is to be seen in the two ranges of this period in the *Clare College* quad, *Cambridge*, the east range built 1638–41 and the south 1640–2. The work is by *Thomas Grumbold*, who was also responsible for the beautiful *Clare Bridge* over the Cam, 1638–40, the oldest of the Cam bridges at the University.

Domestic Building 1650–1690: Dutch Palladianism and the 'Wren' Style

Between 1650 and 1670 a more symmetrical and purely classical house was evolved. This is often termed a 'Wren-style' house, incorrectly because the design was developed before Wren was practising as an architect and also because he designed little domestic work. Of the architects who contributed towards the purer classical trend in house design were *John Webb* (1611–74), a pupil and assistant to Inigo Jones, *Sir Roger Pratt* (1620–84) and *Hugh May* (1622–84). Much of Webb's work was for Inigo Jones' projects and his work closely followed that of his master; *Thorpe Hall*, Northamptonshire, c.1665 is one example (276, 280). Pratt's most famous house was *Coleshill*, Berkshire (1650–2), which was tragically destroyed by fire in 1952 (274). Hugh May's best known house is *Eltham Lodge* (275) in Kent, built in 1663–4, which closely resembles the Mauritshuis in the Hague (1633). Indeed, this style of building originated in the Netherlands and is in essence Dutch Palladianism. The style is so-called because the basis of design is that of Andrea Palladio. These seventeenth-century houses were strictly classical in theme, but with classical orders and ornament adapted to Flemish, and so later English, domestic needs.

Such houses were built of stone or of brick with stone dressings. In broad lines the Italian classical pattern was adhered to, with stress on the horizontal emphasis and a complete symmetry on each elevation and in the whole concept. The plan was a rectangle with an entrance in the centre of each of the long façades (274). There was a semi-basement floor and, above this, divided from it by a string course, was the principal floor called by the Italians the *piano nobile*; this was given prominence in position and proportions. Above was a further main floor and then a cornice and central pediment, balustrade and hipped roof with dormers and plain classical chimneystacks. The centrally placed entrance doorway was approached by a flight of steps to first floor level and led into the entrance hall (276, 284). An order might or might not be used, in column and pilaster form; it generally spanned two storeys (275). Larger houses had projecting side wings added to the rectangular block and a slightly advanced porch and central feature. The skyline was then sometimes broken by a lantern or cupola. *Belton House*, Lincolnshire, 1685–9, is a classic example of such a design (282).

The garden was by now becoming an essential part of the house scheme and the preference for an apparently casual, natural landscaping was beginning to be followed, in contrast to the formal layouts of the Continent, especially in France and Italy. Larger gardens could include a vegetable and orchard section as well as trees and flowers.

In the *house interior* the hall and main reception rooms (280) were placed on the *piano nobile*, with the long gallery and bedrooms above (285). Bedrooms were now chambers in their own right and no longer part of the passage; they were larger and had more furniture as well as a fireplace for heating. Kitchens were also now part of the house, even though generally situated a long way from the dining room, in whatever part of the house they could be fitted. The principal apartments had priority of position and their aesthetic appearance, on the exterior as well as the interior, was of prime consideration to the architect, who rated his clients' comfort and convenience, as well as that of their staff, as of secondary consideration.

The design and treatment of ceilings and walls had changed from Jacobean models. The ceiling and frieze were still of plaster, but a centrepiece – oval, circular or rectangular in shape – had replaced the all-over panels and strapwork. Ornament in this centrepiece was classical and naturalistic, using leaves, fruit, swags, *putti* and animals all in high relief. The cornice was enriched with classical ornament and the area between this and the centrepiece was often coved (280, 285). The central and other ceiling panels were, in large houses, painted with allegorical or historical scenes.

281 *Uppark, Sussex, south front centrepiece, 1688–90, William Talman*

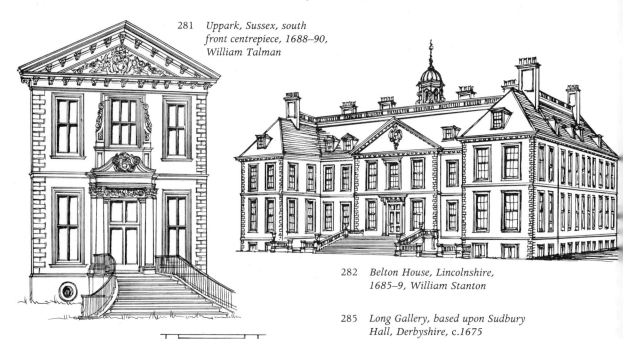

282 *Belton House, Lincolnshire, 1685–9, William Stanton*

285 *Long Gallery, based upon Sudbury Hall, Derbyshire, c.1675*

283 *Petworth House, Sussex, window, 1688–9*

284 *Manor House, Princes Risborough, Buckinghamshire*

Panelling still covered most wall surfaces but, by 1660, the whole room was designed as a single classical unit. The panelling was in oak, cedar or fir and was treated as an architectural order in correct proportion and detail. Columns and pilasters were sometimes used, in which case they were spaced round the room and extended from dado rail to cornice, with plinth below and entablature above. Doors, windows* and chimneypiece were inserted into the scheme, generally flanked by columns or pilasters and decorated in the classical manner. Between these features were rectangular panels, sometimes raised from the background by bolection moulding frames (280, 285). The woodwork was left its natural colour or was painted in white or light shades. Mouldings were carved with classical ornament, most usually egg and dart, acanthus leaf or bead and reel designs (see glossary). There was much decorative carving in the Grinling Gibbons manner framing mirrors, paintings, panels and doorways (299, 300).

The heavy oak staircase was built until the later seventeenth century, though in the middle years a continuous carved scroll and acanthus balustrade replaced the solid balusters (293). *Ham House* in Surrey has a particularly fine example (1638) as also does *Eltham Lodge*, Kent (1664–5). From the 1670s this scroll type of balustrade was replaced by slenderer, barley-sugar twisted balusters (286). Carving in panels and finials was rich and varied all the century (289, 290, 298). Interesting houses of the period include *Fawley Court*, Oxfordshire, 1684–8, *Fenton House*, Hampstead, 1693, *Honington Hall*, Warwickshire, 1685, *Petworth House*, Sussex, 1688–9 (283), and *Uppark*, Sussex, 1688–9 (281, 297).

The union of Scotland and England under one crown from 1603, when James I of England and VI of Scotland, son of Mary Queen of Scots, succeeded Elizabeth, had little effect on architecture. Classical design had only briefly touched Scottish building traditions and, despite a slow abandonment of defensive features, there was no enthusiasm for the symmetrical, rectangular house. Scottish designers

held firmly to the courtyard house in the years before the Restoration. Greater consideration was given to symmetry and there was a new mode in decoration which, like the Elizabethan of the previous century, was based upon mannerist ornament found in German and Flemish pattern books. Both on exterior and interior surfaces there appeared strapwork, cartouches, grotesques and heavily ornamented orders.

The outstanding building of the Scottish Renaissance style, a prototype for later structures here, is *Heriot's Hospital* in *Edinburgh*, built between 1628 and 1650. A square construction built round a square court, this is a strong, impressive building, Renaissance in symmetry and decoration, based, it is likely, on an Italian pattern-book drawing but retaining its Scottish baronial turrets and some Gothic fenestration in the hall and chapel ranges. Another large building, constructed later in 1679–90, but on a similar plan and grouping, is *Drumlanrig Castle*, Dumfriesshire (303). The entrance façade is more richly ornamented than Heriot's Hospital. It is approached by a curving double staircase, like that at Fontainebleau, and the house is carried on an arcaded lower storey, above which giant Corinthian pilasters extend through the first and second floors. Scottish-style turrets are still to be seen on the square corner towers.

It was not until after the Restoration that a purer form of classical architecture penetrated to Scotland and the architect, in the Inigo Jones sense of the term, made his appearance here. The later seventeenth century did not produce any architects of the stature of Inigo Jones or Wren, but the work of *Sir William Bruce* was competent and interesting in that he was able to combine a purer classicism with the Scottish vernacular so that the results were not merely vapid tracings of the Italian Renaissance. In 1671 Bruce was appointed King's Surveyor; his most important work in this office was the reconstruction of the *Palace of Holyroodhouse* in *Edinburgh*. This was not an easy task as he had to incorporate Medieval structures like the remains of the beautiful old church as well as parts of the later palace. Set against the background of King Arthur's seat and the Holyrood Park, the palace is now an impressive building, symmetrical, with its great corner towers still capped by conical turrets, but with a classical coupled-column entrance (302). Inside is the open, arcaded classical court on Roman Renaissance pattern. A further Scottish feature is in

---

* The casement window continued in use until late in the seventeenth century, but the frame, transom and mullion were of wood and built into the brickwork or stone surround. By 1680 the sash window was well established and rapidly superseded the casement pattern in general use.

286   Carved wood staircase, 1670–5

287   St Andrew-by-the-Wardrobe, London, doorway, Wren

288   Balls Park, Hertfordshire, doorway, c.1640

289/290   Staircase finials

291   St Lawrence Jewry, London, window, Wren

292   St Paul's Cathedral, London, window, Wren

293   Carved scroll-balustrade staircase

294   St Margaret Lothbury, London, doorway, Wren

296   *St Martin Ludgate, London, door-head, Wren*

295   *Hampton Court Palace, section of screen on Thames-side, Jean Tijou*

298   *Eltham Lodge, Kent, staircase panel, 1665*

297   *Uppark, Sussex, doorway detail, 1688–9*

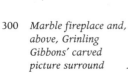

299   *Carved decoration, Grinling Gibbons*

300   *Marble fireplace and, above, Grinling Gibbons' carved picture surround*

301   *St John's College, Oxford. Canterbury Quad, frontispiece, 1631–6*

302   *Palace of Holyroodhouse. Architect, Sir William Bruce. Builder, Robert Mylne 1671–8*

303   *Drumlanrig Castle, Dumfriesshire, 1679–90*

evidence in the dormers and chimneystacks which break the courtyard skyline.

Another impressive classical building can be seen in the house which Bruce built on his own estate of *Kinross* in 1681. He was also responsible for much of the new great mansion of *Hopetoun* near Edinburgh, but his work here has been obscured by the later reconstruction by the Adam family (pages 149, 174).

Sir Christopher Wren 1632–1723

The Restoration of the Monarchy under Charles II in 1660 caused a vigorous reaction in England. The return of a young monarch who was half French and had spent much of his life up to this time on the Continent inevitably introduced an influence which violently contrasted with the Puritanism of the Commonwealth administration. The new court and aristocracy were outward-looking, young and lively. The resulting effect on the arts, painting, sculpture, architecture, music and literature, was considerable. An English Baroque expression in these arts was tentative but perceptible. The current trends in Italy and France now introduced into Britain were having an effect. It was also an age of men of outstanding quality of genius, in science as well as the arts. In the years 1660–90 such men included, apart from Wren, John Milton, Isaac Newton, Robert Hooke, Grinling Gibbons, John Dryden, Henry Purcell, John Thornhill and Robert Boyle.

The name of *Sir Christopher Wren*, Britain's leading architect, is more familiar to the public than that of any other architect and his reputation, unlike that of any of his successors, has stood uniformly high ever since his death. To say that his work dominated the architecture of Britain during the second half of the seventeenth century is no exaggeration, for he was the vital force in all the important architectural schemes of the period, directing, influencing, controlling both the design and execution of large projects such as the rebuilding of London after the fire of 1666 and the layouts at Hampton Court, Greenwich, Chelsea and the universities. He was fortunate also in that when he was beginning to practise, great opportunities opened up before him, largely due to the Great Fire of London. He obtained commissions for civic and ecclesiastical building as a result and he was able early to establish his reputation for original design. Other architects, such as Inigo Jones and

Robert Adam, had the ill-fortune to miss such opportunities. It has been mentioned that Inigo Jones was the first British architect in the modern sense of the term, and Wren followed in this tradition and fully established it, that is, as the designer of a building project who supervises all aspects of the work from its early sketches to final completion.

Christopher Wren was born at East Knoyle in Wiltshire on 20 October 1632. His father was rector of Knoyle while his uncle, Dr Matthew Wren, was also a churchman, later being consecrated Bishop of Ely. The young man was brought up in a High Church tradition with a university background. From an education at Westminster School he went on to Oxford University, where he graduated in 1651 and obtained his master's degree in 1653.

It was soon apparent that the young man was outstandingly brilliant. 'That miracle of a youth', as John Evelyn described him in 1654, was chiefly interested at this time in science. It was here that he found full expression for his inventive mind, developing theories and experiments while still at college on some 50 different problems in the fields of astronomy, physics and engineering. This was a time when experimental science was becoming of interest all over Europe. The Royal Academy of Science was established in Paris. In England, Wren joined with Robert Boyle, the physicist, Dr Wilkins, Warden of Wadham College, Oxford, Dr Scarburgh, the mathematician and others to form the Philosophic Club of Wadham. This club applied itself to a study of science and philosophy and soon its members included Isaac Newton, John Evelyn and Robert Hooke; later, it became the Royal Society.

Wren was over 30 when he launched himself, almost casually, into architecture. At 25 he had been appointed to the chair of Astronomy at Gresham College, London and at 26 returned to Oxford to become Savilian Professor of Astronomy. This background was an unusual one, even in the seventeenth century, as preparation for an architect and his scientific training had a profound effect upon his approach to architecture. He had the faculty of envisaging an extensive scheme as a whole before work was begun and, to the constructional problems of roofing large spans, providing sound structures for support and buttressing, he brought his fresh, technical approach.

It is not known exactly when Wren became

interested in architecture. In 1661 Charles II invited him to supervise the fortification of Tangier. This he declined. His first essay into architecture was to design and build a traditional classical chapel for *Pembroke College, Cambridge* (1663), at the request of his uncle, now the Bishop of Ely. It is a competent building, illustrating a certain inexperience. His second attempt was much more original, the *Sheldonian Theatre* at *Oxford*, 1664 (334). He based his design upon a Roman theatre which he had studied in Serlio's book on architecture. The prototype had been open to the sky and Wren had problems in covering the English counterpart without using supporting columns which would obstruct the view, He solved this, typically, and with the aid of his colleague, the Professor of Geometry, Dr Wallis, by means of a timber trussed roof to carry the ceiling.

Unlike Inigo Jones, Wren made only one short trip abroad. His first-hand knowledge of Continental architecture was limited and, although he studied Italian and French designs, his aim always was to produce classical buildings suited especially to his own country and this is clearly displayed in the essential Englishness of Wren's work. His great fertility of imagination enabled him to design endless variations upon the classical theme to meet this need. In 1665 he went to France on holiday and spent some months visiting châteaux and staying in Paris. In the city he met Bernini who was there to present his designs for the Louvre. Wren also saw the Palace of Versailles and, in Paris, was especially impressed by Le Vau's Collège des Quatres Nations. Wren never reached Italy but brought back a quantity of books and engravings. He had extended his architectural horizons and enriched his appreciation. In 1666 came the turning point and opportunity of his life, the event which was probably what sparked off his decision to make architecture his career.

The Rebuilding of London

In his diary, John Evelyn records for 2 September 1666 – 'This fatal night, about 10, began the deplorable fire near Fish Street in London'. Many attempts had been made since the Act of 1189 to enforce diverse laws making it compulsory to use stone, at least for party walls, in London buildings. By 1666 most of the houses, at least, were still of timber; the streets were narrow and the upper storeys projected almost to meet in the centre of the road. The local outbreak in the baker's shop in Pudding Lane was burning brightly by 1 a.m.; augmented by a strong wind and following upon a long, hot, dry spell of weather, the city was overwhelmed by a rapid conflagration. The fire moved swiftly, encouraged by the early spread among the crowded timber houses towards the Thames wharves, which were stocked by inflammable goods, also by the destruction of the water-wheel by London Bridge, which cut off the water supply to the neighbouring city areas.

London burned for four days, at the end of which time, as is shown in the City Surveyor's report, 273 acres had been destroyed within the city walls and 63 acres without. Among the buildings lost were 87 churches and 13,200 houses in 400 streets and courts. Only one-fifth of the walled city still stood.

Charles II set up a royal commission to organise the rebuilding of London. On 13 September the Royal Proclamation announced that the city would be rebuilt in brick and stone on a new plan with wider streets. Wren was appointed principal architect to be assisted by Hugh May and Sir Roger Pratt in conjunction with the city delegates, Robert Hooke, Peter Mills and Edward Jerman. Wren's plan for the new city, which had earned him the task of carrying it out, was a classical one which not only incorporated ideas from Ancient Rome but also features from his recent observations in Paris. It was a geometrical gridiron plan with focal centres (*rond-points*) to pinpoint important buildings such as St Paul's, the Guildhall and the Mint. These were linked by main thoroughfares which gave vistas to and from them. The city churches were given suitable positions and in front of St Paul's Cathedral was to be a long, wedge-shaped open space. A key point of the plan was a wide embankment quay along the Thames from Blackfriars to the Tower based on that bordering the Seine in Paris (304).

The plan was approved by King and Parliament, but foundered on the commercial interests of the city which refused to yield up part of its rights for the good of London. Only a dictatorship or an absolute monarchy, as in Napoleon's Paris, could have pushed through a scheme which ran counter to so many individual interests. The city buildings were re-erected on the same blackened sites and the narrow

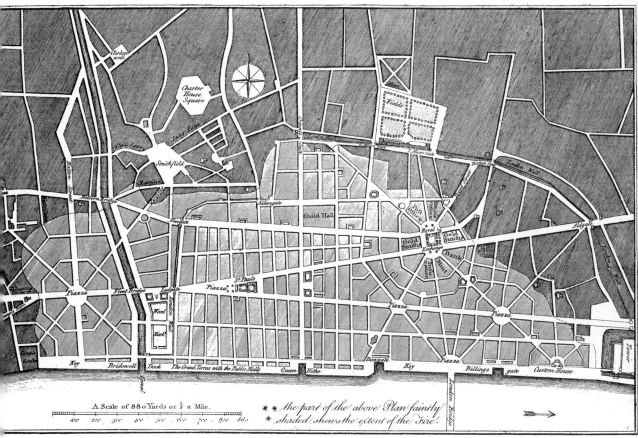

A Scale of 880 Yards or ½ a Mile.

⁎⁎ *the part of the above Plan faintly*
⁎ *shaded shews the extent of the Fire.*

Sʳ Cristopher Wren's Plan for Rebuilding the City of London after the dreadfull Conflagration in 1666.

304   *Wren's plan for London, 1666*

streets remained unaltered.*

Despite the abandonment of his plan, Wren's part in the rebuilding of London was a large one. Some of his colleagues fell by the wayside but, assisted ably by Robert Hooke, he spent many years on the task of reconstruction, notably on 53 churches, which replaced the 87 lost, and on St Paul's Cathedral. Though his city layout was frustrated, a great advance in building construction was effected as a result of the fire. A new structural standard was set up for domestic building in brick and the timber-gabled pattern was abandoned. This was widely

reflected in other towns in Britain and, over a long period, was profoundly effective.

The City Churches

In 1670 a tax was ordained by Parliament to be collected on sea coal arriving at the Port of London. The income derived from this tax was designed to pay for the rebuilding of the city churches and St Paul's Cathedral. In the years 1675–1705, which roughly covered the building enterprise, the money raised paid for the fabric of the churches, while the parishes assumed responsibility for the interior decoration and fittings.

Even in a career so full of great schemes and original architecture, Wren's city churches are out-

---

* Students of twentieth-century architecture might care to draw a parallel with the fate of Sir Patrick Abercrombie's plans after the Second World War.

305   *St Andrew-by-the-Wardrobe*

306   *Plan, St Stephen Walbrook*

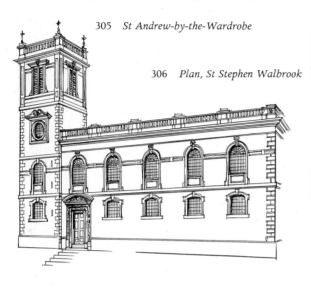

307   *Plan, St Martin Ludgate*

308   *St Bride, Fleet Street, 1670–84*

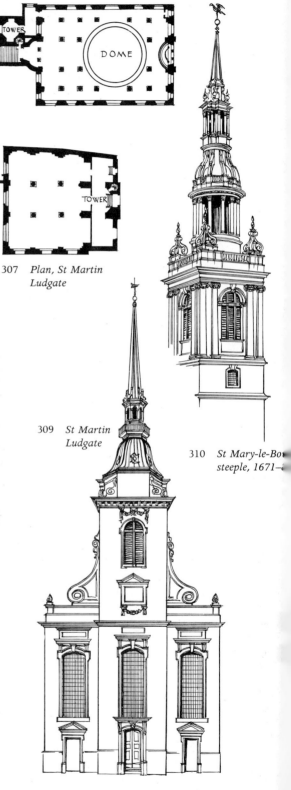

309   *St Martin Ludgate*

310   *St Mary-le-Bow steeple, 1671–*

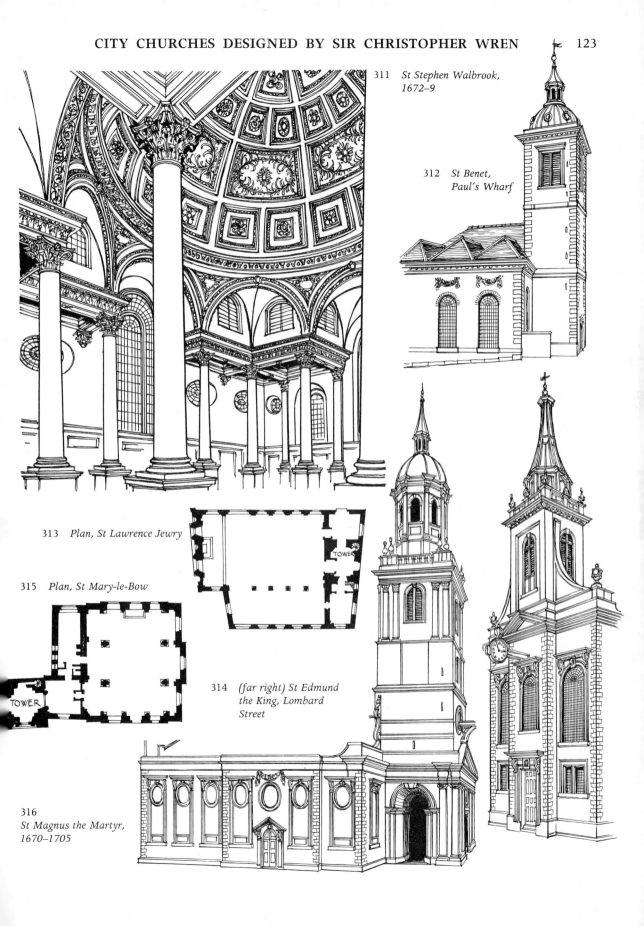

311   *St Stephen Walbrook, 1672–9*

312   *St Benet, Paul's Wharf*

313   *Plan, St Lawrence Jewry*

315   *Plan, St Mary-le-Bow*

314   *(far right) St Edmund the King, Lombard Street*

316
St Magnus the Martyr, 1670–1705

standing. They illustrate, perhaps more clearly than any other examples of his work, his fertility of imagination, his ability to solve the most intractable of problems of site, limitation of space and variation of style. None of the churches is quite like any other; they are nearly all classical in conception, though one or two were designed in Gothic to harmonise with remains. The sites are most varied and few are level or possess any parallel sides of equal length (306, 307, 313, 315). *St Benet Fink*, for example, was decagonal in plan, few churches possessed a right-angled corner, and at *St Benet, Paul's Wharf* the site was so steeply inclined that even in this small area there was a variation of 10 feet in height (312).

Wren's qualities of versatility and inventiveness are nowhere shown more clearly than in his designs for the church steeples. He had no English classical precedent to work upon and many of the designs are in classical form and ornament based upon Gothic construction. Of the tall steeples *St Mary-le-Bow* is probably the most beautiful (310, 315). The gradual build-up from square, pilastered tower and decorative parapet via a central, colonnaded drum to a slender obelisk is perfectly proportioned and gives to London an impressive, though delicate, landmark. Of scarcely less originality is the wedding-cake steeple of *St Bride* in Fleet Street (308) and the design of *Christ Church*, Newgate Street, with its diminuendo in four-faced pattern. Interesting and unusual are the tall towers surmounted by bell towers and lanterns. These vary from the lofty *St Magnus the Martyr* (316) and the delicate *St Martin Ludgate* (296, 307, 309) to the plainer *St Margaret Lothbury* (294) and *St Edmund the King* (314). Many churches have simple towers such as *St Clement Eastcheap*, *St Benet, Paul's Wharf* (312), *St Andrew-by-the-Wardrobe* (287, 305) and *St Andrew Holborn.**

Wren varied his building materials to give colour and interest to the churches. He used Portland stone and brick, together and separately, and most churches had lead belfries and gilded vanes and crosses. In general, he designed the churches on the lines of the Roman basilica, for which he drew freely upon

---

* It is thought that Wren possibly realised that in later years his church steeples would be hemmed in by commercial structures. Certainly his focal interest in the designs and the principal ornamentation is on the upper, final stages and the lower storeys of the tower are plain.

Vitruvius and Serlio. He bore in mind that these were Protestant churches being erected on what had been mainly Catholic sites. He wanted the pulpit to be visible and audible from all parts of the building in order to establish a rapport between preacher and congregation. Also, and partly for this reason, most of these churches have light interiors with large, flat-topped or round-headed classical windows filled with plain glass in contrast to the darker, more mystical Catholic equivalents.

Some of the churches are large and richly decorated, others are small and simple. Some are finer than others, partly on account of the amount of money available, but also because Wren was more closely connected with the supervision of some churches. He gathered a team of craftsmen to work with him and some of the carving, glass and ironwork is superb. Two of the richest interiors were *St Lawrence Jewry* (291, 313), the Guildhall church, and *St Bride* (308) both, sadly, gutted in the Second World War and both now restored. *St Stephen Walbrook*, near the Mansion House, was one of the larger, richer city churches and apparently used by Wren as a 'trial run' for St Paul's. His design incorporates a central dome as well as a corner steeple. The dome is carried on eight arches supported on columns (311).

The rebuilding of the city churches occupied many years and much of Wren's long life. The first church to be restored and re-opened was *St Mary-at-Hill* in 1678, the last was *St Michael Cornhill* in 1721. Wren was then 89 years old.

St Paul's Cathedral

The Medieval cathedral was not destroyed in the Fire, as were so many churches, but the damage caused to an already ailing, neglected building was, in the end, fatal. The Church Commissioners insisted on repair of the fabric but, after the collapse of extensive sections of masonry, they had to give in and asked Wren to design a new cathedral.

St Paul's is Britain's only Renaissance Cathedral. Wren made several designs for it. He was determined that it should be classical and he was strongly influenced by Michelangelo's work on St Peter's in Rome (317, 319). His favourite design, undoubtedly of greater aesthetic and dramatic quality than the final building, was the Great Model Design, made in 1673 (320, 323). It was of Greek cross pattern, with four equal arms, raised on a podium, totally symmetrical and with an immense central dome, 120 feet in diameter, crowning the structure. The project was rejected by the Church Commissioners as breaking too radically with the tradition of cathedral building in England. They wanted a cathedral with a tall spire like the previous one. Also, ecclesiastically, they wanted a Protestant cathedral not one which savoured so much of Rome. They complained that the floor space was inadequate and that there must be a long nave and choir.*

Wren made further attempts and in the final design compromised with an impressive, high, exterior dome on a colonnaded drum. The cathedral is built on orthodox Latin cross plan with long nave and the dome set over the crossing (292, 318), though a break with tradition was made in the large space under this dome (321). The west façade is symmetrical and classical, using coupled Corinthian columns in two stages with central pediment (324). The façade is nonetheless traditionally British in its twin western towers which, despite the Medieval theme, are Baroque in treatment (page 134).

Although Renaissance classical architecture had been introduced into Britain by Inigo Jones, *St Paul's Cathedral* was the first importance instance in the country of domical construction. The dome, as a structural and decorative feature, is the only major factor in the Renaissance architecture of Europe not to have been revived from Roman origins. The Romans had extensively developed stone and concrete vaulting but had not pursued the possibilities of the dome. The Pantheon dome for example is built on walls of circular plan and the problems of constructing a circular dome upon a square supporting structure were not investigated. In Renaissance and, even more widely, in Baroque European architecture, the dome was a vital structural and decorative feature. It was taken from the Byzantine development of the dome, which was one of the most important contributions of this eastern empire centred on Constantinople. The Byzantine domical structural design was, in turn, evolved from much earlier buildings in the Middle East, in Anatolia, Persia and Syria.

The Byzantine contribution was the *pendentive*, which is a satisfactory method of carrying a circular dome upon piers which stand on a square plan, and the system will support large domes. The classic early example in Istanbul is that of Santa Sophia. It was on this pattern that Italian Renaissance architects based their domes; St Peter's in Rome is of this type (317). Fig. 325 illustrates the evolution of the pendentive from the early squinch methods. In 'A' is shown the construction of a circular dome on circular walling as at the Roman Pantheon built by the Romans. This presents few problems. In 'B' the dome is supported on walls on a square plan. Here an octagonal base is provided by building across the angles of the square. The squinch method in 'C' is where an arch or series arches span the angles. This method is used in many Roman and Byzantine examples, but none of these will support a large dome or one constructed upon piers or columns.

In a pendentive method of construction the triangular spaces between the square section and the circular base of the dome are built as if they are parts of a lower and larger dome so that their section is like that of an arch carried across the diagonal of the square space to be covered. This lower dome possesses a horizontal section which is concentric with the plan of the intended dome. As the lower dome is too large to fill the square space, it is cut off in vertical planes formed by the four walls of the square. When the four remaining parts of the lower dome have been built high enough to form a complete circle within the walls of the square, this circle provides the basis for supporting the actual dome. This is shown in 'D', while in 'E' the dome is set in position above its lower dome, that is, the spherical triangles which are called pendentives. In 'F' is shown the typical Renaissance or Baroque dome, carried on a drum (pierced by windows), standing on the pendentives. Internally, pendentives are decorated by paintings or mosaics as in St Peter's (317) and in St Paul's in London (322).

In *St Paul's Cathedral* the dome is set over the crossing of a traditional, Latin cross plan. It is upheld by eight massive piers standing on the floor which, in turn, support the eight arches from which spring the pendentives and dome upon its drum. Each pier is faced with pilasters in the Corinthian Order which is used throughout the cathedral (322). Wren designed

---

* It is interesting to compare Wren's Greek cross plan (320) with that of Michelangelo for St Peter's (319). Here also, after Michelangelo's death, the nave arm was lengthened, on ecclesiastical insistence, to make the design a Latin cross one.

317   *St Peter's Basilica, Rome. Transept and crossing,*
       mainly by Michelangelo, 1547–64

319   *Michelangelo's plan,*
       St Peter's, 1547

320
Wren's Great Model
plan, St Paul's, 1673

318   *St Paul's Cathedral,*
       London, from the
       south-east. 1675–1710.
       Wren

322 *St Paul's Cathedral, London, the crossing,
Sir Christopher Wren*

323 *The Great Model design for St Paul's, 1673*

324 *St Paul's Cathedral, west front, 1675–1710*

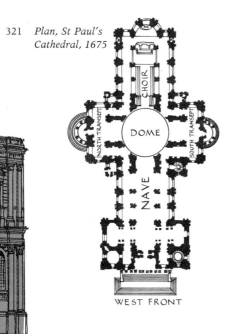

321 *Plan, St Paul's
Cathedral, 1675*

CHOIR

NORTH TRANSEPT

DOME

SOUTH TRANSEPT

NAVE

WEST FRONT

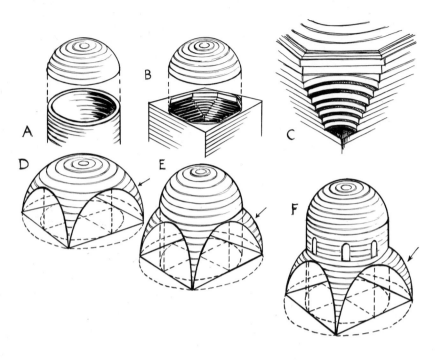

325 *Development of the Byzantine
system of Dome Construction*
A *Dome over circular drum*
B *Dome over square – squinch
across corners to make
octagon*
C *Squinch*
D *Pendentives used – single
dome with pendentive and
dome part of same
hemisphere*
E *Dome, a hemisphere set
above pendentives –
compound design*
F *Dome raised on drum
above pendentives –
compound design*

an impressive exterior dome surmounting a drum surrounded by a colonnade of Corinthian columns. This created for him a difficult construction problem as a hemispherical dome appears, on the interior, to be dark and too lofty. He dealt with the difficulty by building two domes,* an outer, taller one and an inner, shallower one, with a framework between. A brick cone surmounts the inner dome and supports the heavy lantern, the cross of which is 365 feet above the ground (318, 324).

The standard of craftsmanship in St Paul's is of a high order. The workers in different fields were selected from the best available in the 35 years of construction of the cathedral. These craftsmen also worked with Wren on the city churches, at Hampton Court and at Greenwich. Chief amongst the craftsmen of St Paul's are *James Thornhill* (painter), *Jean Tijou* (ironworker), *Joshua Marshall* (mason) and the carvers and sculptors *Jonathan Maine, Francis Bird, Caius Gabriel Cibber* and *Grinling Gibbons*.

---

* The idea of a double dome was not new. It was used in Byzantine building and in Renaissance Italy as at Brunelleschi's cathedral dome in Florence and Michelangelo's St Peter's in Rome. Wren's supporting structure was somewhat different.

Wren's Secular Designs

Apart from university work, there were three other great schemes of these years with which Wren was concerned: at Hampton Court, Greenwich and Chelsea. *Hampton Court Palace* had been built in Tudor brickwork for Henry VIII (page 72) but by the late seventeenth century was in a neglected condition. William and Mary decided to use the palace once more and asked Wren to rebuild and enlarge it. Due to the queen's death and also shortage of funds, the original scheme for demolition was fortunately amended, so the retention of the Tudor palace, incorporated into Wren's designs, has resulted, despite the blend of styles, in a harmonious whole. Wren's contribution to Hampton Court, carried out between 1689 and 1701, includes the grand entrance hall and staircase and new suites of chambers. The exterior of these façades are treated in his familiar manner of rose-coloured brick, with Portland stone for parapets, windows, columns and carving. Wren had used this attractive combination of materials so far only experimentally on one or two of his churches. This was the first example on a large scale and it was a great success (326).

The outstanding craftsmen of the day are seen at

their best at Hampton Court. There is Tijou's wonderful staircase in the entrance hall, his gates and grilles and, particularly, his Thames-side screen (295). *Jean Tijou* was a French ornamental ironworker who came to England in 1689, having fled from France in the Huguenot exodus. He was a prime mover in the revival of interest in ironwork in England in the seventeenth century. In the extensive schemes in hand at St Paul's, the city churches and Hampton Court Palace, he found full scope for expression in his medium. His influence on English ironwork was great. His own work was often ornate and freely scrolled; later, eighteenth-century ironworkers followed his lead, though in a more restrained manner suited to the age. Apart from Hampton Court Palace, Tijou's best work can be seen in St Paul's Cathedral in the circular stair in the west tower, the wrought-iron window coverings and in a number of screens and grilles.

The grand staircase hall at Hampton Court Palace is also noted for the frescoes on its walls and ceiling by *Antonio Verrio* and his colleagues. There are, too, some fine examples of the woodcarving of *Grinling Gibbons*. The story of how, in 1670, John Evelyn discovered this young man in a cottage carving a version of Tintoretto's crucifixion, is well known. Grinling Gibbons was one of the most gifted of all the craftsmen who worked with Wren. He carved in stone and worked in bronze, but his métier was really wood. In this medium he established a unique style in which he strove to recapture the realism and vitality of natural forms as portrayed by the great flower painters of the day. His work revolutionised the carving which was then being done in St Paul's and elsewhere. Hitherto the floral designs had been tightly packed and formally arranged. Gibbons carved almost in the round, with projecting sprays of leaves, flowers and fruit, rapturously flowing and laid with apparent casualness here and there, each being clearly detached from the other. This high relief work threw deep shadows on to the background and on to the other carved forms so that the whole design came alive and was vividly real (299, 300). This shows most clearly in his carving on the stalls and organ case in St Paul's.

The *Royal Hospital* at *Greenwich*, 1660–1714 (later the Royal Naval College), benefited from the experience of the greatest architects of the seventeenth century in Britain. The overall design was by Wren, but Hawksmoor and Vanbrugh (page 136) carried out

a considerable part of the scheme and showed their respect for their colleague by interpreting the design in his manner, not their own. William and Mary decided to build at Greenwich a naval counterpart to Chelsea Hospital. They gave the site and commissioned Wren to design the project, which was to be on an ambitious scale as a fitting tribute to Britain's sea power.

Wren faced the problem that he had to incorporate in his scheme both Inigo Jones' Queen's House (page 108) and the Charles II block already built by John Webb in 1665. The final design was planned with buildings on two sides of an open vista which terminated in the Queen's House (see plan 328). Wren was not fully satisfied with his scheme, for he felt, as have many later critics, that the Queen's House was too small in scale to terminate the vista suitably. Wren, assisted by Hawksmoor, supervised the work until 1702, when Vanbrugh took over. The hall dome and colonnade was completed by 1704 and the chapel side in 1716 (329). Despite criticisms of Greenwich Hospital, such as that the imposing colonnade vista leads nowhere and the unsatisfactory design of the dome drums, there is a grandeur and spaciousness about the complete scheme which strikes the beholder, especially when disembarking from the Thames pier. The approach by river towards the elegant domes and colonnades, retreating in perspective towards the distant classical prototype of the Queen's House, is a dramatic one. The layout spans English classical architecture from its first exponent, Inigo Jones, to the leader of the Baroque school, Sir John Vanbrugh.

The work of *Sir James Thornhill*, the painter, is displayed in the grand manner at Greenwich, where he painted the walls and ceiling of the great hall. His style was sympathetic to the large-scale allegory and his work was predominantly Baroque. At Greenwich the scale was especially suited to him, as was also the dome of St Paul's, where he painted scenes from the life of St Paul. He found full expression for his preference for Baroque when he later worked on the great hall at Blenheim (page 136).

Sir Stephen Fox, while Paymaster-General of the Army, was the chief promoter of the scheme to build the *Royal Hospital, Chelsea*, an idea suggested by Les Invalides in Paris, which had been founded in 1670. Here Wren, who was commissioned to design the scheme, had no restrictions of space or existing

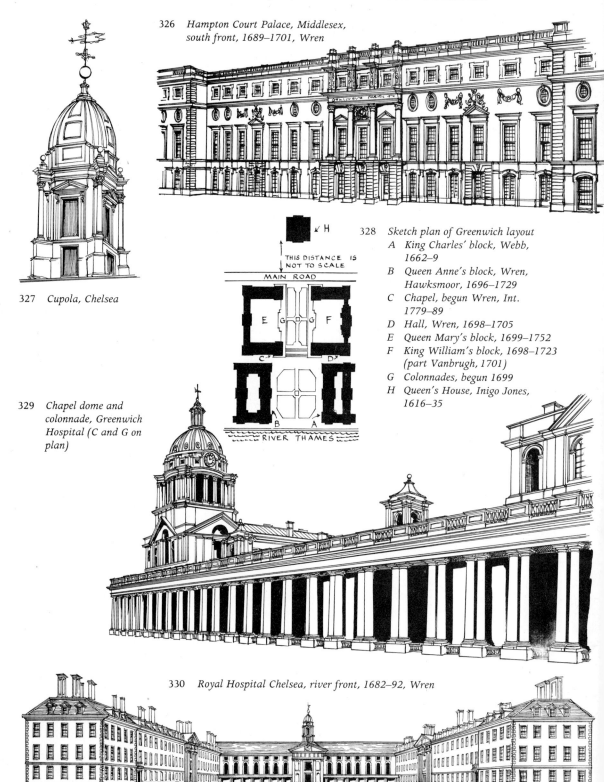

326   *Hampton Court Palace, Middlesex, south front, 1689–1701, Wren*

327   *Cupola, Chelsea*

H

THIS DISTANCE IS NOT TO SCALE

MAIN ROAD

E   G   G   F

C   D

B   A

RIVER THAMES

328   *Sketch plan of Greenwich layout*
A   *King Charles' block, Webb, 1662–9*
B   *Queen Anne's block, Wren, Hawksmoor, 1696–1729*
C   *Chapel, begun Wren, Int. 1779–89*
D   *Hall, Wren, 1698–1705*
E   *Queen Mary's block, 1699–1752*
F   *King William's block, 1698–1723 (part Vanbrugh, 1701)*
G   *Colonnades, begun 1699*
H   *Queen's House, Inigo Jones, 1616–35*

329   *Chapel dome and colonnade, Greenwich Hospital (C and G on plan)*

330   *Royal Hospital Chelsea, river front, 1682–92, Wren*

331 *Nevile's Court, Trinity College, Cambridge. The Library, 1676–84, Wren*

333 *St John's Bridge over the Cam, Cambridge, late 17th century*

332 *The Tower of the Five Orders, Bodleian Library, Oxford, 1613–36*

334 *The Sheldonian Theatre, Oxford, 1669, Wren*

335 *White Horse Close,*
Canongate, Edinburgh.
17th century, redeveloped
1965

336 *Town Hall,*
Abingdon,
Berkshire,
1677–80

337 *Custom House,*
King's Lynn,
1681, Henry Bell

338 *Market House, Tetbury, Gloucestershire, 1700*

buildings and was presented with a site which extended uninterruptedly to the river. The layout of this army hospital, which was built in the decade 1682–92, is simple. It forms three sides of a quadrangle open to the river. In the centre block are the hall and chapel with a cupola set over all (327). The Doric Order, in giant form, is used in the central portico. The whole design is quiet and restrained, carried out in red brick and stone (330).

The Universities 1660–1690

Wren also made the chief impact in this field of work during these years. Apart from Pembroke College Chapel and the Sheldonian Theatre, already mentioned (page 120), he completed Tom Tower at *Christ Church*, *Oxford* in 1681–2 in Gothic style (214) and designed the chapel and other building at *Emmanuel College, Cambridge*, 1666–73. His finest work at Cambridge is the *Library*, occupying one side of Nevile's Court at *Trinity College*. Built 1676–84, the library is a masterpiece of simple perfection in composition. It is a long rectangular building of two storeys surmounted by a parapet. The Doric Order is used in the lower storey, which has an open arcade, and the Ionic Order above it, flanking the window openings. The statues surmounting the parapet of the façade representing Divinity, Law, Physics and Mathematics, are the work of the sculptor *Caius Gabriel Cibber*, a Dane who also worked with Wren at St Paul's and elsewhere (331).

The interior, completed in 1695, is superbly decorated by Grinling Gibbons' carving, especially on the bookcase panels.

CHAPTER SEVEN

The English Baroque 1690–1730

In art and architecture, Italy was the source of the Baroque as it had been for the Renaissance. The underlying force of the Baroque movement was also based upon a new process of thinking, this time not towards Humanism but from Humanism back towards the Church. A deep feeling had arisen: a desire for a re-introduction of spiritual values; evidence of man's need for belief in something greater than himself. Among other Orders in the sixteenth century, the Jesuits were instrumental in re-establishing a Christian way of life more suited to the contemporary world than the outgrown Medieval concept. The Roman Catholic church, aided by the revitalised gaiety and pageantry of its building, made much of the opportunity to attract people back to its fold. Bernini, the greatest of the Baroque artists, was a master of the dramatic form and lighting effects so typical of the Baroque interpretation of the current Christian approach.

From Italy the Baroque architectural forms spread throughout Europe, but the style was suited chiefly to the southern, Latin peoples of Catholic faith. This was partly for its religious significance and partly because it is an extrovert, rich, colourful form. In the greyer, Protestant north – in Britain, northern Germany, Holland and Scandinavia – it gained only a foothold; there classical architecture remained for much of the eighteenth century, cool and aloof, in straight lines and pure tones. Apart from Italy, Baroque architecture is found in its more vigorous and characteristic manner in Southern Germany, Austria, Switzerland, Czechoslovakia, Hungary, Spain and Portugal.

One of its predominant characteristics is a free use of curves (within the classical framework of orders and ornament). These curves, often of whole walls and ceilings, advance from convex to concave. It was Robert Adam (page 173) who, describing Baroque design as a feeling for 'movement', quoted St Peter's in Rome as the prime example. He referred to the balance and contrast of the convexity of Michelangelo's dome in relation to Bernini's concave piazza colonnade. Another important feature of Baroque architecture, especially of the interior, is the dramatic lighting effects in painting, sculpture and architecture, since all three arts are always fused in Baroque to blend into a unified creation. The favourite ground plan is oval as this lends itself to a maximum feeling for movement. Rich, sensuous vitality in colour, form and light is the keynote of Baroque work in all media.

Although several theories have been put forward for the origin of the term Baroque it is thought that the most likely is that it derives from the Portuguese word *barocco*, meaning an ill-formed, imperfect or grotesque pearl. It was first applied in a derogatory sense rather in the same way that the word Gothic was coined earlier (page 37). This was a reference to the strange, curving, sometimes bulbous shapes to be seen in this type of architecture. In the nineteenth century such design was looked down upon as being simply a late, decadent form of Renaissance classicism. It is less than 100 years since Baroque design was recognised as a style in its own right.

Baroque architecture in England takes a diverse form. The curves are only occasionally to be seen, but the movement, violent and discordant, is present, evidenced in the strong massing of shapes, dramatic light and shade and large scale grandeur. The Baroque school was short-lived here; by 1730 it was over and the British returned to a Palladianism first introduced by Inigo Jones, its order and tranquillity more suited to the temperament of the people than the emotional violence and voluptuousness of Baroque.

Different in interpretation though it may be, the later work of Wren, that of Talman and, especially, the designs of Vanbrugh, Hawksmoor and Archer cannot be termed anything other than Baroque for the buildings display the chief characteristics of the concept. Wren's designs showed a tendency towards Baroque in his late seventeenth-century work. The west towers of *St Paul's Cathedral*, for instance (324) and, even more, the domes and colonnades at *Greenwich* (329) are plastic and vibrantly alive. But Wren's Baroque was always restrained and controlled; classicism was paramount over extravagance. The designs never got out of hand. In this, as always, Wren was essentially English.

The end of Wren's career was unhappily beset by jealousies and intrigues. The old man had lived too long; new ideas in architecture were being put forward and the next generation of architects wanted a different approach. In 1714, when Queen Anne died, Wren was 82. He had led the architectural field in all principal appointments for nearly 50 years and younger men, who had worked for and with him, such as Nicholas Hawksmoor, were breaking new ground. George I, who acceded in 1714, preferred the newer approach. As Wren did not resign his Survey-orship, he was somewhat shabbily relieved of his post in 1718 on the pretext of a minor disagreement about the completion of St Paul's. His dignified acceptance of the situation was made in these words: 'having worn out by God's Mercy a long life in the Royal Service and made some Figure in the World, I hope it will be allowed me to die in peace'. This he did at the age of 91 in 1723.

Sir John Vanbrugh 1664–1726

Of the new generation of architects who worked in the English Baroque style, so different from the restrained and delicate classicism of Wren, Vanbrugh was the most colourful. Like Wren he came to architecture in his thirties, but his training and experience for it were in total contrast. Vanbrugh was of Flemish descent and this comes through in his work, seen in the extrovert robustness, elaboration and a tendency to coarseness of architectural form. In his youth he studied art in France, then spent some

time in the army, after which he launched himself into a successful career as a playwright.

In 1699, at the age of 35, Vanbrugh turned to architecture. He had studied building on the Continent and his first attempt at design was the stupendous mansion which he built for the Earl of Carlisle, *Castle Howard* in Yorkshire. Work was begun in 1701 and, like all Vanbrugh's conceptions, was in the grand manner with an enormous frontage and impressive hall. Castle Howard set the pattern for his designs, which were not rigidly defined blocks as in the seventeenth century, but grouped buildings of forceful, powerful masses, often discordantly contrasting with one another. Some of the work is coarse, particularly the detail, but Vanbrugh was a master of three-dimensional form in stone, adept at creating exciting, if violent, patterns in light and shade in settings of grandeur. His Flemish ancestry shows in his Baroque treatment of classicism, in the robustness of his porticoes, towers and wall articulation.

At *Castle Howard* the central block is surmounted by a large drum and cupola which dominate the structure (339). Inside, the great hall (341) is square, its giant Corinthian pilasters supporting the arches upon which the drum rises. The hall itself is spacious and imposing but the interior dome above is lofty and narrow (only 27 feet in diameter and 77 feet above floor level); the price that has been paid to achieve the impressive exterior silhouette.* On the north elevation of the house (346) curving arcades advance to bound a great open court on either side of which are extensive groups of buildings which accommodate kitchens,† stables, laundry, etc.

The creation of *Blenheim Palace*, Oxfordshire, 1705–22, was Vanbrugh's supreme triumph. A present from a grateful nation to the Duke of Marlborough, this immense structure seemed to be designed especially for display, rather than comfort and convenience. With Castle Howard and the later Seaton Delaval (1720–9), these houses were the last of these gigantic residences which became obsolete because of their sheer size and cost; they represent domestic architecture in the palatial grand manner.

This combined palace and castle also presented

---

* Wren's solution of this problem is discussed on page 128.

† As can be seen in 346, the kitchens were almost as far as possible from the dining rooms. In an age of ample supplies of servants this was not regarded as a problem.

339 *North front, 1699–1712, Sir John Vanbrugh*

340 *Park gateway*

341 *Entrance hall*

Vanbrugh with his greatest difficulties. The militant Duchess of Marlborough made no secret of her disapproval of the choice of architect and the design. Her relations with Vanbrugh steadily deteriorated during the years of building until Vanbrugh was finally excluded from his own work and the house was completed by Hawksmoor after the original architect's death.

Blenheim Palace as it stands today, in the superb setting of its park at Woodstock (342), is a remarkable house, both for its colossal scale and the superb Baroque treatment of its weighty and conflicting masses. The great centre block with its Corinthian portico is theatrical, even ostentatious, but its scale is absorbed in the greater compass of the complete frontage, extending to 856 feet (344). The centrepiece is connected to the massively castellar side pavilions by curved colonnades of Doric columns. Beyond these, forming the side wings of the *cour d'honneur*, are the stable and kitchen courts surrounded by their groups of buildings (342). Though quite different from the Italian Baroque of Borromini or Bernini – for there are few curves or undulations – the conception of Blenheim could be described by no other term than Baroque. Surprisingly, in contrast to the Baroque treatment of rustication, pediments, portico and colonnades, the detail is often simple as, for example, in the plain window openings (350). Inside are the superbly decorated great hall and reception rooms, decoration which includes especially the magnificent ceiling and wall paintings by *Sir James Thornhill* and *Louis Laguerre*.

Vanbrugh's architectural career was less than 30 years, much shorter than Wren's. Apart from Castle Howard and Blenheim, he was appointed to succeed Wren as Surveyor at *Greenwich Hospital* in 1716 and worked there until he died 10 years later. In the same years, apart from continuing at Blenheim, he built *Seaton Delaval*, the house at *Eastbury* in Dorset and his own house at Greenwich. This, *Vanbrugh Castle*, was begun in 1716 and is a Baroque version, very personally Vanbrugh, of a Medieval castle with towers and machicolations. In this, his own house, Vanbrugh had no fractious client to placate and he was able to explore his own ideas without hindrance.

House Design 1690–1730

Though such palatial residences as Castle Howard and Blenheim were not typical of the larger country house of these years, they exercised a certain influence. From 1700 the rectangular block with slightly projecting wings, typical of the Dutch Palladian house, gave place to a main rectangular block which was extended towards a three-sided forecourt by curving or straight colonnades which, in turn, connected to side wings or grouped buildings. The principal floor, the *piano nobile*, was given precedence of space and size and much of the plan of the rest of the house was sacrificed to the height and nobility of the reception rooms on this floor. Here were to be found the hall and saloon; an exterior staircase led to the front door at this level.

The outstanding example of the large house of these years is *Chatsworth* in Derbyshire. Here the work of the main block, encompassing the courtyard, was carried out in stages and by different architects. The south façade (1686–96), by *William Talman** is correctly classical while *Thomas Archer's* north front (1705) is more Baroque, with a semi-elliptical bow section. In plan, Chatsworth comprises a great block of apartments disposed round an inner courtyard. Inside there can be seen some of the finest staterooms in England, also a chapel. No expense was spared to obtain the services of the most eminent artists and craftsmen. There are magnificent wall and ceiling paintings by *Antonio Verrio, Louis Laguerre* and *Sir James Thornhill*, while the woodcarving in particular is superb. The whole richly decorated and finished interior was carried out with great care over a long period (345, 347).

Typical of the smaller *town house* design is the rectangular block of *Mompesson House* in Salisbury. Here is a two-storeyed house with equal prominence given to the windows of both floors. Above is a cornice and hipped roof with dormers and chimneystacks. The decorative classical doorway provides the centre focus. Another example is the Headquarters of the National Trust, *No. 42, Queen Anne's Gate in London* (348).

The interior decoration of the main reception rooms and hall of such medium-sized houses had become plainer. The plaster ceiling was now enriched by simple low relief ribs and the walls were plainly

---

* Talman is also known for his work at Dyrham Park, Gloucestershire, where he rebuilt the earlier manor house between 1692 and 1704.

342 *Aerial view of house and park, 1705–22, Sir John Vanbrugh*

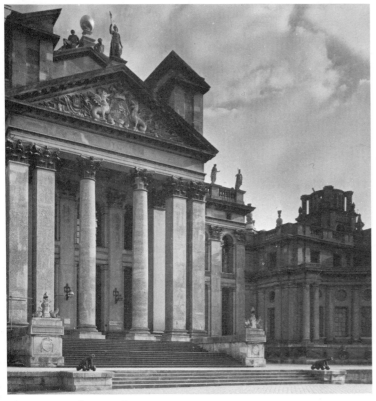

344 *Entrance front portico*

343 *Frontispiece gateway*

345   *Chatsworth House, Derbyshire. The west front*

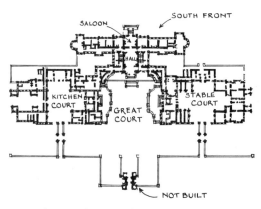

346   *Plan, Castle Howard*

347   *The State Bedroom, Chatsworth*

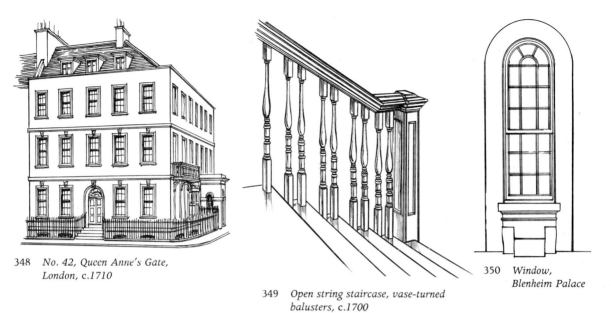

348   *No. 42, Queen Anne's Gate,
      London, c.1710*

350   *Window,
      Blenheim Palace*

349   *Open string staircase, vase-turned
      balusters, c.1700*

351   *Queen Anne Dining Room, 1702–10*

panelled. Some examples were designed with an order, others were without. The polished wood floor was now adorned by a rug or two, though these were still imported and costly,* but furniture was becoming more varied and there was a greater variety of pieces. The windows were of sash design and the doors wood-panelled (351). Staircases, still of wood, had more delicate balusters, vase-turned or barley-sugar twisted. The balustrate was now of open string design, that is, the balusters were set immediately into the stairs instead of the earlier model where they were inserted into a baulk of timber called the string; this was a closed string design. The handrail was now finely moulded and finials were rarely seen (349).

Nicholas Hawksmoor 1661–1736

Hawksmoor spent his whole life in the study of building and architecture. At the age of 18 he came to London and began to work for Wren, at that time as his domestic clerk. He assisted Wren on many projects and quickly absorbed the skill and knowledge needed to make his help invaluable. He was engaged on work at *Chelsea Hospital* (page 129), *the city churches* (page 121), *St Paul's Cathedral* (page 124), *Hampton Court Palace* and *Greenwich Hospital* (page 128/9). In 1705 he became the Deputy-Surveyor of Works for Greenwich. About 1700 Hawksmoor came into close association with Vanbrugh and worked with him on the Vanbrugh great houses.

Despite this long and close association, first with Wren and then with Vanbrugh, Hawksmoor developed his own style and in the first 35 years of the eighteenth century carried out a great deal of his own work, chiefly in ecclesiastical and university projects. Though entirely English in origin, Hawksmoor's Baroque designs were as controversial and forceful as Vanbrugh's. By the time he came to build his famous London churches and university courts he was an architect of great experience and long training. His Baroque work is entirely original; no-one having seen and studied a Hawksmoor church could possibly mistake this style for that of any other architect. Some of his churches, also his university work at All Souls, for instance, have a strong Gothic flavour. Indeed,

this Medievalism is an integral component of English Baroque, unique to this country.

In 1706 Hawksmoor designed the stone house at *Easton Neston* near Towcester. This, his one large domestic building, was articulated with a giant order of Corinthian pilasters standing upon a rusticated base. There is a beautiful staircase inside; also some wall paintings by Thornhill.

In 1711 an Act of Parliament was passed providing for the building of 50 new churches to minister to parishioners in the expanding suburbs of London. This was the first large-scale church building scheme since Wren's rebuilding of the city churches. These were to be new structures in the contemporary architectural idiom. In the first 30 years of the eighteenth century only a dozen churches were built under the Surveyorship of Hawksmoor and William Dickinson, though the latter was soon replaced by Gibbs (page 147) and then by James (page 159 and 360). The largest contribution, six churches, was made by Hawksmoor and his reputation as an architect stands in no small measure upon these highly original, individualistic designs. They are all different and all show vitality and power. They lack grace and delicacy, it is difficult to see beauty, but they are compelling and arouse admiration (albeit sometimes reluctant) and refuse to be ignored. As four of them are in London's East End and one in the City, it was inevitable that they should have received severe damage from bombing in the Second World War. Due to their massiveness of design and construction, much of the exteriors survived except for *St Alphege, Greenwich*, 1712–14, which was reduced to a shell.

St Mary Woolnoth, 1716–27 (353), is the only city church among the six. It is a most original design set upon a square plan. It has a solid-looking rectangular tower with Corinthian columns in the centre stage. Much of the lower section of the church is rusticated. *St Anne's Limehouse*, 1712–14, has a tall semi-circular porch at one end. The tower rises by diminishing stages to a final, multi-sided upper feature. *St George-in-the-East*, 1715–23, whose interior was badly damaged, also has a multi-sided top feature. *Christ Church, Spitalfields*, 1723–9 (354) is the most individualistic of the East End churches. Here a rectangular, classical tower of great width ascends to a Medieval-type spire. The projecting porch below is of powerful design in the Doric Order, the entablature

---

* Carpet weaving was carried on in England from 1700 onwards and Wilton carpets began to be made.

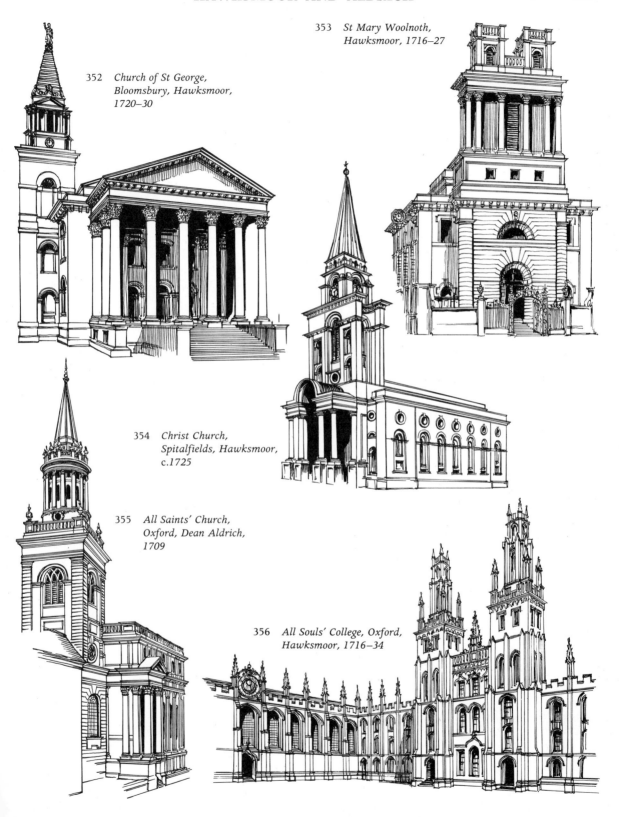

353 *St Mary Woolnoth, Hawksmoor, 1716–27*

352 *Church of St George, Bloomsbury, Hawksmoor, 1720–30*

354 *Christ Church, Spitalfields, Hawksmoor, c.1725*

355 *All Saints' Church, Oxford, Dean Aldrich, 1709*

356 *All Souls' College, Oxford, Hawksmoor, 1716–34*

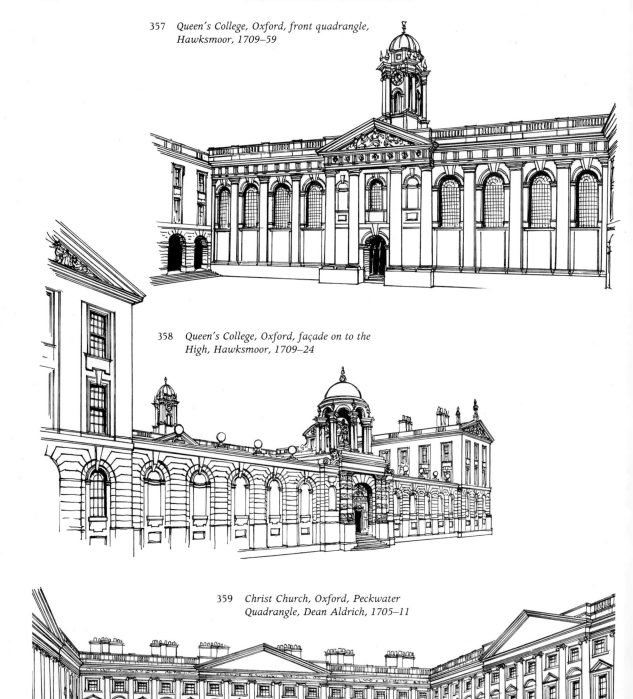

357   *Queen's College, Oxford, front quadrangle, Hawksmoor, 1709–59*

358   *Queen's College, Oxford, façade on to the High, Hawksmoor, 1709–24*

359   *Christ Church, Oxford, Peckwater Quadrangle, Dean Aldrich, 1705–11*

broken by a semi-circular arch. All of these Hawksmoor churches are very large buildings and *St George, Bloomsbury*, 1720–30 (352) the only church of the six in London's West End, is no exception. Erected on a square plan, it has a giant Corinthian portico raised on a podium, approached by steps. The tower is set at the side of the church and the steeple rises in stepped pyramidal form to the statue of King George at the top.

Hawksmoor's ecclesiastical work was obviously so original and of such telling standard that, when Wren died in 1723, Hawksmoor was appointed Surveyor at *Westminster Abbey*. Under his Surveyorship the western towers, long under discussion, were at last designed and built. The towers are hardly pure in style but they have now become a familiar and affectionately regarded London landmark.

University Building

Dr Henry Aldrich made extensive architectural contributions to *Oxford* while Dean of Christ Church. At *Trinity College* he designed the chapel (c.1690), a successful and charming work much in the style of Wren. Inside is some exquisite carving by Grinling Gibbons. In addition to the Fellows' Building at *Corpus Christi* (1706–12), Aldrich also designed the *Peckwater Quad* at *Christ Church* in 1705–6. Here, he planned three almost identical sides, pilastered in the Ionic Order. Each side has a centrepiece with pediment above. The result is dignified and monumental, if a little monotonous (359). The fourth side was completed after his death in 1710.

In Oxford he was also responsible for the *Church of All Saints* (355). Built 1707–10, this church is not of the stature of Wren's or Hawksmoor's work but does provide a link between the two periods of ecclesiastical building. The steeple is reminiscent of St Mary-le-Bow though the lower part of the church has a tall portico nearer to Hawksmoor. The rectangular, galleried interior has suffered from nineteenth-century restoration.

The most important Baroque work carried out at the Universities in these years was Hawksmoor's extensive rebuilding of *Queen's College*. By 1670 the Medieval buildings here had become dilapidated and, as the college was now wealthy, it was decided to rebuild on an ambitious scale. *Nicholas Hawksmoor*, entrusted with the task, began by building a fine

Library, which was influenced to no small degree by Wren's Library at Trinity College, Cambridge, but it is differently proportioned. The library at Queen's has a central pedimented feature with the order confined to this while the remainder of the façade is astylar.

In 1709 Hawksmoor continued his work at Queen's by beginning the scheme for rebuilding the *front quad*. The plan conceived the erection of a hall and chapel as a symmetrical block with a residential wing on each side advancing towards the High Street; the fourth side of the quad, fronting the High was then completed by a screen and gateway. The hall and chapel block has a central pedimented feature in the Doric Order and Doric pilasters are continued across the whole elevation. In the centre rises a cupola reminiscent of Wren's design at Chelsea Hospital (357). The screen fronting the High has tall terminal pavilions, each pedimented, and these pavilions are connected by a rusticated screen, punctuated by ten niches. The centre gateway, flanked by coupled, rusticated Doric columns, is covered overall by a large cupola (358).

Another work by Hawksmoor at Oxford is the *Clarendon Building*, built as the University Printing House in 1713–14. It is a robust classical structure on Roman lines with a giant Doric portico.

Hawksmoor was also responsible for the rebuilding of *All Souls' College* in the years 1716–34. Christopher Codrington, Fellow of the College, left his library and money for housing it to his college. It was decided to rebuild the quadrangle with the library on the north side and a hall and chapel on a different elevation. Hawksmoor was asked to make and carry out designs for this, but whereas at Queen's College the Medieval buildings had been demolished to make way for a classical scheme, at All Souls' he was asked to design in Gothic to fit the existing work. This he did, so the whole quadrangle is in Gothic pattern. An arcaded screen with central gateway fronts the High while, on the fourth side, he designed two large towers planned on the model of a Medieval gateway, but there is no gateway here. This is not Gothic architecture, but the Medieval spirit with Baroque display and scale of power. The design has no Medieval humility but is majestic architecture on cathedral scale (356).

360 *St George's, Hanover Square, London, John James, 1713–14*

361 *St Paul's Deptford, London, Thomas Archer, 1730*

362 *St John's Church, Westminster, Thomas Archer, 1714–28*

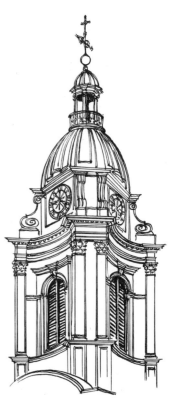

363 *Birmingham Cathedral tower, Thomas Archer, 1709–25*

Thomas Archer 1668–1743

The last member of the triumvirate of English Baroque architects had a different preparation for his career from either Vanbrugh or Hawksmoor. Archer's training was the classic approach followed by most eighteenth-century architects. He was educated at Oxford, then studied on the Continent for four years, seeing at first hand in Italy the ancient classical buildings as well as the work of contemporary Italian architects. This preparation gave him advantages in breadth of vision and knowledge of the wide spectrum of classical design. Unfortunately much of his work has been lost or altered but we still have his north elevation at Chatsworth with its pilastered bow front.

The chief remains of Archer's work are in ecclesiastical architecture and here he displays a greater variety and sensitivity in design, though less self-conscious individuality, than his two colleagues. In 1709–15 he designed the Church of St Philip in *Birmingham*, now the *Cathedral*. This is a large, simplified Baroque structure, still finely sited in the centre of the city. The tower is of especial interest. Its four faces are concave with belfry openings flanked by coupled Corinthian pilasters; the cupola above is gracefully proportioned (363).

The other two churches for which Archer is known are in marked contrast to one another. *St Paul's Church, Deptford*, 1730, is a graceful building of considerable beauty standing in pleasant garden surroundings in a drab district of London. The body of the church is solid and powerful, fronted by a Baroque Doric portico, but above rises a slender, delicate steeple after the style of Wren (361). The *Church of St John* in Smith Square, *Westminster* was less fortunate in that, unlike St Paul's, it did not escape the bombs of the Second World War. It was gutted in 1940 and stood a stark, burnt-out shell for many years before it was rescued and restored to its original condition in 1964–9. It is now used as a concert hall. There is nothing delicate or reminiscent of Wren about St John's. It is a massive, uncompromising Baroque church standing four-square, with its corner towers and matching elevations filling completely the London square which it occupies. Like Vanbrugh's Blenheim and Hawksmoor's Christ Church, Spitalfields, St John's is an individual, powerful building, handled with vitality (362). Inside the church is more traditional, designed and decorated in the Roman Baroque manner with barrel vaulted ceiling supported on giant Corinthian columns. The wood side galleries are carried on Ionic columns.

CHAPTER EIGHT

Gibbs and the English Palladians 1710–1760

Judged by the standards of today, the eighteenth century appears a time of great contrasts. Magnificent mansions and houses were built in gracious parkland, but sanitation, hygiene and convenience received scant attention. The sons of the wealthy took the Grand Tour to enlarge their appreciation of the arts; the majority of the population had little education at all. Medical science made slow headway against the people's strong belief in superstition, witchcraft, magic charms and home remedies which were thought to cure anything from rheumatism to venereal disease. Vast quantities of food were consumed by the upper classes, but the poor in town slums starved. Improvements in agriculture were producing better bread, more meat and a better standard of food for the majority of people, yet over-eating by the wealthy caused them indigestion and, in many cases, shortened their lives.

Yet, in domestic architecture and the arts, the eighteenth century was Britain's 'golden age'. It is not easy to explain exactly why these years were so propitious to the creation of beautiful buildings, superbly decorated with such a high quality of craftsmanship in all fields. It was not simply because Britain was wealthy and under no threat. Victorian Britain was even wealthier and at peace for most of the nineteenth century, yet few art historians would suggest that here was a 'golden age' in their subject. Partly it was an accident of time in that the condition of architecture and the visual arts had reached this stage of high achievement after climbing up to this peak over the previous centuries. There had been a steady development in the classical arts since the

time of Elizabeth I, but probably the most important factor in creating the most suitable climate for the flowering of these arts was the patronage of the aristocracy.

In Britain, the aristocracy functioned better as patron of the visual arts than even the monarchy had done in earlier years, for the monarch and his court had one viewpoint; the aristocracy was multiple. Some monarchs had good taste and were knowledgeable and interested in the arts; others had not and were not. The aristocracy, at their stage of development in the eighteenth century, were, on the whole, knowledgeable and had good taste. They were numerous and so could employ large numbers of architects, artists and craftsmen in all the allied trades and, due to their extensive European travels, knew exactly what they wished to create and possess. They demanded the highest standards, wishing to emulate the great palaces and houses which they had seen abroad and each to build one in the latest fashion greater than that of his acquaintances. To get what they wanted, unlike the middle classes and bureaucratic governments of the twentieth century, they did not count the cost. Indeed, it was not unknown for the head of an eighteenth-century aristocratic family to almost bankrupt the estate in order to create the mansion set in its parkland.

This supremacy in standards set an example to the less wealthy professional and middle classes. Their houses, decoration and contents were not so ambitious or costly, but their quality, though plainer, was in good taste. In a Britain where the industrial revolution had not yet swept skilled workers into the towns, country craftsmen of intelligence worked with care and devotion to produce things of beauty, whether in furniture, furnishings, pictures, silverware or ceramics. The simple builder based his designs for windows, doorways and ceilings upon the handbooks of architecture and decoration produced by the great architects of the day. The proportions and detail of these were laid down for him, meticulously worked out and evolved from 100 years of English experimentation in classical architecture.

James Gibbs 1682–1754

Gibbs was one of the architects whose books influenced later architects and builders, not only in Britain but also in America. His own work was not mainstream, for that was developing into Palladianism by 1720. Neither was he an English Baroque architect of the Vanbrugh/Hawksmoor school. Gibbs was always an individualist, his work influenced by different schools and especially by Wren, but he remained all his life, architecturally, 'the man who walked alone'. Paradoxically, it was Gibbs' books which had the widest influence, especially on the other side of the Atlantic where, on the eastern seaboard, 'Gibbs' churches, houses and colleges abound, though generally built in wood rather than stone. The two books which were especially known were his *A Book of Architecture*, published 1728, and *Rules for Drawing the several parts of Architecture*, 1732.

James Gibbs was one of the outstanding architects of these years. Though not an innovator, he showed brilliance of technical skill in the handling of his materials and in architectural design. He left his native Scotland when still a young man and spent some time travelling on the Continent. Later he was accepted in Rome at the Studio of Fontana, who was then at work on St Peter's. Gibbs worked in Rome during the years 1707–9 and this gave him the advantage over his British colleagues in that he had studied both in practice and theory at the fountain head.

In his first important commission after his return to Britain, the *Church of St Mary-le-Strand* in *London*, Gibbs' design showed his debt both to Roman Baroque and to Sir Christopher Wren. The body of the church was influenced by the years in Rome and the steeple reflects Gibbs' admiration for Wren's city

churches (366). Gibbs continued his ecclesiastical work by completing the neighbouring church of *St Clement Dane* (a Wren church to which Gibbs added the steeple) and by designing the smaller church of *St Peter* in Vere Street, *London*.

In 1722–6 he built his masterpiece, *St Martin-in-the-Fields* in *Trafalgar Square*, which was one of the most important buildings of the time and certainly the finest church. Its influence was deep and widespread; copies and designs obviously inspired by it can be seen in England, but even more so in the United States, where a number of churches in different States were erected to Gibbs' designs. St Martin-in-the-Fields is fronted by a magnificent Corinthian portico and this order is continued round the building in pilaster form. Gibbs broke with tradition here in his construction of the steeple. In order to save space and provide a compact design, he built the tower inside the west wall so that it emerges from the roof immediately behind the portico. This is in contradistinction to Wren and Hawksmoor, who always designed the tower to stand with its base visibly upon the ground. Gibbs had first experimented with a similar scheme in St Mary-le-Strand, where the steeple appears to grow out of the body of the church. Both this building and St Martin's were strongly criticised by the classical purists, but Gibbs' churches are structurally sound and have been judged aesthetically satisfactory by later generations. In the steeple itself, the Ionic and Corinthian Orders are used; the handling owes much to Wren's designs (365). Inside, the church has five bays and is aisled. The ceiling has an elliptical barrel vault, the decoration of which was carried out by the Italian stuccoists *Artari* and *Bugatti* (364).

James Gibbs' contribution to domestic architecture was not extensive. He designed the attractive *Sudbrooke Lodge* in *Petersham*, Surrey in 1718 and the larger house at *Ditchley* in Oxfordshire in 1720. His main field of work, apart from his churches, is *university building*. In his *Radcliffe Camera* at *Oxford*, built between 1739 and 1749, he returned to Roman Baroque in a bold, exuberant cylindrical structure surmounted by a cupola (371). At *Cambridge* Gibbs, like his later colleague Robert Adam (page 183), devoted much time and effort in an attempt to complete the great quadrangle at *King's College*. In both cases – Gibbs in the 1720s and 1730s and Adam in the 1780s – the architect was commissioned to design a comprehensive scheme for the great quadrangle and a

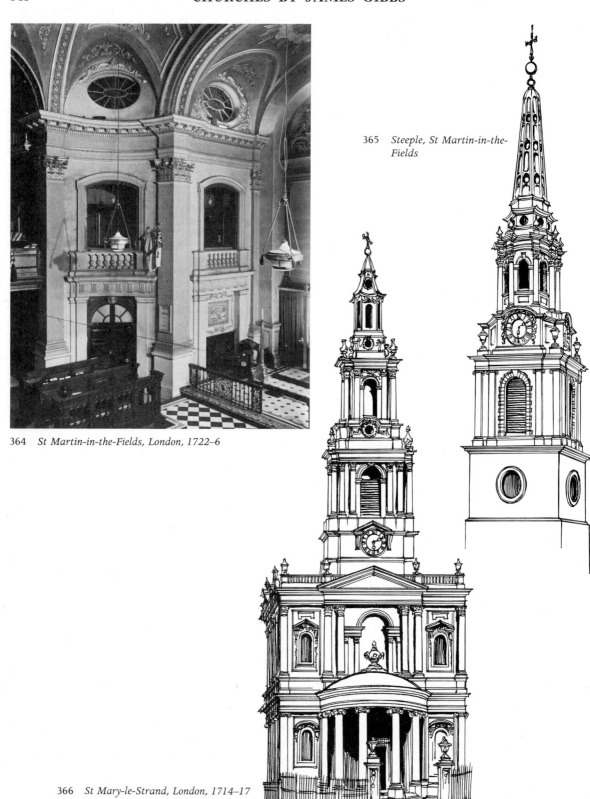

364 *St Martin-in-the-Fields, London, 1722–6*

365 *Steeple, St Martin-in-the-Fields*

366 *St Mary-le-Strand, London, 1714–17*

university library and administrative centre. These were two different schemes but, since the sites were close together, it was considered advantageous for the architectural layouts to have homogeneity.

For both architects the problem was the great Medieval chapel. Since the fifteenth century the large quadrangle had been dominated by this building, regarded by architects and university authorities as sacrosanct, yet how to marry it with an eighteenth-century classical scheme? (373). The chapel is on the north side of the quadrangle; Gibbs' solution was to design the hall opposite, on the south, with a great portico to face the chapel. On the east and west sides he would build classical, plainer blocks. His adjacent layout was for an open court lined by blocks on three sides to serve as administrative buildings and the university library. Only the Senate House, 1722 (368) was built in this latter court and the Fellows' Building, 1724, on the west side of the great quadrangle (372, 373), both restrained classical structures of high standard. Due to endless university wrangling, nothing further was achieved and the architect was shabbily treated (as was Adam later). Gibbs received only £100 in lieu of fees for the Senate House, which cost £13,000 to build.

Scotland

The paths of England and her northern neighbour had continued their separate ways despite the union of the Crowns under James I and VI. The political Union of 1707 was different. This was a watershed and, though until after the 1745 rebellion the changes were not marked, in the second half of the century the prosperity of Scotland began to revive.

Eighteenth-century Scotland produced some fine architects, but in the years until 1760 most of them still found career prospects to be more advantageous in England. James Gibbs was one of these, though he did return to his home town of Aberdeen towards the end of his life to build the West Kirk on the site of the nave of the Medieval Church of St Nicholas. Another Scottish architect was Colen Campbell, the designer of Palladian buildings (page 156) in England, whose publication Vitruvius Britannicus had a widespread influence in advising upon correct classical proportion and detail.

Meanwhile, in Scotland, in the years 1710–60 architects continued to pursue their own indigenous course. Sir William Bruce was followed by James Smith and Alexander MacGill, but the chief architect of this time was William Adam (1689–1748), father of the famous architect of the later eighteenth century, Robert Adam (page 173). William Adam was the son of a stone mason and, after initial training from his father worked for Sir William Bruce. Adam was energetic, a business man who made himself proficient as an architect, becoming in his middle years the man best known in his profession in Scotland. Most of the nobility and gentry went to him for new houses and alteration to existing ones. He was appointed Master Mason in North Britain to the Board of Ordnance and carried out a great deal of work in the building of forts in the Highlands.

Most of William Adam's civic work has been destroyed or altered; it is in his country houses that his style of building can still be seen. This is based chiefly upon the English work by Vanbrugh and Gibbs. Adam was attracted by powerful designs, Baroque in their massiveness and curves, also their monumentality. He used Palladian ornament and façade treatment, but in general the English Palladian school was too formal and prescribed for him. His best and most typical work can be seen at Hopetoun, the Drum, and Duff House.

Hopetoun House had been built for the Earl of Hopetoun by Sir William Bruce and Adam had assisted there as a young man. After Bruce's death Lord Hopetoun asked Adam to extend the building and bring it up to date in the modern architectural idiom. This Adam did, though the work was accomplished so slowly that both architect and patron died before it was completed. The remodelled Hopetoun House is on the grand scale, with an entrance elevation extending over 500 feet and fronted by green lawns and gravel drives. The approach view (376) offers an impressive pile-up of grey masonry; a great centre block, quadrant colonnades and terminal pavilions. A giant Corinthian Order spans the piano nobile and the second storey, taken up in Doric form in the pavilions. This is in the Palladian manner, but the skyline and the sweeping convex and concave contrasting curves of bays and quadrants are Vanbrugh-inspired Baroque, as is the weightiness of the whole composition. Most of the exterior was finished in the 1740s. The interior work, of the highest quality, is by Robert Adam, who took over in 1750.

367 *The Horse Guards, London,
William Kent, 1745–58*

368 *King's Parade, Cambridge. Note
'A', The Senate House, James
Gibbs, 1722–30 and 'B' The
Church of St Mary the Great,
1478*

372 *Fellows' Building,
King's College,
Cambridge, James
Gibbs, 1724–30*

373 *Panorama of buildings of King's and Clare
Colleges seen from the banks of the River Cam,
Cambridge. 'A' Clare College. 'B' The Chapel,
1466–1515. 'C' The Fellows' Building, James
Gibbs, 1724–30*

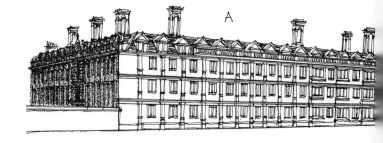

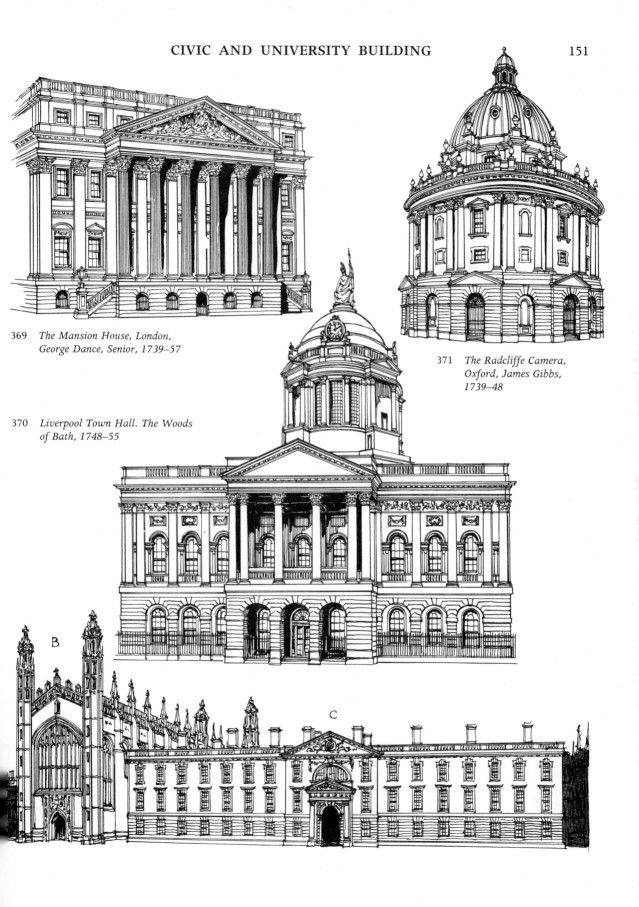

369 *The Mansion House, London, George Dance, Senior, 1739–57*

371 *The Radcliffe Camera, Oxford, James Gibbs, 1739–48*

370 *Liverpool Town Hall. The Woods of Bath, 1748–55*

B

C

374   *Duff House, Banff, William Adam,*
       1730–9

375   *Exterior staircase balustrade in iron.*
       Stoneleigh Abbey, Warwickshire,
       Francis Smith, c.1720

376   *Hopetoun House near Edinburgh,*
       William, John and Robert Adam,
       c.1723–54

William Adam was engaged at the same time on *Duff House*, near Banff. Despite the present state of the house* and the fact that the screen walls and pavilions were never built, Duff House remains the most impressive of Adam's works. Its vast block stands monumental and richly articulated in its dignity and grandeur (374). The house was designed in 1730 as a central, four-storeyed block with corner towers in the Scottish tradition, with central pediment and double curved approach staircase. It was intended to be connected to two-storeyed pavilions by quadrant screen walls. The uncompromising single large block, about 100 by 80 feet in plan, cost over £70,000, mainly because of the ready-worked stone brought by sea from the Firth of Forth. There is a rusticated lower storey; a giant Corinthian Order in pilaster form spans the next two floors with attic and balustraded parapet above.

The Palladians

Baroque architecture in Britain had been an implant, anglicised, but still of foreign origin. In the 1720s it was replaced by something much more English: *Palladianism*. The architectural pendulum had swung back to the correct Roman precepts of Palladio and away from the romantic English concepts of Wren and the rumbustious massing of form and ornament of Vanbrugh and his colleagues in Baroque art. All these variations of classical design were based upon Italian and Ancient Roman classicism but, whereas Wren, Vanbrugh and Gibbs had broken away from the rigid classical rules and had imprinted their own individuality and nationality, thus using the style and not permitting it to govern them, the Palladian school, which held the field in England from 1720 until 1760, returned to the more austere rendering of their ideal. This was a quiet, restrained classical form with little decorative enrichment apart from the orders; its lack of ostentation and dignified treatment were clearly attuned to the English taste.

This had a three-fold basis. First the work of

Andrea Palladio, the sixteenth-century architect of Renaissance Italy after whom the movement was named; secondly, the designs of *Vitruvius*, the architect of Republican Rome on whose precepts Palladio had based his work; and thirdly, *Inigo Jones*, the seventeenth-century English interpreter of the architectural expression. Palladian architecture was not quite like any of these, as a later copy is rarely the same as its prototype. In exteriors it was generally colder and more austere, but interior schemes often reached heights of splendour reminiscent of the great Roman baths and halls which inspired them.

The outstanding contribution of the Palladian school was in *country house* building. The exterior of these houses was generally plain and monumental, almost severe. A rectangular central block would be connected to side pavilions by low galleries and colonnades. The whole scheme was symmetrical, with careful attention to Roman classical proportion, orders and detail. The ground floor was rusticated and, above this, as in Inigo Jones' time, the *piano nobile*, the main floor, was much taller than the others. The entrance front generally faced north or east and on the opposite long side was the garden façade. Both long elevations generally had a central classical portico, commonly in the Corinthian Order, with a pediment above the entablature. This austere, symmetrical exterior was decorated only by rectangular sash windows and a balustrated parapet.

Great Palladian houses appear to be four-square, solid and indisputably English. What makes them into masterpieces, on the exterior, is the siting and surroundings, for the parkland and gardens are in contrast and thus complementary to the architecture. The Palladian house was carefully set on rising ground or at the foot of a vista or by a stream or lake. The peculiarly English park* was then laid out round it, with sweeping lawns, great spreading trees and studiously natural landscape, decorated by pseudo-classical temples and sculpture. *William Kent* and, later, *Lancelot (Capability) Brown*, became famous as the chief exponents of this type of landscaping – Brown made lakes from streams, and moved whole hillsides to where he needed them to create his effect. This treatment is indigenous, very different from French or Italian gardens based on the geometrical formalities at Versailles. It was envied and copied

---

* The building now belongs to the Ministry of Works, who are restoring it to its former condition. In the last 50 years Duff House has been used as a hospital and later by the army. Little remains of Adam's decorative interior schemes, though the structure is largely sound. The original staircase balustrade has disappeared, also all the furniture and nearly all the fireplaces.

* A rarity in Scotland in these years.

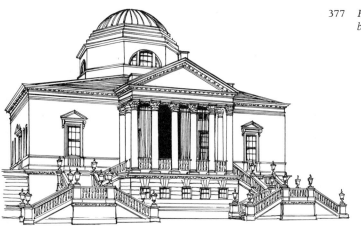

377 *Holkham Hall, Norfolk, William Kent,*
begun 1734. The garden front

378 *Chiswick House, London, Lord Burlington,*
1727–36

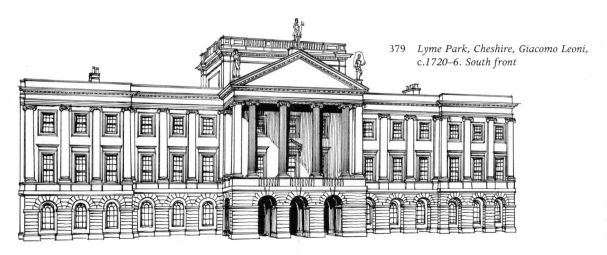

379 *Lyme Park, Cheshire, Giacomo Leoni,*
c.1720–6. South front

381 *Nostell Priory, James Paine, 1733–50.*
East front

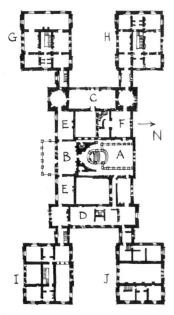

380 *Holkham Hall, plan principal floor. A Hall. B Saloon. C Gallery. D State Bedroom. E Drawing Room. F Dining Room. G Library Wing. H Guest Wing. I Chapel Wing. J Kitchen Wing.*

382 *Holkham Hall, the hall*

later by other European nations, notably by Catherine the Great of Russia.

All over England, in towns but more so in the country, Palladian houses were built – from large mansions to small houses and terraces. Most of the work was by builders who based their designs on houses they had seen or on drawings from books on architecture by men like Campbell (*Vitruvius Britannicus*), Kent (*Designs of Inigo Jones*), Lord Burlington (*Fabbriche Antiche*) and Vardy (*Designs of Inigo Jones and William Kent*), also a translation by Dubois, illustrated by Leoni, of Palladio's *Quattro Libri dell' Architettura*. There were not, as yet, many architects, but there was an informed aristocracy who sent their sons on the Grand Tour of Europe to study its classical sites and buildings for two or three years. On their return these men became patrons of practising artists and architects. One of the great noblemen of this type, leader of the Palladian movement, was Lord Burlington. He designed some buildings himself and was the patron of several of the most outstanding Palladian architects, including *William Kent* and *Colen Campbell*.

The *Earl of Burlington* (1694–1753) went to Italy as a young man in 1714–15 and, on his return, became extremely interested in the work of Palladio as he studied Campbell's *Vitruvius Britannicus*. He returned to Italy in 1719 and spent some months in Vicenza to see Palladio's work *in situ*. He met William Kent in Rome, brought him back to England and employed him at Burlington House in Piccadilly to carry out decorative painting. He employed Campbell there also to transform the house design.* The two best-known examples of Lord Burlington's own work are the *Assembly Rooms* in *York*, a rendering of a Palladian basilica, and *Chiswick House* in *London*, which he modelled on Palladio's Villa Capra near Vicenza. The Chiswick villa, built 1727–36, has only two porticoes (as opposed to Palladio's four) and the chief of these is approached by an Italianate exterior double stair-case. The dome, which covers the hall, is shallow, carried on a hexagonal drum (378).

Colen Campbell (d.1729) also built a version of Palladio's Villa Capra at *Mereworth* in Kent in 1723. This rendering is nearer to the prototype, being a square block with four identical porticoed elevations

and a central drum and dome covering a vast interior hall. The design built by Palladio was suited to the Italian climate, where the idea was to avoid the sun by moving around the hall, to the rooms leading off it, according to the time of day and the shade required. In England the result is magnificent but draughty.

Little is known of Campbell's early life until he was commissioned by Lord Burlington to remodel Burlington House in 1717. In 1715 he had brought out his *Vitruvius Britannicus*, in which he published a series of plates of works by English architects including many of his own designs. It was this publication which attracted Lord Burlington's attention to him. Although his main purpose was to advertise his own work, Campbell performed a considerable service to architecture by the publication of so many plates of important buildings. Among Campbell's other work was *Wanstead House* in Essex, 1720, a large Palladian structure with a 260-foot frontage (demolished 1824) and *Stourhead* (383) in Wiltshire, built 1721–4. His most beautiful house is *Houghton Hall* in Norfolk, designed in 1721 for Sir Robert Walpole and built between then and 1730. This very large house, comprising a central block connected to pavilions by colonnades, extends over a frontage of 450 feet. The architect died before completion and the interior decoration was undertaken by William Kent and the stuccoist Artari. The great stone hall, inspired by Inigo Jones' Queen's House at Greenwich, is in the Roman tradition of splendour, with its first floor gallery, classical doorways, chimneypiece and coved ceiling ornamented with gambolling *putti* (384).

William Kent (1685–1748) was the personality of the Palladian school. A Yorkshireman, he came to London and then went on to Italy to study painting. He lived in Rome for nearly ten years, copying paintings for English patrons until, in 1719, he met Lord Burlington and returned with him to Burlington House to pass the rest of his life there. At first he was employed to carry out decorative painting but under Lord Burlington's guidance he turned to architecture and, through his patron's influence, acquired important commissions and became the fashionable architect of the 1730s and 1740s.

Kent's chief domestic commission was *Holkham Hall* in Norfolk, which he designed in 1734 (380). This, the most famous of all Palladian mansions in England and the home of the Earl of Leicester, lies in magnificent grounds laid out by Capability Brown

---

* Gibbs had worked on the house, also Lord Burlington himself, but much of this was altered in the rebuilding in 1866.

383   *Stourhead, Wiltshire. 1718–22. East front, wings added, c.1800*

384   *Houghton Hall, Norfolk. The stone hall, 1721–30*

385 *The Circus, Bath, John Wood, father and son, begun 1754*

386 *The Circus, detail, ground floor*

387 *The Circus, detail, first floor*

388 *44, Berkeley Square, London, William Kent, 1744–5*

389 *Queen Square, Bath, John Wood Senior, 1728–35*

with lawns, trees and a lake. The exterior of the house is severe and symmetrical (377), but the interior is in complete contrast. The main achievement of Palladian domestic architecture (apart from the setting) was in the interiors and Holkham shows this in its finest form. The hall (382) is based on Roman basilican plan but, in its decoration and order, owes much to the Temple of Fortuna Virilis in Rome. The hall is built in Derbyshire marble in shades of cream and white, marked in red and has Ionic colonnades standing on a tall plinth broken by a central staircase which approaches the apse; behind this the doorway leads into the magnificent saloon. The plaster ceiling of the hall is beautifully designed and coffered; it has a decorative centrepiece enriched with classical ornament. William Kent believed in the practice, unusual at this date, of the architect designing not only the structure of a building but also all the detail of doorways, windows, ceiling, chimneypieces, furniture and furnishings. Holkham is a superb example and is so finely proportioned that it is difficult to credit the great size of the doorways, for instance, until someone stands in the opening and the height can be judged. The saloon ceiling and doorcases are excellent examples of Kent's best work. In 1742–4 he designed *No. 44, Berkeley Square* in *London*. This was a successful attempt to make a lavish home inside the greater restrictions of a town terrace house (388).

There were a number of other architects of quality designing in these years, most of whom followed the Palladian line. One of these was the Venetian *Giacomo Leoni*, *c*.1686–1746, who came to England to superintend the publication of an English edition of Palladio, which appeared in 1715–16 in two volumes; Leoni supplied the illustrations to Dubois' translation. In 1726, sponsored by Lord Burlington, Leoni published his three volume translation of Alberti on architecture. Leoni remained in England until his death and designed a number of houses in Palladian style. These include *Clandon Park*, near Guildford, 1731–5, *Queensberry House* near Burlington House in London, 1721, which was altered in 1792 and his south front additions to *Lyme Park* in Cheshire, 1720–30 (379).

Also working in Palladian style were *Isaac Ware*, d.1766, *Henry Flitcroft*, 1697–1769, and *John Vardy*, d.1765. Ware's best-known work is *Wrotham Park*, Middlesex, 1754; he also designed a number of houses in the West End of London. Henry Flitcroft's chief

building is the *Church of St Giles-in-the-Fields* in London, now dwarfed by the adjacent Centrepoint building. St Giles owes much to Gibbs' St Martin-in-the-Fields, also to the Wren city churches. Vardy worked for many years in the King's Works at Greenwich, Hampton Court Palace, Whitehall and Kensington and was closely associated with William Kent. It was in this capacity that he built the Horse Guards in Whitehall to Kent's designs after the latter's death (page 164). By mid-century the Palladian school was consolidated by a second generation of architects led by *Sir Robert Taylor* and *James Paine*, whose work was largely carried out in the 1760s (page 171). Typical of Paine's designs was *Nostell Priory* in Yorkshire, where he built the east front in 1733–50 (381). The wing on the right was added by Adam in 1765.

A further group of architects working at this time were designing in a manner which adhered less strictly to the Palladian code. *John James*, 1672–1746, had carried out work both at Greenwich Hospital and St Paul's. He contributed one church to the 1711 Act group of churches. This was *St George's, Hanover Square* in London, 1713–14 (360). It has a giant portico of Corinthian columns and a cupola-topped tower. James also completed Hawksmoor's Church of St Alphege at Greenwich.

George Dance the Elder, 1698–1748, was Clerk of the City Works in London from 1733 until his death. His best-known building in the city is the *Mansion House*, 1739–53 (369), with its fine portico of Corinthian columns crowned by the sculptured pediment. Dance built a number of churches in *London* which include *St Luke, Old Street*, 1732 (394), *St Leonard Shoreditch*, 1736–40 (392), *St Botolph, Aldgate*, 1749–50, and *St Matthias, Bethnal Green*, 1741. St Leonard's is the most successful design of these, its steeple owing something to St Mary-le-Bow.

Outside London there were a number of architects designing work of good quality, sound construction and varied design. These provincial architects tended to work in a small area, their contribution confined to a certain town or group of towns. Notable among them is *John Bastard* in *Blandford*, Dorset, where he built much of the new town after the old one had been largely destroyed by fire in 1731. The *Church* here, 1731–9, is a good example of his work (391). At *Worcester, Thomas White* designed the *Church of St Nicholas*, 1726–30 (396) and the *Guildhall*, 1719–22,

390   *Carved decoration, 1754–60*

391   *Blandford Church, Dorset,*
John Bastard, 1731–9

392   *Clock ornament, St*
Leonard's Church,
Shoreditch, George Dance
Senior

393   *Daventry Church, William*
and David Hiorn, 1752

396   *St Nicholas' Church,*
Worcester, Thomas White,
1726–30

394   *Doorway, St Luke's*
Church, Old Street,
London, George Dance
Senior, 1727–33

395   *Parapet, Daventry Church*

while *William* and *David Hiorn* worked in *Daventry*, where they built the church in 1752 (393). These provincial architects were influenced in their church design chiefly by Wren and Gibbs rather than Hawksmoor or the Palladians. This is evident especially in the steeples, but also in the interior decoration as at *Great Witley Church*, for example, built 1735.

House Interiors

The principal rooms in the large houses of the period were on the *piano nobile*. The living rooms led off a large, imposing, central hall, which was entered from the portico or main doorway approached by a single or complex exterior staircase (377, 381, 383). These *living rooms* would include a dining room (399), a small and large drawing room or saloon (402), a library, powder closets and, upstairs would be bedrooms (401) and dressing rooms. Kitchens and servants' quarters were relegated to basement and attics or, in large houses, to the wings or terminal pavilions connected by lower ranges to the central rectangular block. The Palladian tradition in great mansions was to house kitchen and service rooms, as well as stables, in these wings. The inconvenience of receiving one's food cold after being carried such distances from kitchen to dining room was not considered of importance; servants were in plentiful supply and the prestige and splendour of the house was the prime consideration.

There was now greater variety in the forms of interior decoration. This was classical in design, generally correctly proportioned and detailed in the Palladian tradition but the *walls* could now be covered and ornamented in several ways. *Wood panelling* was still employed; pinewood, cedar and, later, mahogany, were carved in classical schemes and ornament, the cheaper woods often painted in white or light colours (398, 399). Alternatively, *stucco-ornamented* walls were fashionable, again in classical decorative form, with the plaster enrichment added, then painted and gilded, to the wall surface (402). In the 1750s rococo decorative motifs began to replace the earlier Baroque and Palladian ornament. The newer designs incorporated scrolls and shells, flowers, ribbons and birds in a delicate, elegant composition. In some apartments, especially bedrooms, the walls were draped with *hangings* as far down as wainscot

level. These were plain or richly patterned in velvet, silk or damask (401).

From about 1745 a fourth alternative wall covering was provided by the introduction of *wallpaper*. At first this was imported from the East, being mainly of Chinese origin. It was sent in strips about four feet wide, several of which made a complete landscape or garden picture. Early English wallpapers were painted or stencilled attempts to imitate the more costly damask or velvet hangings of formal floral design. After 1754 printed patterns were in use; *John B. Jackson* of Battersea was a pioneer in this field. He published a report of his experimental work in 1754, giving data on his wood-block printing method. Many of his designs were representations of sculptured classical figures, made in monochrome, for those who could not afford the marble realities. Later wallpaper designs were of landscapes, floral designs and imitations of famous landscape paintings by artists such as Canaletto, Poussin or Lorraine. Wallpapers were not stuck to the wall. As they were so costly, they were mounted on canvas to a wood frame, attached to the wall by wooden wedges so that new paper could be put up without destroying the old. Some of these papers have been preserved in museums as they were not subject to damp and dirt from the walls.

Floors were of polished wood and *carpets* and rugs were still only seen in the principal reception rooms of large houses as they were as yet very expensive. Most of these carpets, which only covered the centre of the room, were imported, though needlework carpets were made in England. Carpet-knotting had lapsed in England in the later seventeenth century, but was revived as an industry in the middle of the eighteenth century when firms with names such as Wilton, Axminster and Kidderminster were started up (399, 401, 402).

The drawing room (402) or saloon was the main chamber of the house and was decorated and furnished in the most lavish manner. It generally faced south and was used for leisure. A massive cornice ran round the room and the white plaster ceiling was decoratively enriched. The chief feature of one wall was the chimneypiece, which extended from floor to cornice as a two-stage design as the overmantel was replaced by a carved framed mirror or picture. Rococo mirror frames were complex designs, usually gilded and with holders for a number of candles

397   *Marble staircase, iron*
balustrade

398   *Panel wall decoration*
incorporating candle
holders. Carved painted
and gilded wood, c.1756–60

399   *Dining Room, c.1730*

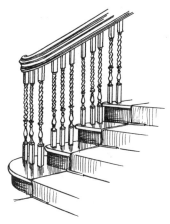

400 *Mahogany staircase, twisted balusters, c.1715*

401 *Bedchamber, 1740–50*

402 *Drawing Room, 1750–60*

whose flames, reflected in the glass panels, increased the illumination of the room (402). Eighteenth-century interior décor made extensive use of large mirrors as well as carefully designed crystal chandeliers for this purpose. Six-panelled doors were most usual, with classical motifs in the carved panel borders. The sash windows reached from cornice to wainscot. They had large rectangular panes in wood frames. They were curtained by velvet or damask, looped up with tassels and cords and hung from a pole often hidden by a pelmet and crowned by an elaborate carved and gilded pediment. The *dining room* was less lavishly decorated but was similarly designed in a classical scheme (399). The principal feature of the bedroom was still the large four-poster bedstead, whose posts were now often in the form of classical columns (401).

A house would have one or two *staircases* according to size. The main staircase would be of stone if stucco decoration was used on the walls of the well and generally of wood if panelling was employed. Balustrades could be of wood or iron. In wooden ones the balusters, in open string design, were turned, usually in barley sugar twists (400). The wrought-iron balustrades were in scrolled design fitted to a mahogany handrail at the top (397). In the vogue for Chinese decoration of the mid-century, fret designs of wood balustrades were popular.

The furniture, furnishings and ornaments in the Palladian house were of a superb standard of craftsmanship. This was the age of beautiful silverware, of pottery and later porcelain and of the emergence of the great cabinet makers. *William Kent* designed much of the furniture used in his houses. This was in large pieces in carved mahogany or gilding and gesso was added to ornament a cheaper carved wood. Heavy marble tops were used on tables.

While William Kent was the chief designer in the years 1727–40, the following twenty years were dominated by *Thomas Chippendale*. Also a Yorkshireman, Chippendale came to London and later set up his shop in St Martin's Lane in 1753. He published his '*Director*' the following year which contained designs for all kinds of furniture in the three basic Chippendale styles based on Gothic, Rococo and Oriental. These were his chief sources of inspiration, but all Chippendale furniture is unmistakably English in design. Chippendale's influence was far-reaching and he established the importance of the designer/cabinet-maker in the eighteenth century. He was

followed in the later decades by other famous designers such as Adam, Hepplewhite and Sheraton.

Building in Towns

The population of Britain was rising slowly. At the beginning of the eighteenth century it is estimated that there were five and a half million inhabitants in England and Wales. Towns were spreading outwards, especially London, whose wealthier citizens were moving westwards from the city and building spacious new houses in the villages of Chelsea and Kensington, as well as northwards and eastwards in Hampstead, West Ham and Walthamstow.

The City was the most densely populated area in Britain. It was not just occupied by day, as in modern times. The merchants and shop-keepers lived at their place of business with their families and servants. It was the nobility and professional men who had moved out, away from their crowded houses to take up residence in Piccadilly, St James's Square, Covent Garden and Westminster.

Town houses in these areas did not follow so closely upon the Palladian theme as the country residences, but some of the fashion trends in design were applied. The town house is, of necessity, restricted in site and so is taller and narrower, but there is the same insistence on predominance for the *piano nobile* where, if an order is used, it extends up from the first floor through two or three storeys to support the entablature above, which might be surmounted by an attic. If there is no order, its non-existence is noted by a string course at first floor level. This Palladian style of town house was in general use in London and other large towns from about 1730 onwards. Examples from these years include *Leoni's Queensberry House*, 1721, and *Kent's 44, Berkeley Square*, 1744–5, (388), both in *London*, and *68, The Close* in *Salisbury*, c.1735–40.

There are not many civic schemes surviving from this period. The outstanding example of Palladian building in this field (apart from the Mansion House, page 159), is the impressive layout of the *Horse Guards* in *Whitehall* (367). It was designed by *William Kent* in 1745, on similar lines to Holkham Hall, though the Horse Guards is largely rusticated and is surmounted by a clock tower. It was completed by Vardy after Kent's death.

Street Planning and Terrace Architecture

The idea of designing town houses by the street, or even round a whole square, had been initiated by Inigo Jones in Covent Garden (page 108). The experiment of making a uniform Palladian treatment of a street of houses tended to lapse after Inigo Jones' time and owners had their town houses built individually on similar, though not identical, patterns. From about 1730, town expansion began to go forward at a speed which made it architecturally desirable to treat the terrace houses as one façade. Ground landlords started to let their sites in a larger block instead of space adequate for only one or two houses. A few streets and squares in London were built with a repetitive Palladian façade as, for example, in Grosvenor Square, but the primary experiment at this time was in Bath.

In the early years of the eighteenth century *Bath* was still a small town. It was between 1720 and 1730 that the value of its waters was re-discovered and they were popularised for their medicinal properties. With royal patronage Bath soon became fashionable as a summer health and amusement resort. The leading figure in the consequent replanning and enlargement of the town to meet the new needs was *John Wood* (1704–54). He had already designed buildings in London and in the north of England, but in 1727 moved to Bath where he spent the rest of his life. By his work he helped to revive the popularity of Bath stone from the local quarries. He had a masterly conception of town planning in terraces, streets and squares. He did not visualise town houses simply as individual units but as part of a complete architectural layout for the city.

Wood's first important project in this manner was in *Queen Square* which he built in 1728–35. The entire square is designed in Palladian manner; the terraces are three-storeyed with rustication on the ground stage and, above the string course the *piano nobile*, its tall windows surmounted by alternating triangular and curved pediments. There is then the second floor with entablature above supported on giant pilasters which span first and second floors. The roof contains an attic stage. In Queen Square Wood did not simply repeat this Palladian formula from end to end of the terrace. He treated the whole façade as a palace with shallowly-projecting end pavilions and a central pedimented feature. These sections are marked by the use of columns instead of pilasters. The houses on each side of Queen Square became, together, the façade of a large country mansion (389).

John Wood carried out further Palladian building in, for example, *South Parade* and the country house of *Prior Park* in Bath, 1735, and, in civic work, *Liverpool Town Hall*, 1748–55 (370). His most spectacular achievement was his design for the *Circus* in Bath. He had discovered something of the Roman history of the city and planned ambitious layouts on Roman lines including a sports arena and a forum. The Circus is based on his ideas for a sports arena. This scheme was abandoned owing to the unsuitability of the English climate, but the form of the layout is the same. Here is a circle of 33 houses divided at three points by incoming streets. The design for the houses is repeated in identical manner all round the circle and comprises three stages using three different orders: Doric on the ground floor, then Ionic and Corinthian at the top (385–7). This simple but great conception was not completed in John Wood's lifetime, but work went on into the 1760s under his son, also John Wood.

The influence of these examples of terrace architecture in Bath was far-reaching. It encouraged architects in London and other towns such as Brighton, Cheltenham, Bristol and Hastings in the later eighteenth and early nineteenth centuries to develop the theme in their rapidly expanding urban areas.

CHAPTER NINE

The Classical Revival
1760–1790

Artistic exposition diversified in the second half of the eighteenth century. Its expression continued to be primarily classical, but eclecticism now had a wider base; the rigid rules of Palladianism were relaxed. This spirit of experimentation with new sources and ideas was the result of the expansion of the time; experienced geographically in extended travel overseas to more distant countries; and in the greater wealth at home which devolved from the current revolutions in both agriculture and industry.

The industrial revolution is sometimes thought of as being a nineteenth-century phenomenon, but even as early as 1760 its impetus was gathering momentum (438). The agricultural revolution in Britain belongs to the same period of development and it is no coincidence that both movements evolved at this time, for both arose in response to the need to provide food and employment for a population now fast increasing. It would have been impossible in the eighteenth century to bring enough food from overseas for this growth of population, stimulated by better conditions of medicine and hygiene. There was a move to farm the great estates more efficiently and smallholders were incorporated into larger units. At the same time thousands of acres of land, previously covered by woodland and heath, were enclosed to become productive arable fields. It is estimated that two million acres were added to the country's farming resources during the century. In addition the introduction of the scientific rotation of crops and pasture led to better yields and fatter stock.

All over the country on these medium-sized and large estates owners were ploughing back their profits into land and buildings. The ambition to own a beautiful house in fine parkland and grounds, prevalent in the years before 1760, culminated in the succeeding thirty years. This was the greatest age of country house building in Britain. The custom grew of sending the sons of great and aristocratic families on the Grand Tour of Europe. Greater distances were covered and two or three years were spent instead of only one in France and Italy, the travellers staying part of the time as guests of friends and relatives and the remainder in inns and rented lodgings. They collected antique and Renaissance sculpture, paintings, books, coins and ceramics and brought them back to decorate their homes. Often it became necessary to build new galleries and libraries to house these treasures.

Travel by the nobility and also by architects and artists led to increased knowledge. Interest was aroused in visiting Greece, Dalmatia and even lands as far away as Syria. In England the *Dilettanti Society* was formed to encourage such original research. It published papers and commissioned and financially supported expeditions by members. Among these was *Robert Wood* who, accompanied by Bouverie and Dawkins, went to Palmyra (Syria). In 1753 he published the result of their studies and drawings made there in *The Ruins of Palmyra*. His second expedition produced *The Ruins of Baalbec* (1757). *James Stuart* and *Nicholas Revett* followed, also under the society's aegis. They went to Pola (now Pula in Yugoslavia), then to Greece where they studied at Corinth and Athens. They returned in 1755 and, in 1762, published their *Antiquities of Athens*.

Other expeditions and other publications came from different countries. Notable were de Caylus' *Recueil d'Antiquités Egyptiennes, Etrusques, Grecques et Romaines* (1752), Le Roy's *Ruines des plus beaux Monuments de la Grèce* (1758), Winckelmann's *History of Ancient Art* (1763) and Dumont's *Temple of Paestum* (1764). This widening of the field for classical research made clear to both patron and architect in western Europe that Greece, not Rome, was the fount of the classical form and that, in many instances, the Greek was purer and more beautiful. The Greek/Roman controversy raged hotly and protagonists in the 'battle of the styles' took up indefatigable stands on one side or the other. In retrospect, the controversy appears to have been much ado about nothing. Both architectural forms were classical, with one derived from, then developed further than, the other. Why not use the better examples from both? This, of course, is what the great architects of the age did.

One factor which excited interest and controversy was the discovery of the *Greek Doric Order*. Ever since Brunelleschi in the fifteenth century, the *Roman Doric* or Tuscan had been the model, based on Vitruvius and the ruins of Roman buildings, then reiterated in succeeding publications through the sixteenth and seventeenth centuries. This order has a much slenderer column than the Greek version and also a moulded base. The drawings now seen, in the books published by those who had studied on the spot, showed the Doric Order of the Parthenon (222, 224), without base, fluted, with a more subtle echinus moulding to the capital than the Roman (which has a semi-circular section) and, most notable, a sturdier column and deeper entablature, giving different proportions of height and width to the order. This Greek Doric version horrified the Palladians and they were even more shocked when they saw drawings of the archaic period temples of Paestum and Sicily, which predate the Parthenon by a hundred years or more. For these earlier temples have even shorter, stockier columns and immensely large capitals supporting a weighty entablature. They are the most powerful-looking Doric buildings in western Europe. The English adherents to the Roman style, in the second half of the eighteenth century, led by Sir William Chambers, thought this work primitive and barbaric.

The pro-Greek faction of the later eighteenth century tended to go too far the other way, feeling that everything Greek was better than anything Roman. But even they did not value, as we do today, the great period of Greek sculpture and decoration. We consider this to be the fifth century BC, rating high the Parthenon sculptures, also earlier archaic work from Olympia and elsewhere. The Greek enthusiasts of the eighteenth century were more impressed by the later Greek work of the second or first century BC. In decorative fields they used designs from Greek vases and, mistakenly believing them to be Etruscan, incorporated their motifs into interior decoration and detail. Wedgwood used these sources, so did Adam. Indeed, the new pottery manufactory established by Wedgwood was named by him 'Etruria' and Adam proudly refers to his new 'Etruscan' motifs and colours of red, yellow earth and black.*

One European country did not acknowledge Greek originality for some time. This, naturally enough, was Italy. As publication after publication appeared, piling up the weight of evidence, the Italians found their champion in *Gianbattista Piranesi*, the Venetian artist who became famous for his drawings of classical ruins. In his publications *Le Antichità di Roma* (1748) and *Della Magnificenza ed Architettura de' Romani* (1763), he attempts the defence of Roman architecture against the Greek, asserting that the latter was more ornate and decadent.

The Greek/Roman controversy occupied the mainstream of architecture in the years 1760–90. On the periphery the widening ripples of the movement towards a climate of change could be discerned in other artistic expression. In mid-century there was, for many years, a fashion for Chinoiserie. This had been seen in Chippendale's furniture (page 164) and even so serious a protagonist of the Roman Palladian school as Sir William Chambers† published his *Designs of Chinese Buildings* and built the Pagoda in Kew Gardens (411).

A more fundamental movement was that of the Romantics. In England this took the form of a rebellion against the rigidity of Roman Palladianism

---

* Another source of these motifs for both men was the Roman art excavated at Herculaneum and Pompeii in the mid-century. Similar colours and decorative forms were found here, inspired originally from Greek sources.

† As a young man Chambers had worked for the East India Company in whose employment he travelled in Bengal and China.

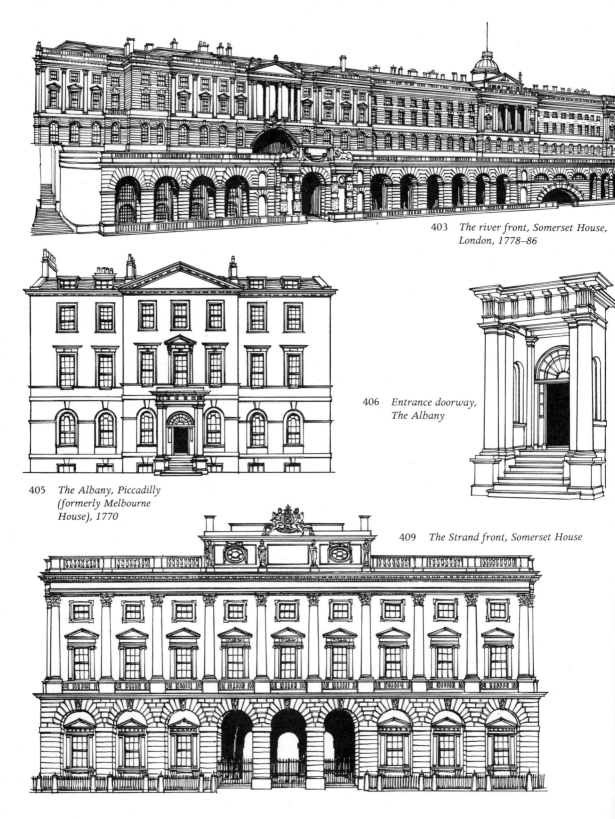

403   *The river front, Somerset House,*
      London, 1778–86

406   *Entrance doorway,*
      The Albany

405   *The Albany, Piccadilly*
      (formerly Melbourne
      House), 1770

409   *The Strand front, Somerset House*

404   *Peper Harow, Surrey, 1765–75*

407   *Window, Somerset House*

408   *Staircase,*
      Peper Harow

411   *The Pagoda,*
      Kew Gardens, 1761

410   *The Royal Bank of Scotland, St Andrew's Square,*
      Edinburgh, 1772

and against the dogma of reason. In the eighteenth century it was largely a literary force; its architectural expression was small. In Britain, Medievalism and the associated Gothic architecture had never completely died. Classical design had dominated the building scene for over two hundred years but the tiny flame had flickered intermittently. There were the few Gothic structures by Wren – Tom Tower at Oxford, some city churches – Vanbrugh's own house at Greenwich, Kent's contribution at Hampton Court Palace and Gloucester Cathedral. Hawksmoor had introduced his own brand of Gothic/Baroque at All Souls' College, Oxford and in the western towers of Westminster Abbey.

All of these examples are in the realm of literary Gothic; they have little in common with the Medieval spirit and lack comprehension of the building style, but they kept the feeling alive and provided the rebel outsiders' expression in a classical age. In the eighteenth century it was *Horace Walpole* who introduced the conception of a Gothic country house. His villa at *Strawberry Hill* where he enlarged and Medievalised the existing cottage in 1750 aroused widespread interest and controversy. In this Strawberry Hill Gothic, as it came to be called, he insisted on authentic Medieval forms for the interior rooms, decorating them with cusped and crocketed arches and panelled ceilings. The results are charming and delicate, full of the essence of good eighteenth-century craftsmanship and elegance but with nothing of the Medieval spirit. Strawberry Hill provides, though, the essential link between the Middle Ages, the Baroque/Gothic form and the final nineteenth-century revival.

Sir William Chambers 1723–1796

Two architects dominated the work of the 30 years after 1760. Both were Scots and they were exactly contemporary, living and dying within a year or so of one another. These men, William Chambers and Robert Adam were, however, in their work and in their personalities, total contrasts. *Sir William Chambers*, though of Scottish stock, was born in Gothenburg in Sweden. He spent much of his boyhood in Yorkshire but returned to Sweden, where he joined the East India Company at the age of 17. After extensive travels, he left the Company when he was 25 and went to Paris to study architecture. He stayed there for a year then continued to Italy where he

spent five years. In 1755 Chambers returned to England and set up practice. He was successful almost from the start of his career, progressing steadily from honour to honour. He became tutor to the Prince of Wales who, later, as George III, in appreciation made him architect to the King. He became Comptroller in 1769, was knighted in 1770 and was appointed Surveyor-General in 1782.

One of Chambers' early commissions was to lay out the *Gardens* at *Kew* and to ornament them with pavilions and temples in classical and oriental manner. Between 1757 and 1763 he did this, designing the Pagoda (411), the classical Orangery, some temples and alcoves. All his life Chambers was a staunch adherent to the Palladian tradition and continued to design, in strictly Roman classical form, work of the highest standard and finest proportions. It is a mark of the age that even Chambers should pay deference to the prevailing mood which demanded a touch of Romanticism in various forms, whether Chinese, Gothic, Indian or Greek; his pagoda was an instance of this.

In 1759 Chambers published his first edition of *A Treatise on Civil Architecture*. He compiled the work from many of his own first-hand studies in addition to works by Italian architects such as Bernini, Peruzzi, Palladio, Vignola and Scamozzi. The work includes whole designs and a wealth of detail on classical forms in doorways, window openings, ceilings and chimney-pieces.

Chambers was a proud, sensitive, reserved and humourless man. He was ambitious and convinced that his views on classical architecture were the correct interpretation for English architects. He resisted all incursion into the Greek form of classicism and rigidly adhered to the pure Roman Palladian form. His detail, ornament and proportions were meticulously correct; his work was sincere, intellectual and of cold, though superbly high quality. His houses, in particular, illustrate his Palladian viewpoint. Among his town houses there exists *Albany, Piccadilly*, formerly Melbourne House, 1771–3 (405, 406), also the two examples in *St Andrew's Square* in *Edinburgh*, one of which now belongs to the Royal Bank of Scotland, 1772 (410). His country house style can be seen at *Peper Harow* in Surrey, 1765–75, where the house, set in beautiful grounds, is now a school. It is a simple three-storeyed design with slightly projecting central block (404, 408). In

Scotland, he designed the mansion of *Duddington* in Midlothian in 1763–8; this house also possesses a beautiful staircase.

Chambers was the leading government architect of his day and in this connection was the architect of *Somerset House* in 1778–86. For a number of years a scheme had been discussed to house several government departments together in one building in the centre of London. The site was decided, that of the old riverside palace, which was demolished, giving a new site with a magnificent south front facing the river of 800 feet in length and a much narrower north elevation facing the Strand of about 135 feet, roughly in the centre of the long façade. This presents a two-storey elevation to the Strand with rusticated arches on the lower stage and the Corinthian Order in column form above. The entrance is placed centrally, comprising three round-arched openings. A balustraded parapet surmounts the cornice (407, 409).

The entrance leads into a central court which has a Corinthian pavilion in the middle of each of three façades. In the central façade, opposite to the main entrance, is a principal feature which also forms the focal centre for the river front; it is surmounted by a pediment and dome.

Somerset House is one of London's finest waterfront monuments, but it presented a number of problems which Chambers solved satisfactorily. One major difficulty of design was the site itself, being of such unusual shape, with one long façade and one short. Also, the river elevation would be lapped by the water as there was then no embankment. Chambers dealt with this difficulty by building a masonry platform above tide level, on which was constructed a basement storey for warehouses and offices. This was then fronted by a rusticated masonry arcade pierced by arches. The façade was divided into three blocks with a central archway and two side watergates so that the tide was controlled by the water's entry into these archways. At that time the building must have had a much more impressive appearance, as contemporary drawings show; now, much of the height has been lost to the modern roadway and embankment.

The river façade has a certain monotony (especially since the addition of the wings in the nineteenth century) and the dome in the central court, while satisfactory when viewed from the court or from the Strand, is inadequate when seen from the riverside.

The building is finely constructed in Portland stone, beautifully finished and with ornament and decoration of high quality. It is an excellent and typical example of Chambers' work.

Palladian and Neo-Classical Architects

In Palladian design, *Sir Robert Taylor* (1714–88) and *James Paine* (1716–89) continued their work in this tradition. Much of Sir Robert's time after 1760 was spent on designs for the *Bank of England*,* for whom he was chief architect. Apart from this, he is noted for his smaller houses: *Ely House*, Dover Street in *London* (1772) and *Asgill House, Richmond*. His chief large country house was *Heveningham Hall* in Suffolk. The north front (412) shows a traditionally Palladian treatment, with its large central block and two side pavilions connected by lower ranges. A giant Corinthian Order spans the two upper storeys, while below the projecting sections are rusticated. The complete elevation is monumental and extensive, handled in faultless Palladian proportion. In 1780 Sir Robert Taylor was responsible for the design of the bridge at *Maidenhead* in Surrey. It is a long stone bridge with balustraded parapet, mellowed attractively in its Thames-side setting.

Like Taylor, *James Paine* was a Palladian in the Burlington tradition. After Nostell Priory (page 159), he designed *Thorndon Hall*, Essex (1763–9) and *Wardour* in Wiltshire (1770–6). Towards the end of his life, while High Sheriff for Surrey, Paine designed a number of *Thames bridges*: those at Richmond, Chertsey, Walton and Kew. The first two of these have survived and that at *Richmond* is especially fine. It was built in 1780–3 of Portland stone and has five arches (435).

Although considered a provincial architect, for most of his extensive practice was carried on in the north of England, the work of *John Carr of York* was in no way inferior to that of the London architects of this group. He began his career as a mason but entered architectural practice soon after 1750. Like Taylor and Paine he was a Palladian architect and had worked under Lord Burlington for some time. Much of his work is in the domestic field of country houses. He designed *Harewood House* in Yorkshire (1760) and built the north front before Adam took over; he built

---

* Little of this work has survived.

412 *Heveningham Hall, Suffolk, north front, 1778, Sir Robert Taylor*

413 *Denton Hall, Yorkshire, 1770–80, John Carr of York*

414 *Fairfax House, York, 1770, John Carr of York*

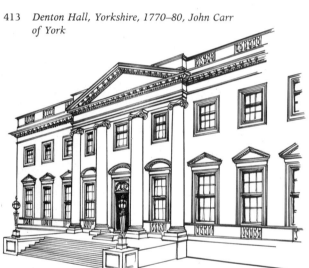

415 *The Assize Courts, York, 1777, John Carr of York*

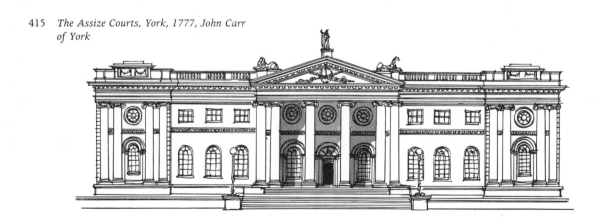

the east front of *Wentworth Woodhouse* in the same county (1770) and *Lytham Hall* in Lancashire (1751–64). Among his smaller houses are *Denton Hall*, Yorkshire 1770–80 (413) and, in *York*, his own house *Fairfax House* 1770 (414). Also in York is his *Assize Courts* 1776–7 (415). Among his churches is *Horbury Church*, Yorkshire (1791), which has a tall, classical steeple, and Ionic lateral porch. Carr's work was always well-proportioned in sound classical tradition and he performed a great service in building so much architecture of high standard in northern cities.

George Dance II (1741–1825) was one of a younger group of architects. Son of George Dance the Elder (page 159), he succeeded his father as Clerk of the City Works in London. He was an original architect following closely neither of the main classical factions of his day, but designing according to the individual commission in hand. Much of his work has been lost, especially in London. The two chief examples were the Church of *All Hallows*, London Wall, which was badly damaged in 1940–1 and *Newgate Prison* which he designed in 1769. This building was one of the most original of the eighteenth century. Built over the years 1770–82, it was an impressive structure with dramatic though austere and even grim qualities. The main composition consisted of unbroken, windowless walls, entirely rusticated; this gave an awesome appearance to the place. In the centre was the keeper's house with entrance lodges on either side. The windows here gave contrast to the enormous area of wall between. The prison was burnt by the Gordon rioters in 1780, later rebuilt but finally demolished in 1902 to make way for the Central Criminal Courts.

In *Scotland* the Palladian, and later the neo-classical, line was being followed, as in England, but still with the incorporation of vernacular features; *Culloden House*, Inverness-shire, c.1788 is typical. The neo-classical approach is to be seen in *James Playfair's Cairness House* in Aberdeenshire, built from 1791. Father of W. H. Playfair of Edinburgh's New Town (chapter 10), James Playfair was noted, as in this instance, for his bold eclecticism in classical elements combined with Egyptian forms.

Robert Adam 1728–1792

Although the work of Robert Adam is two centuries old, it has taken the greater part of this time for a balanced assessment of it to evolve. The fluctuations of critical opinion have been extreme and long lasting. For much of the nineteenth century his name was reviled or ignored. He was mistakenly believed to have based his ideas only upon his studies of the Palace of the Emperor Diocletian at Split. He was also erroneously credited with the inferior work of his host of imitators. In a violent reversal of taste, the *fin de siècle* re-discovered him. Everything was then by Adam, all the work of his contemporaries and successors. In the 1920s he was thought to be a firm of decorators referred to as 'Adams' and there was confusion; was there one Adam or several?

Today the name of Adam is a household word. Everyone interested in the arts, interior decoration and furnishing has heard of him. The public are not so clear about what he did. He is thought to have designed thousands of fireplaces, painted ceilings, made furniture, fire irons and door knobs. How has the reputation of one of Britain's greatest architects become inextricably associated with door knobs and fireplaces?

It is a tribute to Adam's popularity and importance that his services were sought by the richest and most influential people in the land. Such families have so far, in the main, survived the vicissitudes of world wars and penal taxation in death duties and Adam rooms are still in their possession. Since most of the houses are now open to the public we can see for ourselves what his contribution to architecture and decoration was. It is a sobering thought that he decorated all these great houses – some 37 of them – not including the ones which have been demolished – in only 30 years. His tremendous capacity for concentrated work was equalled only by his almost invariably high level of artistry.

Adam began practice in London in 1759 and from then onwards he poured out a tremendous number of very personal designs. He was an eclectic, using many classical sources, fusing them into a quality entirely Adam. His concept of 'movement' came from the Baroque features of Borromini and Bernini. He absorbed Kent's, Gibbs', Vanbrugh's plastic massing of blocks and columns. His early ceiling designs, especially, were rococo. From the beginning, even before he set out on his Grand Tour, he knew himself to be (as he was) an innovator not a copyist. His sense of the romantic, his feeling for elegance were instinctive. They led him to gauge unerringly what the aristocratic owners of houses in Britain would want in the 1760s and he used this personal intuition to combine the architectural themes with motifs from his own archaeological studies in Italy and Dalmatia. He added to these the experience of other men, favouring especially Wood's drawings of Palmyra.

Robert Adam was born at Kirkaldy in Fifeshire on 3 July 1728, the second son of William and Mary Adam. He spent his early childhood in this coastal town on the Firth of Forth then, when he was 11, the family moved to Edinburgh, where William Adam established his architectural practice (Chapter 8). In a family of 10 children there were four Adam brothers, all of whom followed their father into the practice of architecture. The eldest, John, remained all his life in Edinburgh, working first for his father, then competently taking over the practice on the latter's death in 1748.

William Adam sent his sons to the local high school in Edinburgh and Robert and James to university there. Robert attended from 1743, when he was 15, but his studies were interrupted by the '45 rebellion, after which he was ill and never returned to the university nor graduated. He began work with his father's firm and, between 1750 and 1754, carried out architectural commissions in Scotland with John and James. It is interesting to see the work which the brothers achieved in completing the interiors at *Hopetoun House*, which William had been working upon; also in building *Dumfries House* in Ayrshire (1754). The exterior here is straightforwardly Palladian, but inside, as in the red and yellow drawing rooms at Hopetoun House, the décor is already, despite the inexperience of the young architects, beginning to display the breakaway from Palladianism towards a lighter, rococo touch.

In 1754 Robert Adam set off on his Grand Tour with Lord Hopetoun's younger brother, the Hon. Charles Hope. Adam was away for over three years in France and Italy*. He carried out an energetic programme of work, never wasting time and knowing that this was his one great opportunity to amass the knowledge in notes and drawings to carry out his lifetime's career.

This first-hand experience added to his outstanding abilities enabled him to create the 'Adam style'.

Robert Adam returned to Britain in 1758, set up practice in London and, within an incredibly short space of time, became the fashionable architect of the day. By 1762–3 his services were in great demand and in the 1760s he produced his finest work.

Partly due to his success and partly to his temperament, which was self-confident, sometimes impatient, always wanting to tackle something new and on the grand scale, the 1770s were less fortunate for him. His phenomenal success had encouraged many imitators, none of whom possessed his fertility of imagination or quality of originality. Submerged under quantities of work, he experimented with mass-production schemes, which lowered his standards, particularly in stucco ornamentation. Financial problems arose from his impatience to get on with the work, allied to inadequate business judgement, as at the Adelphi. This, combined with what was taken to be his patronising attitude in his preface to the *Works in Architecture* of 1773, acquired for him enemies as well as envious colleagues. The last decade of his life saw him designing more and larger commissioned projects, many of them doomed to sterility as they foundered upon financial inadequacy or bureaucratic opposition.

Adam's great ambitions were to create a new, personal style, which he did, and to complete at least one great public building scheme. In this last respect he suffered as Inigo Jones had done (page 108). He evolved scheme after scheme, all manifesting careful thought, professional presentation and a high standard of individual solution. In the 1780s, little of this was carried out and he died at 63 while engaged on a number of such problems.

Visiting Syon House, Osterley, Kenwood or Kedleston one can see different interpretations of classical design. Adam was always searching for something new and suitable for a given commission and environment. Like Sir Christopher Wren, he found new solutions to differing problems but, also like Wren (page 120), his work, though variable, is instantly recognisable as his own. He created a new form of classical design, of world-wide influence, especially in the U.S.A., France and Russia, but particularly suitable for British houses; as British as Capability Brown's landscaped parks.

He was convinced by his research in Italy, as was

---

* For students who are interested to read a first-hand account of Adam's life in France and Italy, H.M. General Register House in Edinburgh is custodian to the letters which Robert Adam wrote home to his family between 1754 and 1758 (about one letter per week) and which belong to Sir John Clerk of Penicuik. The letters may be consulted in the Register House or photostat copies ordered from there.

416 *Sculptural panel, Admiralty Screen, Whitehall, 1760*

417 *Porch, Chandos House, London, c.1770*

419 *Ground Plan, St James's Square house*

418 *No. 20, St James's Square, London, c.1775*

420 *Fitzroy Square, London, from 1790*

Piranesi, that the Romans had never abided by rigid rules such as those which the Palladians followed,* but had adapted their classical orders to need and scale. Adam did this too. He would take an order, re-create its proportions and decoration, alter the accepted rulings and the result would have more of the essence of the source material than anything seen in Britain in the first half of the eighteenth century.

It is widely known that Adam designed everything in a house down to the smallest detail in order to achieve homogeneity, so much so that we tend to remember the detail rather than the whole. His interiors varied from delicate stucco arabesque-covered walls and ceilings to the Roman grandeur of the columned hall at Kedleston or the palatial richness of the ante-room at Syon. He included colour in a number of his designs; many of these can be studied in the Soane Museum and they show a grading of light ground colours with, often, white stucco ornamentation. Gilt is used sparingly.

What Adam admired most in building was movement. He achieved his interpretation of this by lightness: an ethereal quality, especially in his interiors. The fact that there are fewer exteriors by him was because he was so often asked to alter, enlarge or redecorate an existing building. At Bowood, the Admiralty Screen, Fitzroy Square and in Edinburgh he showed himself equally an exterior architect.

To sum up Adam's work in a phrase or with a label is not easy; the most appropriate is probably 'romantic classicism'.

One of Adam's first patrons was Admiral Boscawen, who in 1759 commissioned him to design the stone screen to front the *Admiralty Building* in *Whitehall*; also to redecorate the principal apartments in his own house at *Hatchlands* in Surrey. In these early works Adam did not play safe by designing in the traditional manner. He took this first opportunity to carry out his own ideas; a similar marine element of decoration appears in both commissions (416, 423). The decoration at Hatchlands is immature in comparison with the great interiors of the 1760s, the stucco is still in fairly high relief and the motifs large scale, but the Adam treatment is already recognisable. *Shardeloes*, Buckinghamshire (1758–63) illustrates the next phase,

still using high-quality materials and craftsmanship, but in more delicate vein.

Adam's work can be neatly categorised into three decades, each showing a change of mood and approach. The *1760s* were the years of his greatest success and of his best quality work. This was the decade of the great country houses, of which Syon and Kedleston are the masterpieces; only slightly less superb are Harewood, Osterley and Kenwood; while there is a great deal of fine work surviving at Bowood, Compton Verney, Croome, Mersham-le-Hatch, Newby and Nostell.

Adam drew on many sources for the designs in these houses, believing that the mode should be suited to the commission, which is why his work appears to be varied. For his palatial style he drew on the grandeur of Imperial Rome found in thermal baths and triumphal arches and the late Roman work which he had studied at Diocletian's palace in Split. For more intimate apartments he adapted the delicate stucco and fresco wall decoration he had seen at Herculaneum and which his brother James later recorded at Pompeii. He also used the purity of Greek ornament and orders, Byzantine richness of colouring and, in his exteriors, his feeling of movement from Italian Baroque.

At *Syon House*, Middlesex, there is great variety in the five state apartments which he designed *en suite* round the square courtyard of the former Medieval religious house, but the palatial theme is uppermost (426). The *great hall* is cool Roman grandeur, all in cream, white and black. It is modelled on a Roman basilica, with apses at both ends; one is coffered, the other screened and containing the steps up to the ante-room, made necessary by the differing floor levels. The Roman Doric Order (Adam's favourite for entrance halls) is used.

In each of the five rooms Adam needed to appear to change the actual dimensions since they were quite unsuited to be eighteenth-century aristocratic apartments. In the hall he reduced its apparent length by the apses and the height by the richly decorated, deeply beamed ceiling. The adjoining *ante-room* he adapted to appear a cube by his disposition of the columns outlining a square floor area and by their advanced entablatures with gilded, life-size antique figures above. The eye is so absorbed by the riot of colour in this room, the gold and white of the ceiling,

---

* Palladianism stemmed from Vitruvius who lived in the first century. The Roman Empire lasted until the fifth century and the style developed greatly in these years.

421　*East portico, Osterley House, Middlesex, from 1761*

422　*Sculptural detail, fireplace, 20, St James's Square, London, c.1775*

424　*Doorway, red drawing room, Syon House, Middlesex, from 1762*

423　*Drawing room ceiling detail, Hatchlands, Surrey, 1759–62*

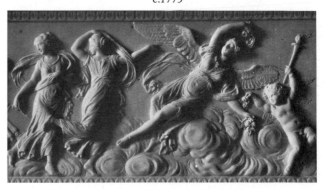

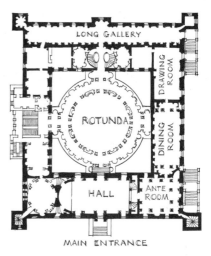

426 *Ground plan of Syon House. The rotunda and other parts (left white) not built*

425 *Ceiling detail, gallery, Harewood House, Yorkshire, 1759–71*

427 *Dining Room based upon Syon House, Middlesex, 1761–70*

the brilliant scagliola floor,* the gilding and the *verde antico* marble of the columns that it does not notice that the room is actually 36 × 30 feet and only 21 feet high.

A further illusion was created by Adam in the gallery. This Jacobean long gallery, 136 feet long by 14 feet wide and 14 feet high, was an absurd shape for a Georgian apartment. It could not be altered so Adam equipped it as a library but decorated it for use in its original capacity, for entertainment, chat and gaiety. His ceiling design of circles, octagons and squares makes the apartment appear wider and shorter. The wall articulation, treated classically in the Corinthian Order throughout, also seems to shorten the excessive length. The whole apartment is decorated in very low relief.

The other two great rooms at Syon, the gold and white *dining room* (427) and the richly red *drawing room* (424) are both superb Adam interiors.

At *Kedleston*, Derbyshire, the house had been designed and partly built by *James Paine*, who had completed the north entrance front. The plan of this Palladian house was a central rectangular block with four pavilions connected to it by curved arms (429). On the north façade Paine had built the house largely according to plan, with a heavy Corinthian portico above a rusticated basement. Adam was called in to design the south front and decorate the apartments.

Here, he pursued his theme of 'architectural movement'. The single block again has a rusticated basement, but with curving stairways to the entrance on the piano nobile. The central feature is a triumphal arch, modelled on that of Constantine in Rome, and the low dome of the saloon rises unobtrusively behind it (431). The design can only be seen in truncated form† for Adam had planned curving colonnades to corner pavilions, balancing those on the north side. His idea was to obtain his 'movement' by the Baroque

theme of convexity moving into concavity, here based upon St Peter's in Rome.

There are many fine state rooms at Kedleston, the *library*, the great *drawing room, dining room, music room* and *state bedroom*, all Adam interiors of high quality. What are remarkable though, and quite unique, are the vast Roman hall and the circular saloon. The *great hall*, on the *piano nobile*, is designed on the lines of a Roman atrium, dedicated to honouring the ancestors of the house and decorated with their statues, arms and trophies. It is an enormous apartment, lit solely from above, like the Pantheon in Rome; there are three elliptical oculi in the ceiling. The 16 vast monolithic columns and four half-columns are of local alabaster, which is cream with reddish-brown markings. Their Corthinthian capitals are in white marble and support a white entablature with dark green frieze. There are two magnificent wall fireplaces in the hall, each of white marble with, above, stucco relief sculptural decoration framing a circular painting. The grate, fire-irons and fender, in burnished brass and steel, are of Adam's finest quality.

The circular *saloon*, leading out of the hall, is 42 feet in diameter and 55 feet high. It is beautifully proportioned and decorated, from the octagonal coffering of the dome to the walls, doorways and paintings. The cast-iron stoves are, in particular, exquisitely ornamented; they are part of Adam's hot-air heating system.

Harewood House in Yorkshire also displays the Adam grand manner. The house was largely built by *John Carr* of York and Adam's exterior work on the south front was altered by Barry in the nineteenth century. Some fine interiors remain which include the hall, gallery and music room. This is one of Adam's best Doric halls, though quite different from Syon; it is smaller and more warmly treated. The entablature has a striking frieze of ox skulls and the walls are decorated with some beautiful relief panels.

As at Syon, the gallery is long and narrow: 77 × 24 feet and 21 feet high. Again, the cleverly patterned ceiling, comprising octagons, lunettes and circles all ornamented in Adam low relief stucco in motifs of griffins and arabesques with painted and sculptured panels (425), helps to detract from the apparent length of the apartment. The gallery is especially noted for the successful co-operation between Chippendale and Adam. Chippendale made most of the furniture and the three great Venetian windows have curtain boxes

---

* A favourite Adam theme was to repeat or create a similar design in floor covering to that of the ceiling above. At Syon in the ante-room this is in scagliola. At Saltram and Harewood, for example, it is in the form of a carpet woven to Adam's design.

† The high cost of the interior apartments which, at Syon, curtailed the building of Adam's rotunda over the central courtyard, at Kedleston forced the cancellation of the building of the wings and pavilions. Exterior work at Kedleston does, however, include the beautiful three-arched bridge (436).

428   *Dining Room based upon Saltram,*
       Devon, 1768–9

429   *Ground plan of Kedleston Hall*

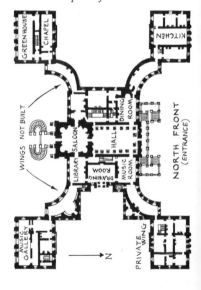

430   *Town House Reception Room,*
       1771–4

431

431 *South front, Kedleston Hall, Derbyshire, 1760 8*

432 *Door furniture, Saltram*

433 *Apse decoration, the library, Kenwood House, London, 1767–8*

434 *Fireplace detail, saloon, Nostell Priory, Yorkshire, from 1766*

432

433

434

and valances carved in wood. They are so realistic that they are generally thought to be curtaining. The pier glasses between the windows, with console tables beneath, are superb.

The *music room* is charming and still possesses its original carpet which echoes the ceiling design. It shows a circle within the square room and a central star surrounded by paterae and swags. These circular paterae reflect the Kauffmann medallions in the ceiling. The wall decoration here is classic Adam: rectangular panels of stucco design alternating with Zucchi paintings of Piranesi-type ruins.

Osterley and Kenwood show Adam in more intimate mood. *Osterley Park* is only a few miles from Syon. Here also the architect took over an existing house, this time Elizabethan. His contribution to the outside is the magnificent portico on the east (421), which is thought to owe something to the Temple of the Sun at Palmyra while the detail is like that of the Erechtheion in Athens. The Osterley portico is approached by a grand staircase of 20 steps which raise the open courtyard beyond the colonnade to *piano nobile* level in the house. The whole of the interior of Osterley, except the gallery, was decorated by Adam and there are many apartments arranged round the courtyard. Those of greatest interest are the *hall*, the *drawing room*, the *library*, the *tapestry room* (its walls covered by tapestries), the *Etruscan room* (so-called because it is decorated in Adam's 'Etruscan' manner) and the *state bedroom*. In all the rooms, as well as the fine *staircase*, the decoration of ceilings and walls is elegant and in low relief, the colours are subtle and harmonious and the doorcases, windows and chimneypieces part of the general scheme.

Kenwood House in Hampstead was remodelled in 1767–8. It is the *library* here which is of especial interest; the apartment was designed not only for displaying books but also as a room for entertaining. The rectangular form is shortened by an apse at each end fronted by a screen of Corinthian columns supporting only a bar entablature which does not hide the exquisite decoration of the semi-dome of the apse (433). This apsidal finish to one or both ends of a rectangular room was a favourite Adam device (see Syon dining room, 427), altering proportions as he needed and giving interest and mystery to the apartment. The Kenwood library ceiling is shallowly barrel vaulted and decorated all over with low relief stucco and painted oval and lunette panels. On the exterior,

Adam built the north portico which is derived from that at the Erechtheion, in Athens. The Greek detail is finely designed and carved.

Of the other houses of the 1760s which survive, of especial interest is the Diocletian Wing at *Bowood*, Wiltshire, 1761–71, the saloon at *Nostell Priory*, Yorkshire, 1766 (434), the gallery at *Croome Court*, Worcestershire, c.1760 and the hall, staircase, library tapestry room and sculpture gallery at *Newby*, Yorkshire, 1765–83.

Adam produced two widely known publications, the first the result of his studies in Split in 1758 entitled *Ruins of the Palace of the Emperor Diocletian at Spalatro in Dalmatia* (1764) and, in 1773, Volume One of *Works in Architecture of R. and J. Adam*. Both these were quality productions with fine engravings and careful text (451). The second publication was a presentation of the Adam designs and volume one was followed by others.

The decade of the *1770s* was a less harmonious one for Robert Adam. Pressure of work caused him to lower his superbly high standard of craftsmanship; his work became thinner, the decoration so low relief as to be almost spidery; the plastic quality of 'movement' waned. He carried out a great many commissions of which the chief were his town houses, the Adelphi project and country houses at Saltram and Mellerstain.

Adam's *London houses*, of which only a few remain, were planned to give accommodation for lavish entertainment and maximum privacy for the owner behind a narrow façade. Behind this front was a carefully planned suite of rooms of different shapes and sizes integrated with an originally designed staircase and landings. Such town houses are today converted into clubs, business, office and university accommodation. The two outstanding examples are 20, St James's Square and 20, Portman Square.

The house in *St James's Square* was built in 1772–3. Both this and the adjoining no. 21 belong to the Distillers' Company, who have duplicated Adam's façade across both houses, making an impressive front. The lower storey is rusticated, broken by windows and two beautiful doorways. The first and second floor are then spanned by a Corinthian Order in pilaster form, with attics and dormers above (418). The ground floor plan (419) is typical of the Adam town house and has close affiliations with the Pompeian town house.

Both houses suffered great damage in the Second World War, but have now been restored carefully and accurately to Adam's designs in the Soane Museum. There are many beautiful rooms here, typical of his decoration in this decade. The outstanding parts of the house (no. 20) are the *staircase* (443) and *well* and the first floor *withdrawing room* (now the board room). The hall rises to the full height of the house, but the single staircase ascends, as was eighteenth century custom, only to the first floor,* where it ends in a balustrated landing. The well is lit at the top by a decorative oval fanlight. The staircase balustrate has a mahogany handrail and a delicate iron balustrade. In the withdrawing room there is a segmental barrel vaulted ceiling decorated rather as in the Kenwood library. The doorcases, doors and marble mantlepiece are of fine quality (422).

No. 20, Portman Square, now the Courtauld Institute of the University of London, has a plain astylar exterior in brick and a delicate pedimented Doric porch. The interiors are of high quality, especially the *music room* on the first floor. Of unusual design is the *staircase* which is set in a circular well. It ascends from the ground floor in one central flight, then divides at the half-landing into two branches, which sweep round the well to the first landing. The balustrade is similar to that at St James's Square. On the first floor the walls are decorated with gravure paintings in monochrome; above are sculpture-filled niches and doors leading into the rooms. Higher up is an Ionic colonnade extending to a stucco decorated drum and then a low-domed, delicate, circular lantern with graceful ironwork decoration. The staircase well is tall and not extensive but the Adam design makes the utmost of the available area, giving an impression of much greater spaciousness than actually exists.

Chandos House, at the end of Queen Anne Street, was built 1770–4. Its chief feature is the elegant porch (417).

The two interesting country houses of this decade are *Saltram* in Devon and *Mellerstain* in Berwickshire. At Saltram the *saloon* and *dining room* survive; notable here are the original carpets. They reflect closely the respective ceiling designs (428).

The new house at *Mellerstain* had been begun in 1725 by William Adam, who built the two wings.

These remained separate for 40 years until Robert Adam was asked to complete the work. The house is in fine condition. The *library* is the finest room with an especially beautiful ceiling.

In the *1780s* Adam's enthusiasm and originality returned. The linear, sometimes fussy decoration of the 1770s, together with the low-relief exterior façades disappeared. Adam rediscovered his zeal for architectural plasticity. His exteriors once more displayed movement; they were characterised by the vitality of their monumental designs. Interior schemes were simpler; there was less of the spider's-web tracery of Portman Square and more of the rich interplay of colour and form that had been seen in the 1760s.

This was the decade of the great projects, large schemes which took a great deal of time to work out in detail and many of which were not built. *Cambridge University* was one of these where Adam, like James Gibbs before him (page 147), made designs for completing the great quadrangles at King's College. At *Bath*, a similar story resulted in Pulteney Bridge (page 190), and at *Edinburgh* the New Town worked out so carefully by Adam, was largely built after his death (page 210 in Chapter 10).

For much of the 1780s Adam was a commuter between London and Scotland. He carried out extensive plans and designs for London streets (page 192), but also undertook many commissions in Scotland. In *Edinburgh, H.M. General Register House* was built to designs which he had made in 1772. The Princes Street elevation has only been slightly altered and, inside, the rotunda retains its Adam decoration. He was commissioned to design new buildings for *Edinburgh University* in 1785. His plans here were for a college built round two quadrangles with a monumental entrance and elegant dome above (440). Work was begun in 1789, but only the entrance section was achieved before financial problems and the Napoleonic Wars delayed the project for 20 years. The façade on to South Bridge is much as Adam designed it (441), though the dome is not; this is a typically nineteenth-century version. The rest of the University, completed by W. H. Playfair, was constructed to a much more limited plan differing considerably from Adam's design.

Elsewhere in Scotland Adam's work in the 1780s extended to country houses as far as the Highlands. He built several projects in *Glasgow* and then worked

---

* A secondary staircase continued up to the other floors, generally on the rear side of the house.

435 *Richmond Bridge, Surrey, 1774–7,*
James Paine

436 *Bridge in the grounds of Kedleston Hall,*
Derbyshire, 1758–70, Robert Adam

437 *Pulteney Bridge, Bath, from 1770, Robert*
Adam

438 *Ironbridge, Coalbrookdale, Shropshire, over*
the Severn, 1779. First iron bridge in the
world

439 *Culloden House, Inverness-shire, c.1788*

440 *Adam's design for ground floor of Edinburgh University, 1789*

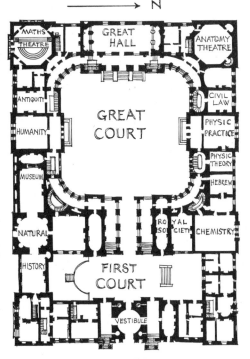

441 *Entrance to Edinburgh University on South Bridge*

on *Yester House* and *Gosford House* in East Lothian and a new house at *Newliston* in West Lothian.

At this time Adam was also designing in a castellar Medieval style related, in a Romantic manner, to the literary Gothic movement combined with the Scottish vernacular theme which had never quite died out. He set a pattern which a number of Scottish architects emulated. The chief example of this type of house is *Culzean Castle* in Ayrshire (1776–92), now the head-quarters of the Scottish National Trust. Here Adam, who was commissioned to enlarge and modernise an existing castle which was of traditional Scottish keep type, designed a boldly massed structure full of 'movement'. Culzean has a magnificent situation, built on the edge of a bluff overlooking the sea which washes the foot of the precipitous basalt cliffs 150 feet below. The architect has produced a fine stately home, romantic Medieval on the exterior and classical Adam within. The outside is dramatic and powerful (442); inside is an unusual layout (445), of which the *circular saloon* and the oval *staircase well* are exceptional. Adam designed the great drum tower on the seaward side of the house as a classic example of 'movement'. He then took advantage of its form to create this unusual circular room. The six tall windows give a breath-taking view of sea and sky with a backcloth of the mountains of the Western Isles. Ceiling and carpet designs are Adam's, not identical but of one theme. The oval stairwell is on Italian Renaissance-villa pattern, with cantilevered stairs and a balustrade curving round the well; the three orders in column and pilaster form are used, one on each floor (444).

Craftsmen of the later eighteenth century

The quality of craftsmanship which decorated the buildings of the second half of the eighteenth century was superb and has never been surpassed in England. The work carried out by painters, stuccoists, metal workers, sculptors, carvers and cabinet-makers was by men who worked with many different architects. Adam employed a number of them and without the high quality of their work he could not have achieved his magnificent interiors. None of them worked solely for Adam; they also decorated apart-ments for Chambers, Taylor, Paine, Wyatt and many other architects. Many of them came from the Continent, some were British.

Of the painters, *Angelica Kauffmann* was the best known and most colourful character. Born in Switzerland, she achieved the unusual honour, for a woman, of becoming a founder member of the Royal Academy. She had wit, charm and gaiety; she married twice, her second husband being *Antonio Zucchi*, also a talented painter. Other painters who carried out a great deal of decorative work included *Giovanni Battista Cipriani*, *Francesco Zuccarelli* and *William Hamilton*.

Some artists worked in several media, for example *Biagio Rebecca* who imitated classical sculptural reliefs as well as painted decoration. *Francesco Bartolozzi* was an expert at reproducing antique designs in engravings. An Italian of great charm, he earned large sums for his superb plates which appeared in many books published by architects. He spent the money as fast as he earned it and consumed vast quantities of alcohol and snuff, yet lived to the ripe old age of 88.

The outstanding stuccoist was *Joseph Rose*, whose superb quality of work can be seen at Syon and Harewood. Among the best sculptors and carvers were *Michael Spang*, *Thomas Carter* and *Joseph Wilton*. The chief craftsman in metal was *Matthew Boulton*; he developed the use of ormolu, widely used by Adam, especially at Syon on chimneypieces and doors.

The name of *Josiah Wedgwood* needs no introduc-tion; Wedgwood pottery is as well-known today as it was in the eighteenth century. Josiah was an energetic visionary, a shrewd businessman and a craftsman dedicated to raising the standard of his product. He aimed at purity of earthenware and made it into a work of art suitable for a queen's table, whereas previously it had been the poor relation of porcelain in the ceramics industry. *John Flaxman*, the sculptor, worked for Wedgwood for many years and modelled the famous classical friezes, medallions and plaques, many of which still ornament Wedgwood jasperware. These plaques were also incorporated in the decor-ation of furniture and chimneypieces in eighteenth-century houses.

Chippendale had set the pattern for the quality designer/cabinet-maker. Adam also designed furni-ture for his interiors and the two men worked together on a number of commissions. *John Linnell* and *William France* also worked in this field, for instance, at Kedleston and Kenwood.

442 *Culzean Castle, Ayrshire, 1771–92*

443 *Staircase, 20, St James's Square, London, c.1775*

444 *The staircase, first floor, Culzean Castle*

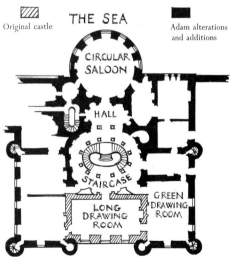

445 *Sketch plan of first floor of Culzean Castle*

448   *The Guildhall, 1775, Thomas Baldwin*

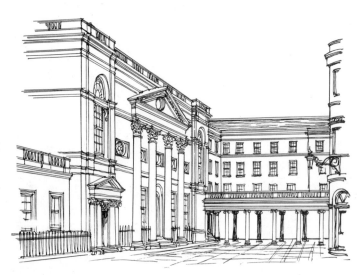

449   *The Pump Room and Colonnade, 1786–99, Baldwin
and Palmer*

446 *Pulteney Street with the Holbourne of Menstrie Museum in centre distance, 1785, Thomas Baldwin*

447 *Bath Street, 18th century, Thomas Baldwin*

450 *Lansdown Crescent, 1789–93, John Palmer*

Terrace Architecture and Town Planning

In 1760 it was still *Bath* which led the way in the design and construction of town houses in streets and crescents. Civic planning on a large scale was carried on here for the remainder of the century. The contours posed problems, with the city centre on the low-lying land flanking the Avon and the hills rising, sometimes steeply, around. The architects who designed the new town not only dealt with this problem, they took advantage of it. There were built curving terraces and crescents on the edges of these hill crowns, giving fine vistas of both city and countryside. In Bath the architecture is Palladian, well built in stone, and the conception is on the grand scale.

The work of John Wood (see Chapter 8) was continued by his son, also *John Wood*, who built the most impressive of the hill-side terraces, that of the *Royal Crescent* (1767–75). Here Wood showed himself like his father and John Carr of York, not only a provincial architect, but one whose work ranked with much of the best building created by London architects. The Crescent forms a gigantic arc following the edge of the crown of the hill, high above the city. The Ionic Order is used, with 114 columns fronting 30 houses, which present a uniform façade constructed on a major axis of 538 feet. The elevation is 47 feet high, comprising three storeys. The giant order of engaged three-quarter columns spans the first and second floors, with entablature and parapet above. The whole Crescent, although now partly internally adjusted to provide more up-to-date accommodation, is almost unchanged on the exterior; it remains one of the finest examples of terrace building in Britain.

A number of other superb terraces and crescents survive in Bath, though not quite so extensive in scale. Of special interest are *Lansdown Crescent*, 1789–93, designed by *John Palmer* (450) and *Camden Crescent*, 1788, by *John Jelly*. There is also some high quality civic work in the centre of the city, built over a number of years but of the same stone and a similar architectural style. The *Pump Room* and colonnade of the famous baths was rebuilt in 1786–8 by *Thomas Baldwin* (449), although the interior was completed by John Palmer a little later. Baldwin also designed the *Guildhall* in 1776 (448). It contains a large banqueting hall of 80 by 40 feet with an elaborate stucco patterned ceiling; the Corinthian Order is used in fluted columns standing on pedestals round the room.

Robert Adam was asked by Sir William Johnstone-Pulteney to design a new town as a suburb of Bath at Bathwick on land owned by his wife. Divided from the city by the River Avon, in the 1760s this could only be crossed by a ferry. Adam designed the *Pulteney Bridge*, which he based upon the Ponte Vecchio in Florence, a roadway lined by shops on either side. This delightful bridge survives, somewhat altered (437), but nothing was built of the rest of the scheme, though the existing Pulteney Street (446) was laid out on the site of Adam's chief artery to the suburb.

In the later decades of the century *London* slowly began to follow Bath's example in laying out town houses in streets and squares. The most impressive instance of this, the Adelphi project, is now lost to us. It was a gigantic speculative enterprise undertaken by all four of the Adam brothers in 1768. The idea arose from Robert's ambition to build a great civic scheme. Not being commissioned to do this, the brothers undertook it on their own, and it proved so vast a project that it was unsuitable financially for private means. Despite near tragedy, the brothers extricated themselves by their own acumen, their personal fortune, a public lottery and the help of influential friends. The accommodation which they built was in great demand from the time that it was finished until its demolition in 1937. The buildings were all continuously occupied for nearly two centuries as the houses and offices for which they were designed.

The Adelphi site was an area bordering the north side of the Thames called Durham Yard. There was in 1768 no embankment and where the Victoria Embankment Gardens are now laid out was a pestilential stinking area of mud which was covered at high tide. The Durham Yard site lay behind this, extending from the present Savoy Place to the Strand and from York Buildings to Shell Mex House. The scheme was to embank or drain the Thames edge and build up a Royal Terrace above vaulted arches which would be used as warehouse storage. It was hoped that the government would take over these vaults and it was their failure to do this which caused the financial crisis.

The scheme was carried out fully between 1768 and 1774. It was designed in the form of palace façades to the river, high up to give a magnificent view and to provide houses and offices there of great beauty and amenity, including stabling, water supply, heating,

451   *The Royal Terrace as it was in 1774*

452   *Doorway, No. 7, Adam Street*

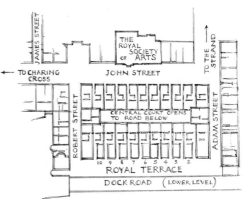

453   *Simplified sketch plan, upper level, 1774*

etc. There were two streets parallel to the Strand and cross streets at the ends (453). This was to be a great Roman palace and the similarity of its theme to the southern colonnaded wall of the Palace of Diocletian in Split was obvious to everyone, even though the architectural style was quite different (451).

The streets were all named after the Adam brothers; the name Adelphi, chosen by them, is derived from the Greek word ἀδελφοι (brothers). The cost was incredible. Architecturally the Adelphi set a pattern for town terrace building for the rest of the century. The Adam style of ornament was applied to the exterior of the building in the form of low relief projection of pilaster and entablature also in ornamental forms of carved and terracotta enrichment.

Almost the whole scheme was demolished in 1937. This act was summed up by Sacheverell Sitwell[*]: 'The Adelphi wilfully and of cupidity was pulled down. Willing hands did more damage to London than a German land-mine'; and by Dr Pevsner[†]: 'In London, the principle of the palace façade for a whole row of houses was introduced by Robert Adam in his Adelphi (that magnificent composition of streets with its Thames front known all over Europe, which was destroyed, not by bombs, but by mercenary land-owners just before the War)'.

The Royal Society of Arts building survives in John Street and the façade of No. 7 Adam Street shows the typical pilaster and ornamental treatment used on the façades of the less important houses (452).

The Adam brothers also undertook two other schemes in *London* of speculative building by streets and squares. In *Portland Place* Robert Adam planned a *Grande Place* on the Continental pattern surrounded by individual palaces, each different and specially designed for a wealthy patron. He interested a number of the wealthy aristocracy, but the American War of Independence, which began in 1775, curtailed the desire for financial speculation and the scheme was shelved. The houses, which were built a decade later, on either side of Portland Place, still a stately thoroughfare, were handled by James Adam. They are monotonous in their repetition and, due to inadequate supervision, they came as near as Adam work ever did to slap-dash standards.

Fitzroy Square was designed by Robert Adam in 1790, but was built after his death. The south and east sides (420) were constructed largely to his designs, which show a bold massing in the central block and terminal pavilions. The interiors have been altered.

---

[*] Sacheverell Sitwell, *British Architects and Craftsmen*, Batsford, 1948.
[†] Nikolaus Pevsner, *An Outline of European Architecture*, Penguin Books, 1961.

CHAPTER TEN

Late Georgian and Regency 1775–1830

The term 'Regency' in Britain is, like that of 'Queen Anne', a misleading one for it is used in the arts and architecture to describe the years from about 1790 to 1830, that is, the intermediate time between the end of Georgian Britain and the beginning of Victorian. The actual Regency – that of the Prince of Wales, later George IV – lasted only from 1811 until 1820, but the term is used here in its architectural sense. This is very much a transitional period between two different social structures. Georgian Britain had an agricultural economy, controlled by a privileged aristocracy; Victorian Britain saw the growth of industrialisation, the rapid spread of towns and the consequent depopulation of the countryside. Architecturally, as well as economically and socially, the Regency is a time of transition and a pause between two divergent ideologies. In Georgian Britain classical architecture was built for the well-to-do patron and displayed superb design and craftsmanship. Victorian Britain saw the establishment of the speculative builder, suburban expansion and the decay of taste. It also witnessed the end of original architecture in the re-emergence and adaptation of every previous style.

Although it had been developing since the mid-eighteenth century, industrialisation did not, before 1830, produce the full impact of the changes inherent in this revolution. The great engineers – Telford, Stephenson, Rennie and Brunel – were building their bridges and aqueducts, but the railway system had yet to come and the condition of the roads, though improving, still hindered easy travel.

In general, in *industrial building* traditional materials and structural methods were still employed. The silk mill in 457 is typical: a brick construction in simplified classical form. Bridges, too, were mainly of the elegant, classic design, little changed, except in their simplicity, from earlier eighteenth-century examples. The stone bridge at *Cambridge* by *Wilkins* (455) and that by *Soane* at *Tyringham* (456) are two beautiful instances of this.

Ironwork, generally wrought iron, had been used as a building material for a long time, but it was only in the late eighteenth and early nineteenth century that architects and engineers began to use it on a large scale. An early instance is the *Ironbridge* at *Coalbrookdale* (438) in Shropshire, over the River Severn. This was the first bridge in the world to be made almost entirely of iron and reflects Britain's position as the earliest industrialised nation. The bridge was built in 1779 and is now scheduled as an ancient monument. It is constructed of five parallel arch ribs almost 200 feet in length. The spandrels are filled by circles and ogee arch heads while the roadway above is made from cast iron plates of two and a half inch thickness. The bridge, which took only three months to build, weighs 400 tons.

In the early nineteenth century many bridges were made of iron as the development of cast iron proceeded apace. They became less traditional in design and were adapted to the characteristics of the newer material. An early instance is the remarkable structure of the *Pont-Cysylltau aqueduct* in the Vale of Llangollen. Built by Telford in 1805, it has an iron superstructure carried on stone piers, spanning over 1000 feet of countryside (454).

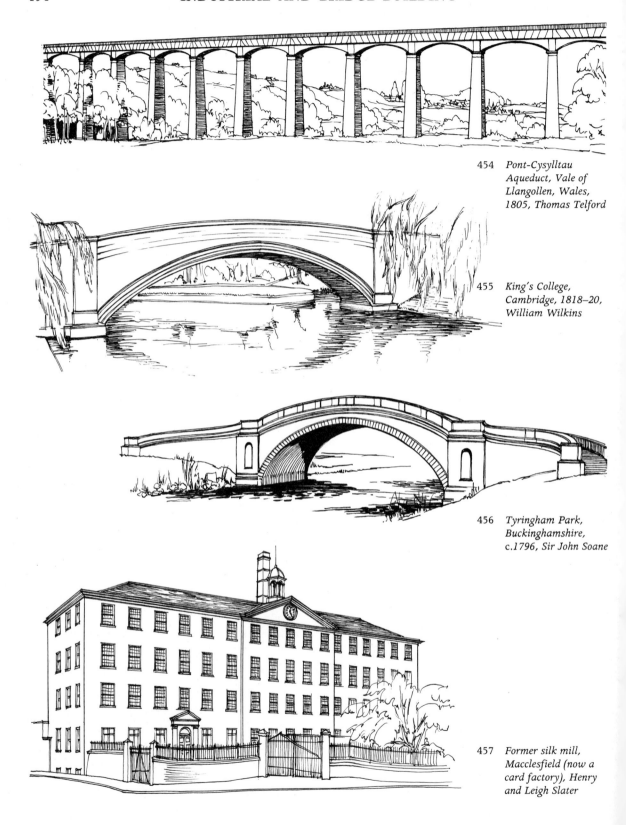

454 *Pont-Cysylltau Aqueduct, Vale of Llangollen, Wales, 1805, Thomas Telford*

455 *King's College, Cambridge, 1818–20, William Wilkins*

456 *Tyringham Park, Buckinghamshire, c.1796, Sir John Soane*

457 *Former silk mill, Macclesfield (now a card factory), Henry and Leigh Slater*

Iron was being used more and more extensively in all kinds of building, both decoratively and structurally, though up to 1830 this was mainly as decoration in canopied balconies, railings and staircase balustrades. It was a prime characteristic in Regency terrace building in particular, and superb examples of the craft survive in many parts of the country, in London, Brighton and Hove, Bristol, Cheltenham and Edinburgh (462, 466, 478, 487–92, 494, 496, 503, 507).

Late Georgian Building

In the 1770s and 1780s there were a number of architects designing in neo-classical form in a similarly elegant and eclectic manner to Robert Adam. Some of these were copyists and adapters of the Adam style, but Holland, Leverton and Wyatt were quality architects in their own right.

Henry Holland (1745–1806) designed entirely in classical style; his work was meticulous in its interpretation and detail and he preferred, in general, the simpler, subtle Greek forms to the more ornate and heavy Roman. Unfortunately most of his work has been lost, in particular his Carlton House in London and Pavilion at Brighton, both of which were commissioned for the Prince of Wales and were redesigned later by Nash. In common with other eighteenth-century architects, Holland undertook speculative building in London where he developed an area of land in *Chelsea* and laid it out in an estate which he called *Hans Town*. This comprised the streets known today as Sloane Street, Hans Place and Cadogan Place.

In 1771 Holland went into partnership with Lancelot (Capability) Brown and built a number of country houses for which Brown laid out the grounds. One of the best of Holland's surviving houses is *Southill* in Bedfordshire, which he built for Samuel Whitbread. It is typical of his work, tasteful and restrained, exquisite in detail and excellently planned. Colonnades of coupled Ionic columns connect the centre block to the two wings, all of which are pedimented, and the Ionic Order is repeated on the south façade of the main block (458).

Thomas Leverton (1743–1824) was a less original architect and patterned his work closely upon Adam and Wyatt. This has a delicate, tasteful quality which can be seen in his town houses and terraces in *London*. Here he created some beautiful interiors in romantic classical manner, with fine stucco decoration and elegant staircases with iron balustrades. Typical are several houses in *Bedford Square* (461) where No. 1, in particular, has a beautiful staircase and domed entrance hall. Of his country houses, *Woodhall Park* in Hertfordshire (1778–82) survives. An interesting feature here was the 'Etruscan' style entrance hall, with fluted ceiling and white walls decorated with painted medallions in red, yellow and red-brown. The curving staircase had a delicate, iron balustrade (462). The stairwell was stuccoed in decorative panels in the Adam manner while the domed ceiling was fluted in a fan design.

James Wyatt 1746–1813

A member of a large family of builders and architects, James was the most gifted and best known. A man of unusual talents, he experimented with all possible styles of architecture and excelled at a number of them; he is considered by some critics to be a mere copyist and by others a brilliant originator. Early in his career Wyatt was hailed as a genius. At this time Robert Adam was at the height of his fame and Wyatt began to design in the Adam manner. Infuriated, Adam complained in his *Works of Architecture* of plagiarism. Wyatt had spent some years in Italy where he had made measured drawings of St Peter's and the Pantheon. He returned to England to win the competition for the rebuilding of the *Pantheon* in Oxford Street in *London*. Designed for concerts and masquerades, it was a large, aisled hall under a giant cupola. It had a hemispherical dome like its prototype in Rome, but the decoration reflected that of Adam. The building* created a sensation when it was opened in 1772. It was a great success architecturally and functionally and established Wyatt's reputation. Aristocratic patronage began to flow in his direction.

Wyatt went on to design a number of country houses in the Adam manner and in Greek Revival form. At *Heveningham Hall* he continued the work of Sir Robert Taylor (page 171) and redecorated the interior, which possesses some fine, delicate craftsmanship (466, 467). His beautiful Orangery here has an elegant semi-circular portico (465). Heveningham is mainly in the Adam manner; in a more Greek vein

---

* The Pantheon was burnt down in 1792. It was roughly on the site now occupied by Marks and Spencer's Stores.

458 *Southill, Bedfordshire, 1796–1803, Henry Holland*

459 *Boodle's Club, London, 1780, John Crunden*

460 *St Pancras' Church, London, 1819–22, W. and H. W. Inwood*

461 *Bedford Square, London, 1774, Thomas Leverton*

462 *Woodhall Park, Hertfordshire, 1778–82, Thomas Leverton*

463 *The Radcliffe Observatory, Oxford, designed by Henry Keene, 1772, completed James Wyatt*

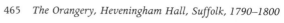

464   *Fonthill Abbey, Wiltshire, 1795–1807*

465   *The Orangery, Heveningham Hall, Suffolk, 1790–1800*

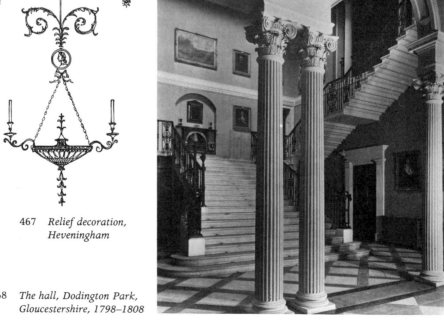

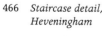

466   *Staircase detail,*
      Heveningham

467   *Relief decoration,*
      Heveningham

468   *The hall, Dodington Park,*
      Gloucestershire, 1798–1808

Wyatt built the *Radcliffe Observatory* at *Oxford*, originally designed by Henry Keene and based upon the Tower of the Winds in Athens (463).

In the early nineteenth century Wyatt turned to both Greek classicism and Romantic literary Gothic. *Dodington Park*, Gloucestershire, is a dignified Greek classical house with a large Corinthian portico and, inside, a great hall (using the Composite Order) and an imposing double staircase (468). The detail work here in ceilings, friezes and doorcases is of high standard in the best Wyatt tradition. He also designed the church at Dodington on Greek cross plan.

Wyatt built a number of Gothic houses which, like Strawberry Hill (page 170), were picturesque and Medievally romantic. *Ashridge Park*, Hertfordshire, the best known of the survivors, has a central hall taking up the whole height of the tower. The most spectacular essay into Gothic must have been *Fonthill Abbey*, Wiltshire, which he designed for the wealthy William Beckford in 1795. This immense house (464) was cruciform in plan and over 300 feet along. The tower, constructed over the crossing, ecclesiastical fashion, rose to 270 feet and, inside, the great hall was 80 feet high. At one end of this a flight of steps ascended to a saloon built under the tower. The Gothic detail (as at Strawberry Hill) was authentic. Mr Beckford was so anxious for the house to be completed that he ordered work to be carried out in shifts round the clock. Due to inadequate supervision, specified support arches to the tower were not built and some years later it collapsed in a gale and the house was afterwards demolished.

Regency Building

From the 1790s onwards the regurgitation of previous architectural styles really begins. But in the years before 1830 this is a light-hearted, still romantic affair; new sources of inspiration are tried out, tossed around and abandoned in favour of something else. It has nothing of the seriousness of Victorian eclecticism. Regency architects experimented with these architectural forms in order to create something of their own and in no case was the Regency version a close copy of the original; it was an idea, a conception to be played with. Because of this the resulting Regency architecture is interesting in its own right, suited to its time and, to us, attractive to look at and functional to use. The sources of material employed

at the time were classical, based on Greece and Rome; Gothic, still of a Romantic type, but becoming more Medieval in spirit; Italian Renaissance and Baroque and Oriental, primarily Indian.

In the years 1790–1820 there were two outstanding architects whose work dominated the time as, a generation earlier, the scene had been dominated by Chambers and Adam. Similarly, these later architects, Soane and Nash, were as great a contrast to one another in both architecture and personality as their predecessors had been.

Sir John Soane 1753–1837

Soane was the son of a bricklayer, born near Reading. He determined early in life to become an architect and this dedication to and love of architecture stayed with him strongly all his 84 years. He was articled to George Dance, then to Henry Holland. He won both gold and silver medals at the Royal Academy Schools and went to Italy on the Travelling Scholarship from 1778–80, where he studied in Rome, Paestum, Pompeii and Sicily.

Soane was the last of the line of completely original architects, which had begun with Inigo Jones. He used many styles for inspiration, mainly neo-classical, generally Greek, but he also took structural ideas and decorative treatment from Byzantine sources. Like Wren and Adam before him, he fused these sources into an architectural style which was personally Soane and characteristically English. In his later work, the austere simplicity of his barely ornamented masses foreshadow modern architecture, but for over 100 years no designer in England took up his lead.

In 1788 Sir Robert Taylor died and Soane was appointed to succeed him as Surveyor to the *Bank of England*. He held this post until 1833, during which time he carried out extensive schemes in London. At the Bank he developed his personal style. The work was monumental, stripped of all superfluous ornament, partly Greek, partly Byzantine, relying on simple, pure lines and fine proportion. Soane was never content with less than perfection; he paid meticulous care to detail as well as design.

His exterior work to the Bank of England was in the *screen wall* with which he surrounded the awkwardly triangular site. The wall had to be secure from attack and so was windowless. Soane avoided monotony, using a stylised Corinthian Order articula-

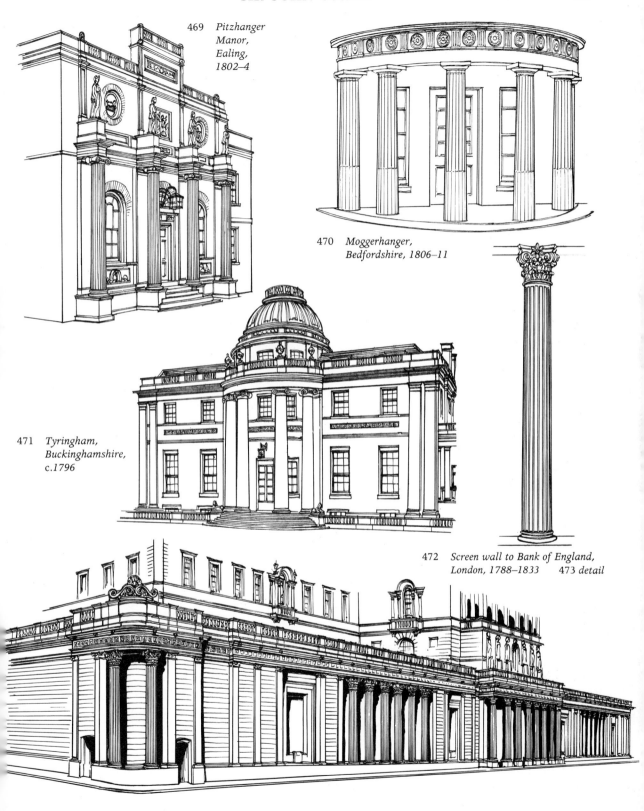

469 *Pitzhanger Manor, Ealing, 1802–4*

470 *Moggerhanger, Bedfordshire, 1806–11*

471 *Tyringham, Buckinghamshire, c.1796*

472 *Screen wall to Bank of England, London, 1788–1833* 473 *detail*

tion in the form of the Temple of Vesta at Tivoli. Even today, when the balance and proportion of the screen wall has been ruined by the vast twentieth-century superstructure, Soane's design has dignity and interest (472, 473).

His greatest originality at the Bank was in the interior halls which he lit from above with glass domes and lunettes, supporting these on austere arches and vaults, their mouldings and ornament reduced to a minimum.

It was no doubt at Paestum and Sicily that Soane began to appreciate the beauty of the monumental, archaic Doric Order. These same, sturdy, fluted columns without base, supporting a heavy abacus and entablature, which had horrified both Adam and Chambers had an austere power which appealed to Soane. He used this on the house at *Moggerhanger* in Bedfordshire (470) in 1806. At *Tyringham* in Buckinghamshire, he preferred a lofty Ionic portico leading the eye upwards to the simple cupola (455, 471).

Of greater originality were Soane's own two houses, the town house at *13, Lincoln's Inn Fields* in *London*, built 1812–14 and now the Soane Museum, and *Pitzhanger Manor, Ealing*, c.1802, his country house, now the public library (469). The former is handled in low relief with typical Soane incised decoration, while the latter is fronted by four Ionic columns with their own entablatures and pedestals. Both houses are ornamented by Soane's favourite draped figures based upon the caryatids from the Erechtheion south porch. The severe *Art Gallery and Mausoleum* at *Dulwich** (1811–14) owes little to classical architecture or, indeed, any earlier style. It is original Soane in brick with austere lines and simple masses. Apart from a rare note of detail here could be a modern building of the inter-war years.

John Nash 1752–1835

An exact contemporary of Soane, Nash was a contrast to him in every way. He was not austere or restrained but an enthusiastic extrovert. Whereas Soane's architecture was personally original, Nash's was not. Like Wyatt, Nash was a man of his age; he designed in all styles of the picturesque and romantic. He dabbled in Gothic, the Italian Renaissance, Palladian

and Greek; he built rustic-cottage country houses, castellated mansions and picturesque villas.

He was also attracted by the possibilities of Indian design and took the opportunity to experiment with his ideas when he was commissioned by the Prince Regent to build the Pavilion at *Brighton*. The royal pavilion here was originally designed by *William Porden* and built 1803–5. This had an Indian flavour, clearly influenced by *Sezincote*, designed a few years earlier for Sir Charles Cockerell who insisted on this style. Porden's building later became the *Dome Concert Hall* and Nash designed the present, colourful *Royal Pavilion*. He began the work in 1816, and, though originally planned to be in Indian style, Nash mixed his sources of design and the building might more accurately be described as 'Indian Gothic' with a flavour of Chinese, especially in the interiors (486).

John Nash's contribution to architecture lies not in his eclectic experimentation nor in the originality of his classical, design but in his brilliance as a town planner. His extensive Regent's Park terraces, the old Regent Street and Carlton House Terrace represent a far-reaching achievement in town planning, of modern dimensions carried out in a picturesque version of eighteenth-century classicism. Here was the logical continuance of the work and schemes of men like John Wood.

Nash was given a unique opportunity in 1811 to design and carry out this extensive London scheme. This was made possible by the availability of the land at the same time as a period of prosperity and energetic support from royal patronage. With this combination of circumstances Nash was enabled, between the ages of 60 and 80, to build a considerable proportion of his great scheme. The layout comprised a large area covering Regent's Park, St James's Park, Regent Street and Trafalgar Square.

In 1811 Marylebone Park property reverted to the Crown. It consisted of farmland which it was intended to develop and the Prince Regent enthusiastically backed the idea of a lavish scheme to enhance his capital. Both Nash and Leverton were asked to design a plan. Leverton's was not very original and consisted of an extension of the eighteenth-century conception of domestic squares. Nash's ideas were far more extensive and revolutionary. He set out a whole garden city for the well-to-do in the centre of the metropolis. The scheme included a park with graceful villas, a lake, a canal, crescents and terraces and focal

---

* Now rebuilt after war-time destruction.

474 *Carlton House Terrace, The Mall, 1827–32*

475 *Cumberland Terrace, Regent's Park, 1827*

476 *The Haymarket Theatre, London, 1820*

477 *All Souls' Church, Langham Place, portico, 1822–4*

478 *Hanover Terrace, Regent's Park, 1822–3*

centres such as Trafalgar Square. The *pièce-de-résistance* was to be a royal route from the Prince Regent's Park, where a summer palace was to be built, to his Carlton House in the Mall via the future Regent Street.

Nash's scheme was accepted and he began work in 1812. When he died, 23 years later, much of his vast concept, in which he energetically participated to the end, had been realised. He was forced, during these years, to forego some of his best ideas such as the double circus, many of the villas and their gardens and the Summer Palace. Regent's Park today represents only a section of his original plan and Regent Street has been totally rebuilt, though it retains its unusual quadrant line. But the terraces have largely survived and are probably appreciated more now than when they were built. In that age of critical architectural appraisal, some of the slap-dash detail and proportions which the builder had carried out from Nash's sketchy drawings, and without adequate supervision, were deplored. Today, restored and adapted to modern use, the Regent's Park Terraces display an architectural splendour against a background of mediocrity of building.

The crescents and terraces were built over a 20-year period. The earliest was *Park Crescent*, begun in 1812. It was planned as a circus but only half was built. It is a simple but impressive layout with its colonnade of coupled Ionic columns. Fronting the park are the palatial, imposing terraces of which *Cumberland Terrace* is the most monumental (475). Also impressive are *Hanover, Cornwall* and *Chester Terraces* (478). In the years 1827–32 Carlton House in the Mall was demolished and Nash replaced it with *Carlton House Terrace* (474), and St James's Park was laid out.

Regent's Park was the northern end of Nash's royal mile and Carlton House the southern. Between the two he designed the great boulevard which, commencing with Park Crescent, would sweep down Adam's Portland Place towards Oxford Circus, continue as Regent Street with the quarter circle (the Quadrant) at the lower end to bring it into line with Lower Regent Street and so to Waterloo Place. There were problems with commercial interests in Regent Street as Nash insisted upon absolute symmetry of architectural design in the Quadrant and in the Lower Regent Street approach to Carlton House. But these were overcome and the scheme was architecturally and financially successful. Nash also built *All Souls'*

Church at the northern end of Regent Street. It is an unusual design and aroused controversy for its circular porch and spiked spire (477).

In 1825 Nash was creating a new scheme aimed to connect Bloomsbury and Whitehall, with a link to the Regent Street scheme by means of Pall Mall. A new square was formed at the north end of Whitehall called, from 1831, *Trafalgar Square*. Except for St Martin-in-the-Fields, the buildings were all erected there after Nash's death by other architects. The development of the square enabled St Martin's to be viewed clearly for the first time.

Of Nash's other work in *London*, the exterior of the *Haymarket Theatre* (476) survives much as he designed it, also the *United Service Club* in Pall Mall (1828). Nothing remains from his ill-fated project of Buckingham Palace except for the beautiful *Marble Arch*, which he had based upon the Arch of Constantine in Rome and planned as a triumphal entrance arch to the palace forecourt.*

William Wilkins 1778–1839 and Sir Robert Smirke 1781–1867

These two architects belong to the next generation. Together they were responsible for the bulk of architectural commissions between 1825 and 1840. They typify their time, their work being sound, authentic in whatever style was considered suited to the individual commission – Gothic or classical in Greek or Roman form, excellently constructed and executed. By eighteenth-century standards their buildings are not inspired; they lack the originality of a Soane and the brilliance and sense for design in the mass and on the grand scale of a Nash. In comparison, though, with Victorian building, their contribution gains in stature and accomplishment.

William Wilkins was the son of an architect. He was educated at Cambridge and returned there later to carry out extensive commissions. After a period of study in Europe he published his *Antiquities of Magna Graecia* and established a reputation as an enthusiastic Greek revivalist. In *London*, Wilkins built *St George's Hospital* at Hyde Park Corner in 1827–8 and, in 1832, his best-known structure, the *National Gallery* in Trafalgar Square (Chapter 11, page 219).

---

* The Marble Arch was set up in its present position in 1851.

Sir Robert Smirke was the son of an artist and began his architectural career as a pupil of Soane. Like Wilkins, he spent some time studying in Europe, after which he began work as a convinced Greek revivalist. He acquired an exceptionally large London practice, much of which was concerned with public building. Smirke's work was almost all based upon Greek classicism; it is academic, well designed and often monumental, but rarely uplifting. His best known building is the *British Museum* (Chapter 11, page 219), but he also designed the *Royal Mint* (1809) and the *College of Physicians* in Trafalgar Square (1824–7). Here he used his favourite Greek Ionic Order as he did also in his *Shire Halls*, for example that at *Gloucester* (1814–16).

Churches

Comparatively little church building had been carried out since the impetus given by the 1711 Act providing for the erection of churches, in which Hawksmoor had been the leading spirit (page 140). By the early nineteenth century the population had increased and had been re-distributed. New centres of population had been formed by the migration of workers from country to town. To meet this situation in 1818, the Church Building Society was formed and, with Parliamentary support, a Church Building Act was passed, which provided that £1,000,000 should be spent to build new churches. The money would be allocated under the supervision of the Church Commissioners, since which time these churches have been referred to, generally in a derogatory manner, as the Commissioners' Churches. Some years later a further £500,000 was allocated and the total number of churches constructed was eventually 214, of which 174 were Gothic (see Chapter 11). The majority of these churches are in the London suburbs and in the industrial areas of Yorkshire, Lancashire and the Midlands. Few of them are aesthetically or architecturally attractive; they are nearly all large, capable of holding big congregations and most were cheaply built. In the years 1818–30 there were no terms of reference as to style and the early examples were in Greek classical form. Later the Gothic Revival movement gained ground, especially for ecclesiastical building (page 221).

The Church Commissioners were advised in their selection by a board of three architects: Nash, Soane and Smirke. All of these built one or more churches, but none of them was very interested or helpful in this project of mass production churches. They were individualists, successful and busy. No real leader emerged and it is inevitable that later generations should compare this situation and its results with the two previous opportunities which had occurred; the first after the Fire of London in 1666, when Wren had designed his 50-odd churches (page 121) and the second in 1711, when Hawksmoor and his fellow architects had stepped into the breach. Now, lamentably, there was no Wren, Gibbs or Hawksmoor and, at the same time, the Commissioners were asking for as large a church as possible to be built for as little of the taxpayers' money as possible. This injunction (so familiar today) was hardly likely to produce a St Bride's or St Martin-in-the-Fields.

A few of the earlier classical churches are exceptions to the general uninspired mass of those built in the first half of the nineteenth century; those designed by the Inwoods are amongst these. In particular, *St Pancras'* Church, London, built 1819–22, is one of the exceptionally fine Greek Revival churches and ranks with St Martin's as a great success (463). The design for the church was by *H. W. Inwood*, who had travelled for a short while in Greece and returned to win the competition at the age of 24. He and his father, W. Inwood, were partners and they built it together. The church has an unusual steeple which is based upon the Tower of the Winds in Athens, the motif being repeated in diminishing scale. The body of the church is based upon the Erechtheion in Athens, with fine detail in the Ionic Order. The design comprises a large hall with an apse at one end and the tower and portico at the other. Inside, the simple, galleried hall has a flat ceiling and rich Greek decoration. The church was costly – some £70,000 – over four times the cost of an average Commissioners' church.

Another delightful Inwood church is *All Saints'* at *Camden Town*, 1822–4. This has a tall, semi-circular portico, still in the Greek Ionic Order, and a slender, cylindrical tower. Here too the detail is delicate and finely executed (480).

Sir John Soane's contribution to the Commissioners' churches does not show his work at its best. He built three in London, *Holy Trinity, Marylebone* 1824–5, *St Peter's, Walworth* and *St John's, Bethnal Green*, 1824–5. Holy Trinity is a classical design with Ionic

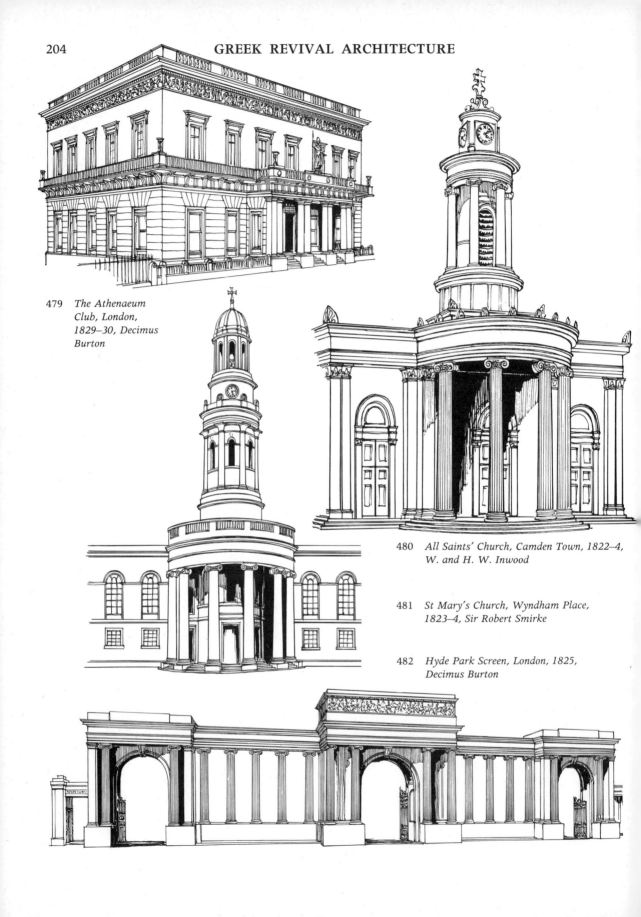

479　*The Athenaeum Club, London, 1829–30, Decimus Burton*

480　*All Saints' Church, Camden Town, 1822–4, W. and H. W. Inwood*

481　*St Mary's Church, Wyndham Place, 1823–4, Sir Robert Smirke*

482　*Hyde Park Screen, London, 1825, Decimus Burton*

porch and a traditional Corinthian tower. St John's is a more original, typically Soane design with tall, simple, round-headed windows of Gothic, plate traceried quality but with a classical doorway; the interior has been altered.

John Nash's church, *All Souls'* in Langham Place, has already been referred to (page 202). The circular porch here is of Roman Ionic design, boldly Baroque in its deep shadows and curves. The drum, below the spire, is encircled by a colonnade of Corinthian columns (477).

Sir Robert Smirke designed a greater number of churches for the Commissioners than his two colleagues. They are all on Greek Revival pattern and remarkably similar to one another. Typical is *St Mary's* in Wyndham Place in *London*, 1823–4 (481). The church is built on a terminal site on the Portman Estate and has a fine semi-circular Ionic portico. The tower is too lofty and somewhat repetitive. Similar are *St Anne's, Wandsworth*, 1820–2, *St Nicholas', Strood* and *St Philip's, Salford*, 1825.

Apart from the work of these architects, *Thomas Hardwick's* parish church of *St Marylebone*, 1813–18, is an imposing classical example, and a more delicate design was provided by *James Savage* in *St James' Church, Bermondsey*, 1827–9. Savage designed several classical churches for the Commissioners and he was also responsible for an early Gothic one, *St Luke's, Chelsea*, 1820–4 (484). Although this shows a certain lack of experience in building in Gothic, it represents a serious attempt to construct a Perpendicular Gothic church with stone, not plaster vaults, and the concomitant abutment system. It is a large, costly church with pleasing silhouette and good detail.

University Building

William Wilkins was the main contributor in this field, designing in both classical and Gothic styles. *London University* was founded at this time and Wilkins designed it in 1827–8. Now University College, the structure is fronted by an impressive Corinthian portico raised on a great podium with approach steps.* The dome is set above and to the rear. This was a new university building, erected in the centre of a great city and a break was made from the Oxford and Cambridge tradition of court plan-

ning. Here was envisaged no chapel but a central, large assembly hall with flanking libraries, museums and other accommodation. The portico was built with its entrance steps and, inside, the vestibule and grand staircase, but, strangely, the assembly hall was not carried out.

Still in classical vein, Wilkins designed the building for the new *Downing College* at *Cambridge*. A Greek Revival work, the Ionic Order from the Erechtheion is used on an austere, rather conventional structure. Not far away is his attractive, single-arched, stone bridge over the Cam at King's College (454).

In the 1820s Wilkins turned to Gothic. At this time architects still approached this style of work in a romantic manner, though it was being taken more seriously than in the eighteenth century. In 1822 Wilkins submitted a design for the completion of the great court at *King's College, Cambridge* which, despite the elaborate plans of Gibbs and, later Adam, had still not been completed (pages 147, 183). Other architects submitted designs, some classical, some Gothic. It was decided to use Gothic in order to harmonise with the Medieval chapel and Wilkins' plan for a long screen fronting the main road with a centrepiece formed by the principal entrance gateway, was accepted (483). He also built the Gothic Hall, where he broke with tradition by setting his great oriel window half-way along the elevation instead of at the daïs end.

At *Corpus Christi College* in Cambridge Wilkins designed the *New Court* in 1823–30 in Perpendicular Gothic style. The whole new quadrangle is laid out as one unified scheme which comprises library, hall and chapel. It is here that Wilkins' Gothic can best be judged as he had a free hand in a new layout. The results are pleasing and the Medieval spirit is not lacking.

Also in Gothic vein is *Rickman*[*] and *Hutchinson's New Court* at *St John's College* nearby, built 1827–31. This is in Perpendicular design too, but is warmer and more romantic than Wilkins' somewhat classical Perpendicular. There is a screen wall with central gateway and terminal features with centrally placed

---

* The side wings were added after Wilkins' time.

[*] This is Thomas Rickman (1776–1841) who published in 1817 *An Attempt to Discriminate the Styles of English Architecture*, where he gave to Medieval building the classifications of Early English, Decorated and Perpendicular (page 40).

483   *King's College, Cambridge, screen and gateway, 1822–4, William Wilkins*

484   *St Luke's Church, Chelsea, 1820–4, James Savage*

485   *St John's College, Cambridge, 1826, Rickman and Hutchinson*

486   *The Royal Pavilion, Brighton, 1816–20, John Nash*

Perpendicular oriel windows. The Perpendicular Gothic bridge, the 'Bridge of Sighs', so-called after its Venetian prototype, is by the same architects. It is a single-arched bridge and the whole scheme, with the court is undoubtedly Rickman's most successful achievement (485).

Town Planning and Terrace Architecture

Already in the later decades of the eighteenth century the Industrial Revolution had begun to cause a slow but steady migration of workers from country to town. In agricultural areas unemployment was forcing whole families to move to towns to find work in the new factories. At the same time better standards of medicine and hygiene were enabling more children to survive to adulthood and the population began to increase sharply; by 1801 it had risen to nine millions. The 20 years of war with revolutionary and Napoleonic France interrupted building programmes for new housing which soon became acutely necessary and municipal corruption and lethargy had never been greater. The slum conditions in large towns, bad in the eighteenth century, because of these varied factors deteriorated further.

Although in these years conditions of living in towns were now extremely bad for the poor, the development of civic planning and housing for the well-to-do was extending rapidly. Throughout this this period the standard of building was high; many acres of land were covered by, in the main, fine, solid graceful structures, laid out in streets and squares. Portland stone was used for larger buildings and brick, covered in stucco and painted the colour of stone, for the terraces and smaller houses. The name of John Nash is closely associated with this increase in stucco-covered façades.

Apart from the need for civic building and housing for the increasing population in London and the manufacturing towns, other small centres of population were expanding rapidly because of leisure interests. These were the spas and seaside resorts. Bath was the chief eighteenth-century example (Chapter 9), but during the Regency it was followed by such spa towns as Cheltenham and Tunbridge Wells. Along the south coast, continuing upon the popularisation of Brighton by the Prince Regent, came the extension of Hove, Hastings and St Leonards.

London

Here, as in other large cities, the quality terrace architecture built in the eighteenth century has been demolished on a widespread scale. Of the few examples which survive, with the exteriors at least mainly as they were built, are part of *Fitzroy Square*, designed by *Adam* (Chapter 9) and *Bedford Square*, where much of *Leverton's* work remains (487). A few of *Holland's* houses exist from his *Hans Town* development, but it is difficult to visualise the original scheme. *The Paragon* at *Blackheath* is a variant on the usual terrace; it consists of classical blocks connected by curving Doric colonnades (493).

It was from 1800 that the steady but accelerating growth of the capital began to transform London from a normal city surrounded by pleasant villages into a sprawling metropolis. In 1800, most of the suburbs which we now think of as near to central London were yet villages: Hampstead, Highgate, Blackheath, Putney, Chelsea. Between 1800 and 1835 were developed much of London's West End, Bloomsbury and Belgravia. The architectural standard was still good and the amenities excellent. The classical form of terrace architecture prevailed. The terraces varied from whole streets to small blocks and were curved or straight.

Apart from John Nash's Regent's Park scheme (page 200), the two men chiefly responsible for the building enterprise of these years were *James Burton* (1761–1837) and *Thomas Cubitt* (1788–1855), both of them speculative builders, not architects. Burton was a most enterprising and successful man. He developed much of *Bloomsbury*, taking over sites and letting out some work to other builders, although supervising the whole himself.

His son, *Decimus Burton*, the architect, designed much of the work for his father and also worked with Nash on the Regent's Park terraces. Decimus Burton is especially known for his *Hyde Park Corner screen*, with its graceful Ionic colonnade (482) and for the arch which he had designed as a triumphal entrance to the park. This was based upon the Arch of Titus in Rome and a sculptured quadriga was intended to surmount it.* Decimus Burton also designed the

---

* The arch was later moved to the top of Constitution Hill and its angle to the screen altered. The present quadriga was set in position in 1912 and replaced the earlier equestrian statue of Wellington.

487 *Bedford Square, London, 1780, partly by Thomas Leverton*

491 *The Promenade, Cheltenham*

492 *New Steyne, Brighton*

493 *The Paragon, Blackheath, c.1790*

494 *Lewes Crescent, Kemp Town, Brighton, H. E. Kendall*

488   *Royal Crescent, Brighton*

489   *Belgrave Square, London, 1825, George Basevi*

490
Lansdown Parade, Cheltenham

495   *Pelham Crescent, South Kensington, 1820–30, George Basevi*

496   *Brunswick Terrace, Hove, 1825, Wilds and Busby*

Athenaeum Club in Pall Mall (479). It is interesting to note here, as well as on the Hyde Park screen and Nash's United Service Club, the Greek sculptured friezes extending round the buildings. These were all inspired by the arrival of sections of the Parthenon frieze (the Elgin marbles), which had been acquired for the nation in 1816.

Thomas Cubitt continued Burton's work from the 1820s onwards. He is, perhaps, more famous particularly as the founder of the first modern-style building firm. Until Cubitt's time, work in different trades had been sub-contracted – bricklaying, masonry, carpentry, etc. – and, whereas the system had worked well enough until 1800, when large-scale development was involved, as the nineteenth century required, it showed itself inefficient and slow. Cubitt bought land and workshops and set up a firm which included all craftsmen necessary to the building trade, on a permanent wage basis. To keep his firm financially solvent he had to provide continuous work for them. This he did by large-scale speculative building. His standards in building and architecture were high, far above those of the men who followed him. Sometimes he had to sacrifice aesthetic needs to financial and domestic ones; here was the beginning of the devaluation of architectural standards, a devaluation which has continued uninterruptedly ever since.

Despite this, Cubitt performed a great service to London. Many of his houses, squares and terraces still stand; as fine, elegant and sound as they were over 100 years ago. They expose as inferior much of the later phases of development which surround them. All his life Cubitt used his influence to combat the abuses of architecture, building and living standards to which speculative building is heir. He was especially interested in drainage and London's sewage arrangements, and constantly worked to improve these. His own houses were soundly built, pleasant to live in and created to last, not just for the moment. He supplied first-class amenities in the way of land drainage, sewage, lighting and roads.

Cubitt began his development at *Highbury Park* and *Stoke Newington*, then moved on to *St Pancras* in Tavistock Square, Woburn Place and Euston Square.* The façades of his houses were in stucco in Greek

---

* Considerable loss was occasioned here in 1961, together with the great Greek Revival Euston Arch, designed by Hardwick 1838, when the new Euston Station was built.

classical style. His most extensive and best-known enterprise was his creation of *Belgravia*. When Buckingham Palace was designed from Buckingham House he realised that the area was suitable for wealthy development. He leased an area of swampy ground from Lord Grosvenor and converted it into aristocratic squares. *Belgrave Square* is typical, designed by *George Basevi*. The square is lined with classical terraces with single, large houses set at the corners (489).

George Basevi (1794–1845) had been a pupil of Soane. In a short working life he designed a great deal of terrace housing in London. Apart from Belgravia, where he worked for Cubitt between 1825 and 1840, he helped to develop South Kensington, where his *Pelham Crescent* survives (495).

Edinburgh

Scottish cities such as Glasgow, Aberdeen, Dundee and Elgin were expanding as were the English ones. At Edinburgh the final achievement of the New Town was, perhaps, the most notable because of the long delay and the extended period in which the city had been restricted to its Medieval compass.

In the mid-eighteenth century Edinburgh was still confined within its city walls, built entirely on the narrow ridge which extended from Holyrood to the Castle and which contained only one main road, the royal mile. The whole of Edinburgh was packed into this strip, one mile long and about a sixth of a mile wide. Because of this the city, in the three previous centuries, had had to extend upwards. Tall, stone tenement blocks, eight to ten storeys high, were squeezed together with narrow passages (wynds), three to five feet wide, between. These wynds are still there in the old town, with their steep steps and slopes and metal handrail up the centre, like their counterparts in Montmartre.

From early in the eighteenth century it had been decided to build a new town north of the city. In order to do this the North Loch had to be drained. This was a lake bordered by marshes, noisome and pestilential and made even less salubrious by the tanneries and slaughterhouses which by tradition lined its edges. It covered the area now occupied by the Waverley Station and Princes Street Gardens as far as the Castle Rock. The loch was finally drained in 1763 and a plan for the town chosen by competition in 1767. This plan by *James Craig* was comprehensive, but work was painfully slow. Between 1780 and 1792 *Robert Adam* carried out countless surveys and designs for the new town, but the municipal delays were endless and frustrating.

From the plan (498) of the centre of present-day Edinburgh, it can be seen that, having drained the North Loch, bridges had to be built to span this area and the Cowgate, which were steep valleys flanking the main ridge of the old city where the royal mile (High Street and Canongate) runs. The *North Bridge* was built to the designs of *Robert Mylne* and *John Adam* in 1772 and the *South Bridge* and the university façade on it to Robert Adam's in 1788.*

With the opening of the bridges the New Town could be built. It was to be laid out on grid-iron pattern in classical style within a rectangle of 4000 by 1100 feet. The main thoroughfare, George Street, was to run east/west along the ridge parallel to Princes Street and the royal mile (498). There would be a square at each end, Charlotte Square on the west and St Andrew's on the east. Most of the town was laid out after Adam's death, but the north side of Charlotte Square was built to his designs (499), as was H.M. General Register House in Princes Street.

Costs were mounting and there were delays due to the Napoleonic Wars. After 1815 the speed of building accelerated and a new generation of architects created the Greek Revival New Town, the 'Athens of the North' as it was termed. Far less fine in individual buildings than Adam's designs and architecture, the New Town nevertheless was a tremendous achievement, creating, as in Bath, a homogeneous scheme in one style and material. The city had, at last, awakened to the advantages of its topography and had utilised this to the full instead of complaining, as people had in the previous century, of not possessing a city built on flat land where it was easy to expand.

St Andrew's Square was completed as was Charlotte Square. Here, unfortunately, St George's Church, which had been planned by Adam to dominate the west side of the square, was finally built by and to the designs of *Robert Reid* (1811–14) and is an anti-climax. The terraces were completed and the Calton Hill – Edinburgh's acropolis – was covered by Greek

---

* The North Bridge was replaced in 1896 and only the engineering of the South Bridge survives; the street façades are modern.

monuments like a weighty northern Athens. On the lower slopes of the hill stands the best Greek Revival building in the city, the *Royal High School* (1829) by Thomas Hamilton (500).

In Princes Street, at the intersection of the Mound, were built Edinburgh's chief Grecian structures, the *Royal Scottish Academy* (1823–36) and the *National Gallery* (1845), both by *W. H. Playfair*, who contributed so greatly to Edinburgh's expansion in these years, including completing the University. A fine vista showing the topography of Edinburgh and the New Town development in juxtaposition with the old can be seen from the top of the Scott Monument in Princes Street (501, also see 498).

Resorts and Spas

The seaside resort of *Brighton* and *Hove*, popularised by the Prince Regent and developed from the village of Brighthelmstone, was laid out between 1800 and 1850. From Hove to Kemp Town, some three miles of sea front stand as a magnificent tribute to the terrace building of these years. There are gaps where later development has intervened, but a great deal survives. Here is the culmination of Nash's Regent's Park terraces; there is no local feeling present. The work is mainly painted stucco-faced, as in London.

Many architects contributed to the Brighton and Hove scheme. Of particular quality and distinction is the great length of *Brunswick Terrace* (496), built by *Charles Busby* and *Amon Wilds*, divided into two sections by *Brunswick Square*, by the same architects. Nearby is *Adelaide Crescent* by *Decimus Burton*, while at the other end of the sea front, are the magnificent terraces and squares at *Kemp Town* (494). Of outstanding quality also is the *Royal Crescent*, on more intimate scale, with its dark brick contrasting harmoniously with the white painted woodwork and iron canopies and railings (488). At *Hastings* and *St Leonards* there was considerable expansion also. *James Burton* and his son *Decimus* designed and built much of the fine architecture here, though less has survived than at Brighton.

Cheltenham was developed as a spa in the early nineteenth century as Bath had been in the eighteenth (490). The architect most closely associated with this was *John Buonarroti Papworth* (1775–1847), much of whose work was for Cheltenham. The son of a builder, he worked in an architect's office in London before

497   *The Regent Bridge*

498   *Simplified plan of c.1790. Shaded area represents the low ground originally covered by the North Loch water and marshlands: now the site of Waverley Station and railway, Princes Street Gardens, the Mound and art galleries. The Mound was created from earth excavated from the New Town*

A   Charlotte Square
B   North side built to Adam's designs
C   St George's Church
D   Adam houses in Queen Street
E   St Andrew's Church
F   St Andrew's Square
G   The Royal Bank of Scotland
H   H.M. General Register House
K   North Bridge
L   The Tron Church
M   St Giles' Cathedral
N   South Bridge
O   The University
T   The Castle

499 *Charlotte Square, 1791, Robert Adam*

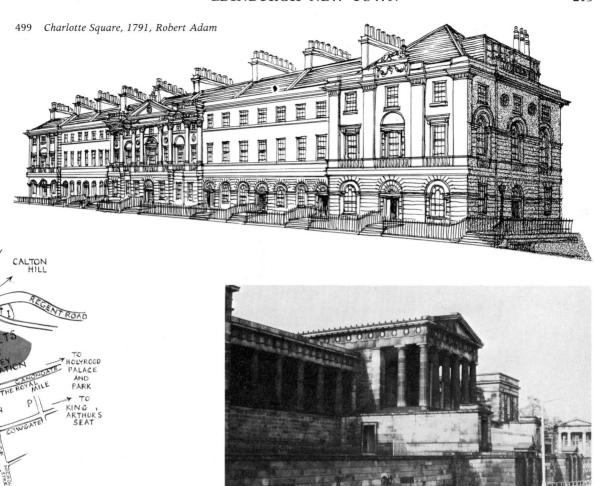

500 *The Royal High School, 1829,*
Thomas Hamilton

501 *Panorama seen from top of Scott Monument*
  A *Church of Tolbooth St John*
  B *Outlook Tower*
  C *New College and Assembly Hall*
  D *Castle*
  E *National Gallery of Scotland*
  F *Royal Scottish Academy*
  G *St Cuthbert's Church*
  H *St Mary's Cathedral*
  I *Princes Street*
  J *St George's Church*

502 *Ickworth, Suffolk,*
     1796–1830, Francis
     Sandys

503 *Staircase with iron*
     balustrade, 1790–1800

504 *Bryanston Square, London*

505 *Dining Room, c.1795.*
     Style of James Wyatt

506 *Seaside terrace house, c.1800*

507 *Serpentine scroll balustrade, c.1800*

508 *Dining Room, 1811–20*

beginning practice there himself, where he became a versatile architect. In Cheltenham he laid out the *Montpellier* and *Lansdown Estates* in mainly Greek classical style. *John B. Forbes* also contributed a great deal to the city's expansion. He initiated the *Pittville Estate*, building the *Pump Room* there in 1825–30, which like Papworth's Montpellier Pump Room is fronted by a colonnade with a rotunda rising behind. It was a great assembly hall based on Roman bath plan, but is Greek Revival in style in the Ionic Order.

At Brighton and Cheltenham, as also at *Tunbridge Wells*, where *Decimus Burton* designed the *Calverley Estate* for his father *James Burton* to build, there are many examples of decorative ironwork, wrought and cast. The variety of design in balconies, railings and canopies is infinite and the craftsmanship excellent (488, 490, 491, 492, 494, 496).

The House Interior

Ceilings and walls were most commonly stucco-decorated with classical motifs, using white and light colour shades. The ornament was similar to that which Adam had initiated, but in low relief, and it became more sparing towards the end of the century (505). Cast iron, used previously for utensils and implements, was employed more widely. It was decoratively handled and appeared in staircase balustrades, fire grates, fireplaces and stoves (507, 508). Coloured and white marbles were still widely employed, as also was scagliola. This was made from gypsum, glue, isinglass and colouring to imitate marble. It was very hard and could be polished. It was cheaper, also more plastic than marble for use as inlay so it could be used in table tops, columns and chimneypieces as well as floors.

In the later eighteenth century *staircases* were more often of stone or marble, with iron balustrade and mahogany handrails (462, 466, 503). The circular or elliptical stairwell plan was fashionable so that the staircase swept down in unbroken line from top to bottom of the house. Adam, Chambers and Wyatt had set the pattern which continued into Regency houses (507).

The doorcase was still of classical design; in large houses it was flanked by columns and surmounted by a pediment. Doors were solid, of polished mahogany, panelled and decorated with brass or ormolu. Early nineteenth-century doors were panelled in low relief. The tall, sash windows had narrow glazing bars (505). Bow windows were fashionable in the Regency (506). Some were round in section, others segmental (508).

There was a feeling of lightness in Regency houses, both in atmosphere and colour. The large windows were draped with light-coloured silk, linen or chintz curtains, often striped or delicately sprigged to echo the gowns of the day. The curtains were held back from the window to permit the light to enter the room. Wallpaper was, by 1800, the most usual wall-covering. Papers were light and gay to blend with curtains and upholstery. Stripes were fashionable, often satin-grounded, also in flock papers as well as some in imitation of marble (508).

Mirrors were still an integral part of the interior décor. They increased the illumination of the room and were decorative. All the furniture designers of the eighteenth century had made them. They had carved frames and a large area of glass divided into smaller panels by the curving frame design and incorporating candle holders. Regency mirrors were typically circular with convex glass. The frame was ornamented by balls and was surmounted by an eagle or scroll (508).

There were a number of famous furniture designers and cabinet makers who followed on from Chippendale and Adam. The two outstanding names were *Thomas Sheraton* (1751–1806) and *George Hepplewhite* (d.1786). Sheraton's furniture is noted for its apparent fragility. He had a preference for inlaid or painted furniture rather than carved decoration. Hepplewhite is known for his shield and oval-backed chairs. His furniture was also delicate and he used similar motifs to those of Adam, though he also included his 'Prince of Wales' feathers'. *Thomas Hope*, the interior decorator and furniture designer, published his *'Household Furniture and Decoration'* in 1807. This reflects his studies and travels in Greece, Sicily and Egypt and, though his work followed French Empire styles, his Regency furniture was strongly influenced by Greek and Egyptian motifs. These included sphinxes decorating the backs and arms of chairs.

PART THREE

THE AGE OF REVIVALS

CHAPTER ELEVEN

The Nineteenth Century
1830–1900

It is only now that a balanced evaluation of Victorian architecture is being made. In the first half of the twentieth century historians were too close to the previous age to assess its contribution fairly. Most condemned the work as derivative, mass-produced and in poor taste. A few, in contrast, praised fulsomely. Certainly the Victorians perpetrated much ugly, tasteless building, permitted largely uncontrolled expansion by private speculators and created for posterity immense areas of slums; but they also constructed buildings which have endured; developed a complex and extensive system of railway, road and canal communications; experimented successfully with methods of mass production in building materials; explored the possibilities of iron, glass, steel and pre-fabrication and last, not least important, created a quantity of fine architecture.

Despite continued demolition of nineteenth-century work, we still possess a great deal because so much was built. Indeed, more buildings were constructed in the nineteenth century than in all the previous ages added together; this is one of the reasons for the low standard of much of the work. It was in the years 1830–1900 that the effects of the Industrial Revolution snowballed; the movement of peoples from country to town accelerated and the higher birth-rate and better medical care raised the total number of people to an undreamt of level. To provide houses, factories, schools, colleges and civic buildings for this increased population a tremendous building drive was necessary.

Two major results of this – problems which still trouble us today – were the mass-production develop-

ment of the building industry and speculative expansion. In the early nineteenth century craftwork and hand-made decoration, furniture, etc., were still common. By 1900, ceiling plaster ornamentation, wainscot mouldings, fireplaces and decorative motifs of all types were mass-produced and applied ready-made to both outside and inside of a building. A hardness of finish and sameness of design invaded more and more the domain previously governed by aesthetic considerations; a process which has culminated in the module-based glass and concrete box architecture of our own day.

At the same time, unscrupulous members of the community, present in every age, were cashing in on the desperate need for housing. Speculators bought land on the outskirts of industrial cities and built houses, packed densely in the familiar back-to-back style of the northern and Midlands towns of the 1860s. Sanitation and amenities were totally inadequate; life was a misery for thousands and their standards of health and hygiene appallingly low. The ravaging of the British landscape by bricks and mortar in ugly shapes and monotonous rows had begun, to continue almost uninterruptedly until the present time. As the buildings rose so smoke from the myriads of coal-burning chimneys blackened their surfaces and polluted the atmosphere to create the 'peasouper' fog for which British cities were known throughout the world.

But not all Victorian town housing was of slum potential. Between the two extremes of large houses and back-to-back dwellings was also created a quantity of middle class homes. These too were often built in terrace rows. Though not usually beautiful, they were well constructed and many of them still stand and make good homes today. They contain large, well-designed and proportioned rooms. Architecturally the better examples followed the current fashions of the time. Of early Victorian schemes in *Islington, Milner Square* by *Gough* and *Roumieu,* 1841–3, (512) is an example of a simplified, classical pattern, while *R. C. Carpenter's* Lonsdale Square,* 1838, is in the current Perpendicular Gothic mode (511). Later in the century, terrace building for the well-to-do was more commonly on a Baroque classical theme with French-style mansard roofs or Flemish gables. In London, *Albert Hall Mansions,* 1879, a brick block of flats and *Grosvenor Place,*† 1865–75, are typical (513).

By 1850 there were appearing, in Europe as well as England, philanthropists, visionaries and architects of social purpose, ahead of their time and current thinking. In Germany there was Krupp at Essen, in England Sir Titus Salt in Yorkshire. Such men built 'ideal townships' for their workers, with housing, shops and amenities near to the factories. These were the pioneers of the new town or garden city concept of the twentieth century.

Saltaire was the first example of a 'New Town' in Britain. *Sir Titus Salt,* the Bradford mill-owner, built a new Italianate mill on the banks of the River Aire a few miles from the city and, around it, houses, a hospital, library, church, institute and almshouses for his workers. Each house had a parlour, kitchen, pantry, cellar, three bedrooms and outside toilet. Built of stone, in terrace form, the streets were named after Sir Titus' large family of children: Titus, Caroline, George, William, Henry, etc. (509). Though lacking some of the 'mod cons' expected in a new town of 1975, these houses were well built. They are pleasantly situated and were palaces compared to the slums in which other Bradford workers lived at the time.

A similar scheme, on a smaller scale, was initiated at *Copley,* a village near Halifax, where a Grecian-style mill and about 100 houses were built to the designs of *W. H. Crossland* in the 1860s. These stone houses are simple, late Gothic in design.

---

* Carpenter's finest work is Lancing College chapel (515), built in Decorated Gothic style in 1854–5.

† Being demolished piece-meal and replaced by modern buildings.

Later, a housing experiment was carried out at *Bedford Park* in *London.* Here was no industrial centre or industrialised founder. In 1876 *Mr J. T. Carr* initiated the construction of a housing estate to be built centred round a church, general stores and club. Several architects worked on the project over many years: *Norman Shaw, Maurice Adams, E. J. May* and *Sir Ernest George.* The houses are of brick, semi-detached and in terraces, suitable for families of moderate income. They have gabled roofs and many are built in Shaw's Queen Anne and Dutch manner (510).

In style the Victorian age was one in which previous designs were revived. There was not a single earlier style which architects did not emulate and adapt to their use. The two fundamental types of building – classical and Gothic – were used in all their forms. Classical architecture was designed in Greek, Roman, Italian and French-Renaissance clothing, while Gothic appeared in all its guises from Romanesque and Lancet to Perpendicular and Tudor. Many architects designed in both classical and Gothic form, suiting the style to the building. Although there was no rule, classical forms were preferred for civic and public building – government offices, town halls, university colleges – and Gothic for ecclesiastical and domestic work. This was particularly so before 1855–60, after which time the Gothic Revival became stronger than the classical faction and Gothic town halls, station façades and academic buildings appeared all over the country.

In the 1830s the leading architects continued to design their important structures in Greek Revival manner. *Sir Robert Smirke's British Museum* (517) is an impressive example, with its tremendous south front of 48 Ionic columns. The building is constructed round an open quadrangle and the Ionic colonnade continues round it. It was *Sidney Smirke,* Sir Robert's younger brother, who covered in the quadrangle with a cast iron dome to create the reading room in the 1850s. *William Wilkins* built the rather less successful National Gallery in Trafalgar Square (1832–8) and *George Basevi* began his *Fitzwilliam Museum* in *Cambridge* in 1837; this has a fine Corinthian portico.

Charles R. Cockerell (1788–1863) succeeded Soane as architect to the *Bank of England* in 1833. Whereas Taylor and Soane had both contributed chiefly to the London headquarters, Cockerell made his reputation in building branch banks in large industrial cities. Of

509   *Titus Street, Saltaire, Yorkshire, 1854–70, Lockwood and Mawson*

510   *Bedford Park, London, from 1876*

511   *Lonsdale Square, Islington, 1838, R. C. Carpenter*

512   *Milner Square, Islington, 1841–3, Gough and Roumieu*

513   *Grosvenor Place, London, c.1867–75*

similar Greek Revival design are those at *Bristol, Plymouth, Manchester* and *Liverpool* (516). Apart from the banks and insurance offices, Cockerell was also responsible for the *Taylorian Museum* (the Ashmolean) at Oxford (1840–5).

The outstanding classical building of the nineteenth century is *St George's Hall* in *Liverpool*, designed by an architect who died of tuberculosis at the early age of 34, *Harvey Lonsdale Elmes*. The structure was planned to incorporate a great central hall for concert performances flanked by the crown court on one side and the civil court on the other. The building occupies a fine site in the centre of a great square in the city and is a remarkable design for a young and inexperienced architect who had never visited Italy or Greece. The exterior is in Greek classical form in the Corinthian Order (514), while the interior is the essence of Roman grandeur based upon the great vaulted Baths of Caracalla.

In Gothic design the most outstanding and most popular structure is the *Palace of Westminster*. It is fortunate that such a building was designed in the 1830s before the Gothic Revival had gathered momentum. In 1834 the old Palace was destroyed by fire. It was decided that the new Palace should be Gothic in style to harmonise with the nearby Westminster Abbey and that it must incorporate the Medieval Westminster Hall and St Stephen's Chapel from the old Palace. *Sir Charles Barry* (1795–1860) won the competition and the first stone was laid in 1840.

At this time the fashionable interpretation of Gothic was in the Perpendicular form. This attracted Barry also because it would harmonise most closely with the Henry VII Chapel of Westminster Abbey opposite and because he was in sympathy with the chaste, rectilinear simplicity of the style. Barry's handling of the design problems was masterly. He retained Westminster Hall and, in the centre of his new building, made an octagonal chamber with lantern above; a chamber which gives direct access through St Stephen's Hall to Westminster Hall. At the southwest corner is set the Victoria Tower and, at the opposite end of the Palace, the more delicate Clock Tower (containing Big Ben). The finest view of the limestone building is from the river (518, 519).

Because of his close connections over so many years with the Palace of Westminster, Barry is often thought of as a Victorian-Gothic architect, but he carried out a great deal of work in the 1830s and much of it was in classical idiom; he was a man of his age and believed in suiting the style to the commission. His *St Peter's Church* at *Brighton* (1823–8) is Gothic, but in the *Royal Institution, Manchester* (1824–35 and now the City Art Gallery), the *Treasury Buildings* in *Whitehall* (1846) and his London clubs, the *Reform* (1837) and the *Travellers'* (1829–31), he used either Greek or Italian Renaissance classical. He also remodelled a number of large houses in classical and Elizabethan design.

Although he lived until 1860, Barry was not a Gothic Revival architect. His work was authentic in style and structure but his attitude to Gothic was nearer that of earlier designers. The Gothic Revival was seriously established in Britain by the idealists and thinkers rather than the architects. The movement was espoused by men who advanced it on moral and theological grounds. They were desperately sincere and had a deep belief that only a man moral and good in heart could design great architecture and that an immoral man could only create inferior work. They also believed that the Middle Ages was the greatest period of human endeavour and of the human spirit and that the arts and architecture which emanated from that time were the most beautiful. They aimed to recreate such architecture. They had a horror of architectural sham and thought that any material which had not existed in the Middle Ages should not be used in Gothic Revival ones. They abhorred the work of the years 1780–1840 when architects had used plaster to surface vaulting and incorporated iron as column structure.

One important influence of this type was the *ecclesiological movement*, which emanated from Oxford and Cambridge. Ecclesiologists believed strongly that, not only was Gothic the true style, especially for ecclesiastical architecture, but it must be late thirteenth-century Gothic or 'Middle Pointed' as they termed it. Another forceful influence was *John Ruskin*, the art critic. He was one of the most fervent prophets of the Gothic Revival and, by his works, especially the *Seven Lamps of Architecture* and the *Stones of Venice*, spread and popularised it.

The third important protagonist was *A. W. N. Pugin*, who was writer, decorator and architect. In his *Contrasts: or a Parallel between the noble edifices of the fourteenth and fifteenth centuries and similar Buildings of the present day. Shewing the present decay of Taste,*

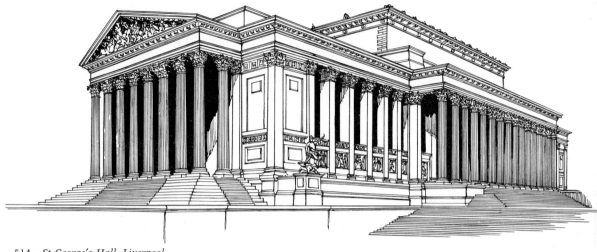

514 *St George's Hall, Liverpool,*
     1839–54, Harvey Lonsdale
     Elmes

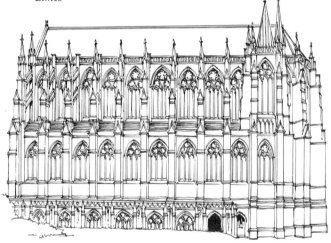

515 *Lancing College Chapel, Sussex,*
     1854, R. C. Carpenter

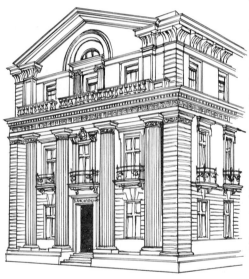

516 *The Bank of England, Liverpool,*
     1845, C. R. Cockerell

517 *The British Museum, London,*
     1825–47, Sir Robert Smirke

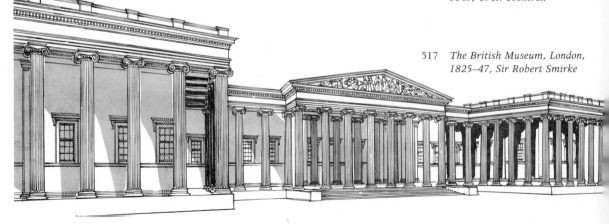

518 *The Palace of Westminster, 1836–65, Sir Charles Barry*

519 *Detail, Palace of Westminster*

520 *Bristol Cathedral, west doorway, 1868–88, G. E. Street*

521 *St James the Less, Westminster, 1858–61, G. E. Street*

he sought to prove the inferiority and immorality of Renaissance architecture by showing drawings, beautifully executed, of a fine Medieval structure side by side with an inferior standard nineteenth-century classical one. Pugin worked unceasingly, writing, drawing and designing. His output was enormous. He followed his *'Contrasts'* with *The True Principles of Pointed or Christian Architecture*, where he tried to show that the decorative features of a Medieval building are essential parts of it, not a veneer. Unlike his early nineteenth-century predecessors he understood fully Medieval structural principles and put these into practice in his churches such as *St George's* (now the Cathedral), *Southwark* (1848), the *Roman Catholic Cathedral of Birmingham* (1839–41), *St Giles', Cheadle* (1841–6) (523), *St Marie's, Derby* (1838) and *St Augustine, Ramsgate* (1846). He designed a number of houses also, but his chief monument is his work on the *Palace of Westminster*, where he collaborated with Barry and made all the designs and supervised the work for the ornament, stained glass, fittings and furniture (519).

Shortly before his death Pugin arranged the *Medieval Court* for the *Great Exhibition* of 1851. He undertook the work with his usual passionate enthusiasm, although he did not scruple to make clear his scorn and contempt for the building itself: 'a greenhouse', he called it.

The question may be asked: 'What is the fundamental difference between the architecture of the Gothic Revival and that of the Middle Ages?' It is clear that there are differences, but these are not easy to define. The chief of them is in the craftsmanship. Medieval work evolved over hundreds of years. A large body of craftsmen spent their lives carving, modelling, painting and working in plaster, glass, iron or wood. In the nineteenth century, after several hundred years of classical design, there were no craftsmen in Gothic architecture. Barry and Pugin had to train a new school of craftsmen to build the Palace of Westminster. Their work was excellent but, after 1850, the pace of work accelerated and demand far exceeded the supply of all forms of craftsmen. So means of mass-production of decorative features had to be developed. It is this which gives the hard, repetitive finish of a nineteenth-century finial or capital. Medieval buildings took many years to erect: nineteenth-century ones could be completed in months.

Another difference is in spirit. Medieval building arose from the religious feeling of its time. In the nineteenth century religious fervour was strong but it was not the sole basis for life. Lord Clark* expresses this feeling vividly: 'Although the saints in a modern Catholic image shop are extremely virtuous, they are obviously the product of an utterly worldly civilisation, whereas the gargoyles of a Medieval cathedral, though monsters of vice, are alive with the spirit of a truly religious age.'

The Gothic Revival in Britain was at its height from 1855–85. Termed the High Victorian Gothic period, its chief designers were Street, Waterhouse, Scott and Butterfield. These architects, and many others, covered the country with Gothic structures: town halls, hotels, administrative centres, university and school buildings and railway stations. The ecclesiological doctrine had now triumphed, indeed the pressure from the society's influential members upon architects to toe the line or else forego the commission had been great. As time passed, earlier Medieval sources were sought; Barry's Palace of Westminster had been derived from Perpendicular Gothic, High Victorian design was based on 'Middle Pointed' and then Lancet and even Romanesque, though many buildings also incorporated a dash of Venetian, Flemish or French flavour.

George Edmund Street (1824–81) was a deeply religious man, an ecclesiologist and a believer in the theory of the indissolubility of a clear conscience and a great architect. His work was strong and uncompromising, with a fondness for colour and polychromatic patterning. His *Church of St James the Less* in *Westminster* is typical, built in red and black brick and with a richly decorated, dark interior (521). Street's best known work is the *Law Courts* in the Strand (1868–82); he spent many years also in Medieval restoration work as at *Bristol Cathedral* (520).

Alfred Waterhouse (1830–1905) carried out many larger projects in industrial cities. They are monumental, polychromatic, boldly three-dimensional and arouse strong feelings in the beholder. The harsh colours of his red, yellow and black bricks, ornamented with terracotta, have matured to a softer blend with the passage of time and structures such as the *Natural History Museum* and *Prudential Assurance*

---

* Kenneth Clark, *The Gothic Revival*, John Murray, 1962.

Building in London and his *Town Hall* in *Manchester* are more tolerantly, even affectionately, regarded than they were 30 years ago (524).

Sir George Gilbert Scott (1811–78) represents the quintessence of the Gothic Revival. Less original than his colleagues, he was responsible for the greatest number of buildings and for popularising the movement. He believed in it implicitly and was a great admirer of Pugin. Hardworking and sincere, he was the founder of an architectural dynasty which spread over a century. His output was tremendous; he was engaged on and responsible for some 730 buildings, many of which were pedestrian. Of particular interest are some of the structures which have aroused controversy over the years but are now returning to favour, such as the *St Pancras Station Hotel* façade (522), the *Albert Memorial* and the *Foreign Office* in *Whitehall*.

William Butterfield (1814–1900) was the architect most revered by the ecclesiologists. A reserved, arrogant, deeply religious man, most of his work was ecclesiastical, in churches and universities. His style was highly individualistic, characterised by strong massing, lofty steeples and stronger and harsher polychrome colouring than that of any other architect. He did not believe in painted colour, but used durable materials for his ornament: mosaic, tile, brick, marble and alabaster. *All Saints', Margaret Street* is typical of his churches and *Keble College, Oxford* his best work (525). The chapel here aroused fierce controversy for many years, but opinion has mellowed as has, fortunately, his harsh polychromy.

A vital, far-reaching contribution to architecture was made by the nineteenth-century development of the potentialities of *steel, iron* and *glass*. The great engineers of the first half of the century such as *Telford, Rennie, Stephenson* and *Brunel* had shown by their bridges and aqueducts what could be done with iron and steel. Pioneering examples which survive include the *Clifton Bridge* over the Avon gorge at Bristol (528) and those at *Conway* (529) and the *Menai Straits*. Not only were these structures great technical achievements, they also rank among the finest aesthetically; as innovators and designers the Victorian engineers led the architects.

The nineteenth century was the *railway age* and in this field engineer and architect worked together to provide a previously undreamt of comprehensive transport system for everyone, as well as creating the railway termini – the 'cathedrals' of their time. The technical advances in the production and use of cast iron spread over into the terminus buildings. Railway architecture was in classical, and later, Gothic style, but its structural basis was iron. Many of the best examples, such as Euston Station, have been demolished, but much of the iron structure at Paddington survives; also the façade at King's Cross (526).

Another famous 'cathedral' of the nineteenth century was the structure of glass and iron designed to house the Great Exhibition of 1851. Dubbed '*The Crystal Palace*' by Punch, it has been known by this name ever since. In 1850 a competition was held which included the proviso that it must be possible to dismantle the building and re-erect it elsewhere. This precluded the use of traditional building materials and the competition was won by *Sir Joseph Paxton*, who was not an architect but a gardener and glasshouse designer. His Crystal Palace was a pre-fabricated glasshouse of vast dimensions (530). It was erected in Hyde Park for the exhibition in less than five months. 1851 feet in length, it contained 900,000 square feet of glass in a metal framework supported on over 3000 iron columns. In 1852 it was dismantled and re-erected at Sydenham where it was in popular use until its destruction by fire in 1936.

The Crystal Palace was bitterly criticised at the time by many architects, as well as by both Pugin and Ruskin, to whom a pre-fabricated building constructed by mass-production methods was anathema. But it was an important innovation both for the use of the materials and the structural methods employed and pointed the way towards modern techniques.

Large country and town *houses* were still being built during the nineteenth century by all the leading architects of the day who designed these in the current mode. *Barry* built and re-designed a number using, for the example, the Elizabethan style at *Highclere Castle* in Hampshire (1842–4) and Italian palace design at *Bridgewater House* in London (1849); *Harlaxton Manor*, Lincolnshire, by *Anthony Salvin* (1831–55) is typical of the Perpendicular Gothic phase and *Pugin's Scarisbrick Hall*, Lancashire (1837) has an ecclesiastical flavour.

At the same time the rapidly growing and well-to-do middle class was building its houses. These were of considerable size, good construction, solid and complacent. The family of substance, from 1855 onwards, seemed to find in the 'Medieval' architec-

522 *St Pancras Station Hotel,
1865–75, Sir George Gilbert Scott*

523 *St Giles' Church, Cheadle,
1841–6, A. W. N. Pugin*

524 *Manchester Town Hall, 1869,
Alfred Waterhouse*

525 *Keble College, Oxford, 1868–82,
William Butterfield*

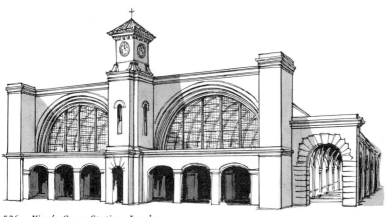

526 *King's Cross Station, London,*
1852, Lewis Cubitt

527 *Seaside Ironwork, Brighton*

528 *Clifton Suspension Bridge, Avon*
Gorge, 702 ft. span, 1836–64,
I. K. Brunel

529 *Conway Road Suspension*
Bridge, 1826, Thomas
Telford

530 *The Crystal Palace, Hyde*
Park, London, 1850–1,
Sir Joseph Paxton

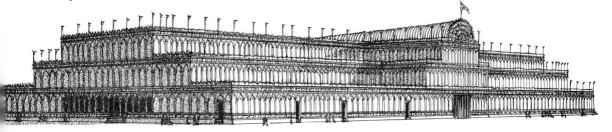

tural style the answer to its desire for romantic building and artistic expression. These Gothic houses were mass-produced, built of ornately decorated polychrome brick and stone. Simplicity of line and ornament was rare. They were often a mixture of Medieval styles; a single house might contain features of early Gothic and Tudor with Flemish sixteenth-century gabling.

Many examples of such houses survive, now divided into several flats, on the inner ring of such cities as London, Oxford, Reading, Manchester or Edinburgh (538). The main floor, the Georgian *piano nobile*, is approached via a flight of steps to the front porch; there is a bay window at one side, extending downwards to the floor below, which is the half-basement or area storey. Generally there are one or two floors above the first and attics and dormers in the roof. Victorian town houses are tall rather than wide and steep gables and chimney stacks break the skyline. Coloured brick is used in yellow, red and black, with brick and stone dressings round the Gothic windows. The Medieval-style capitals, columns and ornament were factory-produced and appear hard and bulbous.

In the 1860s the romantic absorption with the Middle Ages was giving to some painters, designers and architects a longing to get away from Victorian overdecoration, spurious materials and mass-production. *William Morris* (1834–96) particularly abhorred the trend towards mechanisation and tried to re-establish the quality of craftsmanship and simplicity in design. When he married in 1859 he commissioned his friend, the architect *Philip Webb*, to build his home in traditional materials in English farmhouse style. This was the *Red House* at *Bexley Heath* in Kent.

Unable to find the designs of textiles and furniture that he wanted he designed these himself and, with his friends, for instance Edward Burne-Jones, founded the firm of Morris and Co., which became known for quality design and workmanship in the making of textiles, wallpaper, furniture, coloured glass, murals and weaving. The well-to-do flocked to buy the firm's products, but Morris, the Socialist, was bitterly disappointed that the cost of producing articles by the individual craft method could not compete with the mass-produced item and so put his work out of reach of the average buyer.

Morris' ambition to elevate the craftsman again to the position which he had held in Medieval society

failed – the clock could not be put back – but his re-introduction of quality design and the use of genuine materials slowly began to influence a new generation of architects and designers.

Especially in domestic architecture a number of these men began to design in simpler style, using traditional materials. The buildings were still 'revivals', but of a plainer type evidencing quality of taste. *Philip Webb* (1831–1915) was followed by the most versatile of these architects, *Norman Shaw* (1831–1912), who adopted a number of differing styles to suit the client of a town or country house, demonstrating both his astounding adaptability and his instinct for tasteful design and good craftsmanship. In particular, he is noted for his houses based upon sixteenth-century half-timber work (536) and Flemish brick-work with terracotta ornament (532). He also developed a Dutch Palladian style as at *Bryanston* (531) and a Queen Anne town house pattern as at No. 170 Queen's Gate (1888) in South Kensington. Shaw was not only a domestic architect; he carried out a quantity of civic and public building as in, for instance, his insurance blocks in Pall Mall and, the best-known, *New Scotland Yard** where he experimented with Scottish baronial style in polychrome banding of Dartmoor granite with brick (535).

With the last decade of the century the work of Voysey and Mackintosh presaged the development of modern architecture. *C. F. A. Voysey* (1857–1941) was not only an architect, but designed also wallpapers, fabrics and furniture. His work was plain with clean lines in traditional materials. His houses were also traditional, but the plan was informal and the elevations unsymmetrical. The walls were roughcast in white, the ceilings low and the roofs long and sloping with lean-to buttresses. His window openings are characteristic, plain and rectangular casements with leaded lights. Typical are his own home, '*The Orchard*' at *Chorleywood* (533) and the pair of terrace houses in London (537).

Voysey's houses, though modern in their simplicity, were still traditional. The work of the Scottish architect *Charles Rennie Mackintosh* (1869–1928) more nearly heralded the functionalism of the twentieth century. His *Glasgow School of Art* (1896–1909) was designed on stark, uncompromising lines

---

* The Embankment building, not the modern structure in Broadway.

531 *Bryanston House, Dorset, 1890, Norman Shaw*

532 *Ornamental detail, 196 Queen's Gate, London, 1875, Norman Shaw*

533 *'The Orchard', Chorley Wood, Hertfordshire, 1898–9, C. F. A. Voysey*

534 *Bishopsgate Institute, London, 1893–4, C. Harrison Townsend*

535 *New Scotland Yard, London, 1886–90, Norman Shaw*

536 *'Wispers', Midhurst, Sussex, 1875, Norman Shaw*

537   *14–16 Hans Road,*
      Kensington, 1891,
      C. F. A. Voysey

538   *Gothic suburban house,*
      1860–70

539   *Early Victorian drawing*
      room, c.1840–8

which owed nothing to the past. His decorative work and furniture showed the influence of Art Nouveau, as does also the work of C. Harrison Townsend (534).

From 1835 onwards the *rooms* of a house were crowded increasingly with furniture, furnishings and ornaments. Colour schemes became darker and the light was obscured more and more by curtains and fringes. Fig. 539 shows an early Victorian drawing room where this trend has begun. The wallpaper is still light-coloured and striped and the ceiling white and plain but the Victorian furniture is heavier and more ornate than that of the Regency, and the room is more crowded with pieces, including the typical papier mâché work. The room is lit by gas, supplemented by candles and wall mirrors are now small and ornately framed.

By 1855–60 all surfaces were decorated. Carpet, wallpaper and furnishings were designed with large floral motifs in strong, dark colours and the paintwork was usually a heavy brown. The grate was of black-leaded cast iron and the chimneypiece above a complex polished mahogany or painted wood erection draped with fringed and tasselled velvet, its shelves and nooks overflowing with bric-à-brac. Long lace curtains hid the windows and these were flanked by heavy velvet or brocade ones to be drawn at dusk. There was a profusion of brass, porcelain, glass, papier mâché, lace and tatting – all demanding hours of housework, from a large, easily obtainable staff.

In the last decade of the century in the interior of the house, like the exterior, overdecoration was controlled. Eighteenth-century revivals in décor and furniture followed quickly upon one another. There was a vogue for neo-Adam decoration and imitation Sheraton and Hepplewhite furniture. There were still too many pieces filling the available space, but the intolerable clutter and obsessive ornamentation was abating.

PART FOUR

MODERN ARCHITECTURE

CHAPTER TWELVE

The Twentieth Century

British architecture, like that of Western Europe, had been a story told in two styles only: Gothic and classical. The twentieth century has produced something quite different which is international and owes nothing to its predecessors. Modern architecture is the term universally applied to this style of building which evolved in a number of countries after the First World War and which has culminated in the current designs of glass, concrete and steel based on module construction presently being erected all over the world. No-one has yet suggested a better name to describe these structures which appear to have no link with past styles.

There were four primary causes for the emergence of modern architecture:

1. The nineteenth-century population explosion in Europe which, together with the effects of the Industrial Revolution, made urgently necessary an increased rate of building for all purposes.
2. The development of new building materials and methods.
3. The deep desire of architects, designers and artists for a change of style.
4. The extensive destruction in two World Wars which necessitated the rebuilding of whole towns as well as particular sites.

Although the third point is a valid one, the development of modern design became inevitable chiefly from the pressure engendered by points one and four. This pressure hastened the development in materials and technology which made it possible to erect cheaply by mass-production methods and prefabricated systems on a large scale. Together these factors have brought about a transformation in the building scene and have killed for ever the architectural industry founded upon craftsmanship and an aesthetic basis.

Before the emergence of the modern movement, the strange ephemeral episode of *Art Nouveau* manifested itself. Appearing in a number of European countries from 1890, it had burnt itself out by 1914. It was a decorative rather than an architectural movement though it showed itself in early twentieth-century building design. Though short-lived and limited in its scope, it is important historically in architecture as an early attempt to break away from eclecticism. It was not entirely successful in this but manifested a deeply-felt striving to do so. The chief materials used in Art Nouveau were iron and glass, also faïence, terracotta and veneers. In England the decorative forms were applied in interior decoration in fabric design and stained glass. Architectural examples on the fringe of the movement included *C. Harrison Townsend's Whitechapel Art Gallery*, 1900 and *Bishopsgate Institute* (534), both in *London*, and *C. R. Mackintosh's Glasgow School of Art* (page 228).

Art Nouveau was in part an escape for architects who wished to break away from eclecticism but who also shied away from industrialisation and technology. They preferred the world of the individual, the craftsman, the cottage industry. It was an extension of the ideas of Morris and Ruskin. Based upon backward-glancing, it could not last. The First World War finally broke down the illusions and post-1918 architects were either eclectics or modernists.

Apart from the small voice of Art Nouveau, architecture in Britain until 1914 was eclectic, largely a continuation of late Victorian work. Based upon classical or Gothic prototypes, more often the former, some of the best works evidenced a robust baroque theme inspired by the building of the Grand and Petit Palais in Paris at the turn of the century. Of this type, the extensive layout of the *Cardiff City Centre* (543, 544), the *Central Hall, Westminster* (545) and the *town hall* at *Deptford* (540) all by the firm of *Lanchester, Stewart and Rickards* are excellent examples. Well designed and finely detailed, the city centre in Cardiff, in particular, has stood the test of time well.

At the turn of the century, the work of Voysey, Shaw and Mackintosh had put British architecture in the vanguard in Europe. It looked as though Britain would continue to lead when, due to her pre-eminence industrially, she developed an early use of steel frame construction for buildings. But this was not to be and the possibilities of a new architectural style based upon steel girder construction were not followed up. Instead, the traditional stone façade was used to clothe the steel structure so that, in appearance, there was no difference between such buildings and nineteenth-century ones. The *Ritz Hotel* in *Piccadilly* and the *Morning Post Building* in the *Strand* were both built in 1906 by *Mewès and Davis* with steel framing, but the Ritz in particular is faced with a heavy stone façade more Renaissance than modern.

Building impetus gathered force after the First World War and there was great activity in Britain in the years 1920–9. Designs continued to be traditional, the workmanship was of good quality but architects were reticent about moving into new fields. The trend towards a modern architecture was solely in the simplification of the classical or Gothic form. Buildings became plainer with large areas of empty wall scarcely enriched by sculpture or any other ornamentation. Vacuity was mistaken for simplicity. In the classical field the early work had been led by such men as *Sir Aston Webb* (Victoria and Albert Museum, Cromwell Road façade, 1899–1909, Admiralty Arch, 1910, Buckingham Palace façade), *Sir Reginald Blomfield* (the Quadrant, Regent Street) and *Sir Guy Dawber* and *Sir Ernest Newton* in domestic building. This was all competent, traditional classicism in the English vernacular. In the 1920s architects such as *Vincent Harris, Herbert Rowse* and *Sir Herbert Baker* contined the theme, the work still competent but becoming more aridly unoriginal as time passed.

The outstanding figure of the time was *Sir Edwin Lutyens* (1869–1944). His work was also traditional, generally on a classical basis, streamlined and simplified, yet definably personal. He worked in all fields: civic, housing, ecclesiastical. Like Wren, Adam and Shaw he handled the simplified classicism of his day in the specifically English manner, yet placed his own original mark upon it to make it recognisably Lutyens. His earlier work was in country house building where, following in the tradition of Shaw and Voysey, he used brick, half-timber and stone in pleasing, spacious designs suited to the individual commission. Typical are *Heathcote, Ilkley*, 1906, of local stone, *The Deanery, Sonning*, 1899–1901 and *Tigbourne Court, Surrey* (547, 549) in brick.

Lutyens built few town houses (36, Smith Square, Westminster is a survivor), but his work in *Hampstead Garden Suburb*, begun 1908, shows his traditional brickwork. Here he built the pleasing churches and Institute Buildings in the centre of the estate (572). His low-cost council scheme in *Page Street, Westminster* (548) is a more original housing complex. Here he used light grey bricks, Portland stone and white cement to produce a chequer-board pattern in successive rectangular blocks on courtyard layout. The effect is austere, modern and non-eclectic, apart from the white painted sash windows. It is one of his most original works.

In the early 1920s Lutyens turned to large civic schemes and developed his classical theme. One of his best works is *Britannic House* in Finsbury Circus in London (546). Typical of his simpler, more streamlined approach is the *Reuter Building* in Fleet Street. He built a number of these large, plain classical structures, particularly as architect to the *Midland Bank*.

Another traditionalist was *Sir Giles Gilbert Scott* (1880–1960), grandson of the nineteenth-century Sir George. In a large number of churches, work on abbey, cathedral and university chapel restoration and building, Scott evolved a simplified Gothic style as Lutyens had done in classical form.

His outstanding contributions were in widely different fields: the Anglican Cathedral of Liverpool and in power station design. Scott won the competition for *Liverpool Cathedral* in 1901 at the age of 21. It is a fine design: Gothic in modern dress. It is a red sandstone building with a high vault and impressive tower. The high cost and difficulty of finding sufficient funds and skilled labour has delayed its completion, but now the nave is the only part unfinished. The last of the great Gothic-style cathedrals, it is perhaps an anachronism, though a worthy swan song.

541, 542
*London Life Assurance
Building, 1924,
W. Curtis Green*

543   *Cardiff City Centre*

540   *Deptford Town Hall,
London, 1902, Lanchester,
Stewart and Rickards*

544   *Central Wesleyan Hall,
Westminster, 1906–12,
Lanchester and Rickards*

545   *The City Hall, Cardiff City
Centre, 1897–1906,
Lanchester, Stewart and
Rickards*

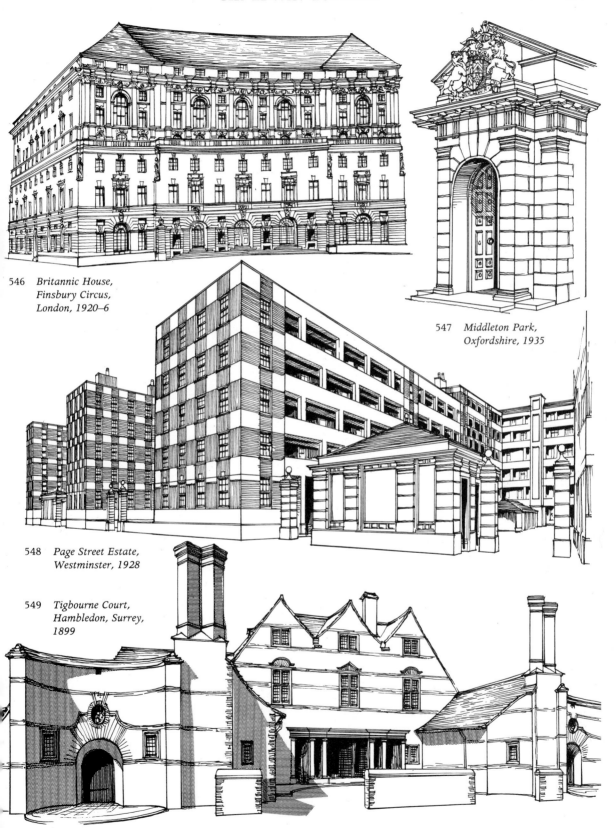

546 *Britannic House,*
Finsbury Circus,
London, 1920–6

547 *Middleton Park,*
Oxfordshire, 1935

548 *Page Street Estate,*
Westminster, 1928

549 *Tigbourne Court,*
Hambledon, Surrey,
1899

Scott's Medieval design in his churches is less interesting, though it is typical of the period (551). Other architects followed in this style of emasculated Gothic from *Sir Edward Maufe's Cathedral* on Stag Hill at *Guildford* (553) and his *Church* of *St Thomas* at *Hanwell* (1933) and the *Church* of *St Wilfred* at *Brighton* by *Goodhart-Rendel*.

In 1929 Scott set the pattern for *power station* design in Britain with his brick building at *Battersea* on the Thames in London. He continued with this type of work till late in life; at the age of 79 he was consulting architect for the nuclear power station at Berkeley. In 1937–52 he built the new *Waterloo Bridge* in London and was later consultant for the Forth Road Bridge near Edinburgh.

Although genuine modern architecture did not appear in England until the 1930s, a few structures showed indications and a slow trend towards its adoption. *Adelaide House* at London Bridge (1924) and the *Kodak Building* in Kingsway (1911), both by Sir John Burnet's firm, are early examples of steel framing with the structure visible and marked in the façades. There followed the plain block architecture, superficially modern in appearance but still with classical window openings, shorn of mouldings and ornament. *Senate House* at *London University* (1933–7), *Shell Mex House* (1929), *Broadcasting House* (1929) and *Bush House* (1925–8) all in *London*, are typical. The best example of this type is *Broadway House*, the headquarters of the Transport Executive by *Sir Charles Holden* (1929), though at *Swansea, Sir Percy Thomas* built a new civic centre as interesting and characteristic of its period as the earlier Baroque layout at Cardiff (559).

The Modern Movement

A few architects were experimenting with new ideas before 1918, but in general it was an inter-war creation. These modern architects rejected ornament; in reaction to nineteenth-century overdecoration and eclecticism they produced buildings which were stark, denuded of softening enrichment. They were concerned with the proper use of material and architectural structure.

It is paradoxical that the centuries where men had the original thought and courage to defy the tradition of the established architectural schools should mainly have been among those which, in the 1920s and 1930s,

submitted to totalitarian government. Such totalitarianism made it impossible for these original artists to work, so they emigrated, suffered in prisons and camps, died or submitted to dictation in their work. These countries – Germany, Italy and the U.S.S.R. – produced more than half of the original thinkers and designers of modern architecture.

Many of the leaders of modern architecture were born in the decade 1880–90. A large proportion of them lived to a considerable age and, like Mies Van der Rohe, Gropius and Le Corbusier, continued working and creating interesting designs until very recently at the end of their lives.

There are many 'isms' to which modern architecture has been subject in its evolution since 1920. These are often incomprehensible to the layman, in themselves difficult to define and explain and represent the stages through which many of the architects passed, often quickly and without regret. Expressionism was current just before and after the First World War, then came Constructivism, but it was Functionalism which was chiefly associated with the movement in the 1920s. This, the need for a building to be designed suitably for its purpose, had always been a tenet of good architecture, but one which had to a certain extent been lost sight of in nineteenth-century eclecticism. The leaders of the modern school were impressed by the theme of structure, of making it visible and unashamed, not covered by a classical or other façade. They were intrigued by the new technology and by engineering projects and the shapes evolved: spheres, cylinders, cones, cubes. They worked out the economics of building in these forms, endlessly repeated to facilitate cheap production. Their careful idealistic schemes became lost under the calculations of accountants, the mass of buildings required, under municipal and parliamentary authorities and the amount of money available, so that everything became subject to the theory that if a building were efficiently designed for its purpose it must, willy-nilly, be beautiful. Early essays on these principles, especially in housing, were disappointing. The results showed plain concrete blocks, relieved only by a railing or a gate. Stark simplicity was characteristic, but before long architects learnt to handle the new materials and to adapt to the new freedom of design. For centuries architectural proportions and form had been governed by structural means. Steel and concrete building meant

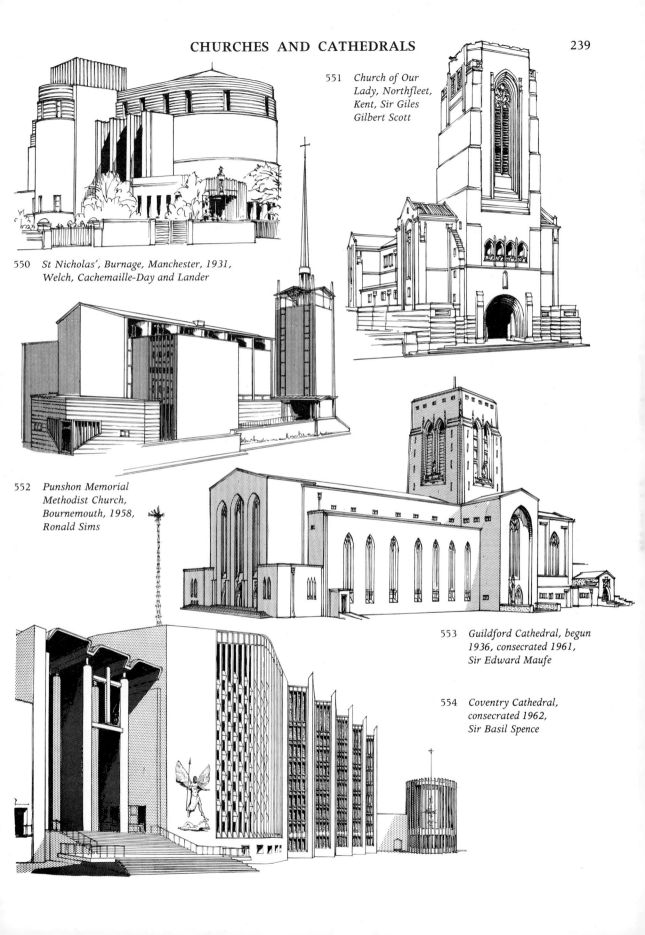

551 *Church of Our Lady, Northfleet, Kent, Sir Giles Gilbert Scott*

550 *St Nicholas', Burnage, Manchester, 1931, Welch, Cachemaille-Day and Lander*

552 *Punshon Memorial Methodist Church, Bournemouth, 1958, Ronald Sims*

553 *Guildford Cathedral, begun 1936, consecrated 1961, Sir Edward Maufe*

554 *Coventry Cathedral, consecrated 1962, Sir Basil Spence*

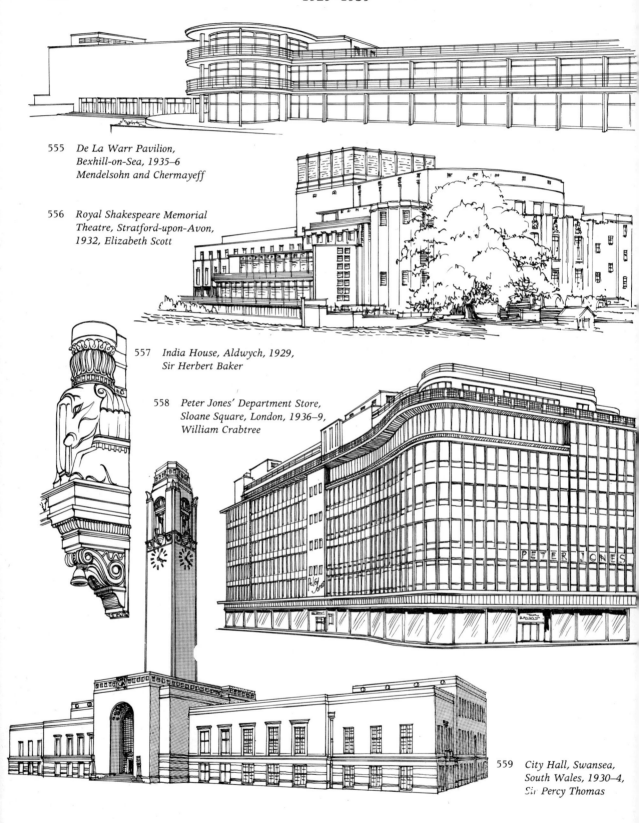

555   *De La Warr Pavilion,*
Bexhill-on-Sea, 1935–6
Mendelsohn and Chermayeff

556   *Royal Shakespeare Memorial*
Theatre, Stratford-upon-Avon,
1932, Elizabeth Scott

557   *India House, Aldwych, 1929,*
Sir Herbert Baker

558   *Peter Jones' Department Store,*
Sloane Square, London, 1936–9,
William Crabtree

559   *City Hall, Swansea,*
South Wales, 1930–4,
Sir Percy Thomas

that many of the old concepts of weight, support and strength were outdated. The architect was now free to design heights, spans and loads far greater than had previously been known. Only slowly did most of them take full advantage of this opportunity.

In the U.S.A. architects such as *Frank Lloyd Wright* and *Louis Sullivan* had been experimenting for some time with these new concepts and structures. In France *Le Corbusier* was developing his *'Urbanisme'* theories; in Italy *Terragni* was at work. In Russia there were *Lissitzsky* and *Melnikov*, in Switzerland, *Moser* and in Holland, *Oud* and *Dudok*. In Europe, probably the most influential centre was the Bauhaus.

It was in 1919 that *Walter Gropius* was appointed at Weimar to head the Art College which developed into the *Staatliches Bauhaus*. Here he was able to put into practice his strongly held ideas. He was so successful that this small college, which trained only a few hundred students in the short years of its existence, became architecturally world famous, a Mecca which attracted architects, artists and students from all over Europe. Artists of such stature as Paul Klee from Switzerland and Vassili Kandinsky from Russia were two who joined this orbit.

Gropius' idea was to set up an institution where students in all the arts and crafts could study and learn one from another. He abhorred the artificial barriers which existed between artists and craftsmen and between artists practising in different media. He saw them all as interdependant. He felt that the manual dexterity in the craft was as vital and necessary as the mental contribution of the designer. So every Bauhaus student, whatever his field of work or talent, took the same workshop training. He saw and studied what was necessary for the complete design. When qualified he was able to comprehend and oversee all the aesthetic and constructional processes in his field.

In these theories Gropius was returning, as William Morris had wanted to do, to the Renaissance architects' comprehension and facility in all the visual arts, but, unlike Morris, he did not want to set the clock back, but embraced with enthusiasm all the advantages of modern technology, adapting and utilising them to the needs of architectural design.

Genuine modern architecture was unusual in Britain before 1945. The few examples which were built were chiefly by the European architects who fled from their own countries in the 1930s and came to seek political asylum in Britain. Although some would have liked to stay in the country, mainly they emigrated further, mostly to the U.S.A., because the architectural opportunities in England for modern architecture were so limited. The British profession was still dominated by the traditionalists.

Walter Gropius himself came in 1934. He designed one or two buildings, notably *Impington Village College*, Cambridgeshire with Maxwell Fry and departed for the U.S.A. in 1937. *Erich Mendelsohn* also came from Germany, in 1933. He built the *De la Warr Pavilion* at *Bexhill-on-Sea* (555) in 1936 with *Serge Chermayeff* (from the Caucasus), then went to Palestine and later to the U.S.A. *Berthold Lubetkin*, also from the Caucausus, founded the firm of *Tecton* which built the *Highpoint Flats* at *Highgate*, also the *Finsbury Health Centre*, both in 1938. *Peter Behrens*, who came from Germany, built one of the first modern houses in Britain as early as 1926. This is *'New Ways'* in *Northampton*, which is a starkly plain block with a triangular metal-framed window extending vertically the full height of the house above the severe canopied doorway.

The lead given by these Continental architects encouraged modern building in Britain. In the 1930s, slowly, some of the younger architects broke away from the traditional school led by Lutyens and Scott to design functionally in steel, concrete and glass. At first a modern design was produced in brick in plain blocks constructed on steel framing. *Sir John Burnet's Royal Masonic Hospital* at Ravenscourt Park (1930–3) is a purpose-built structure of this type; so also were *Sir Charles Holden's* new *London Underground Stations* as, for example, the circular one at Arnos Grove (1932).

Much closer to the Continental functionalist pattern was the new *factory* for *Boots Pure Drug Company* at Beeston by *Sir Owen Williams*. The site of 236 acres was acquired in 1927 near Nottingham on the River Trent. Williams designed two sections of the pharmaceutical factory, the 'wets' and the 'drys', the former for liquids, creams and pastes, the latter for powders and tablets. Completed in 1932 and 1938 respectively, these two structures are based on the unit dimension system in steel and concrete with an immense area of glass curtain walling under a cantilever roof construction.

A parallel structure was designed by *William Crabtree* in *London*. Equally ahead of its time in

Britain this is *Peter Jones' department store* (558). Reminiscent of Mendelsohn's earlier work in Germany, the façade is wrapped round the structure in a curving glass and steel front, almost Perpendicular Gothic in its reticulated panelling.

Architecture since 1945

The pattern had now finally changed. No building had been carried out for six years and vast areas of destroyed and damaged property needed replacing. No longer were traditional architectural methods adequate, so in Britain, as elsewhere in Europe, the international style was accepted and followed. Within a decade a new problem emerged, that of reconciling the needs of pedestrians and motor vehicles for space in the city streets.

Since 1950 a tremendous quantity of building has been carried out. The town planner has become an important factor in the scheme and, both in reconstruction and in new layouts, the scale encompasses wider areas of land and groups of buildings for different but related purpose.

Despite the international character of modern architecture, national traditions still make themselves felt, based, as they always have been, on climate, resources, individual life style and economic necessity. Thus, although modern architecture everywhere is based on module construction and the same materials of glass, steel, and concrete are used, there are differences between the work of countries and areas. For example, due to an advanced steel industry, British modern architecture follows that of the U.S.A. and Germany in steel-framed building, which means designs based upon the rectangular block, then glass curtain-walled or concrete faced. In Italy or Spain, for instance, where steel is less readily available, there is greater stress upon reinforced concrete, often designed in parabolic curves and vaults. Again, in Mediterranean countries, glass curtain-walling is less suited to a hot, sunny climate and the traditional desire for colour is seen in bright mosaic and painted exterior murals.

In order to carry out the immense building programme needed after the War, standardisation of design and form was inevitable. This, together with the quantity of structures completed, has led to monotony. As more and more of the architecture of the past centuries is demolished to make way for present needs this monotony increases. A visit to some of the cities of West Germany, where the original buildings were almost 90% destroyed – West Berlin for example – shows that no matter how high the quality of the modern work, if there is little leavening provided by older structures, there is a chilly uniformity to a city which is entirely newly built.

It is not always easy to blend the architecture of previous centuries with modern work. It was possible to build new structures in the seventeenth and eighteenth centuries side by side with those of the fifteenth and sixteenth. The style may have been different but the material and scale was the same. Nothing can blend successfully a 200-foot modern tower with the intimate Medieval or classical structure. A visit to the City of London, where office blocks rise far above dainty Wren steeples or to St Giles' Circus where Centrepoint stands alone, incongruously overshadowing the pre-war structures limited by the 100-foot cornice line, shows the incompatibility of such a marriage. At least the re-emergent cities of Essen and Düsseldorf do not have this problem.

Typical of major structures erected in the first decade after the war are the Royal Festival Hall and Coventry Cathedral. Neither of these is out of scale with surrounding buildings and, though modern in treatment and structure, there is nothing aggressively different about them. The *Royal Festival Hall* was the permanent building which stemmed from the Festival of Britain held in 1951 to commemorate the Great Exhibition of 100 years earlier. Designed by the L.C.C. architects *Robert Matthew* and *Leslie Martin* (560), the hall has been a great success. Simple, and due to the austerity of the period, perhaps a little clinical in appearance, it is functional and pleasant inside, well heated and ventilated, and with an acoustic system which totally shuts out the noise of the adjacent railway yet retains that of the concert performer. The auditorium (seating nearly 3500) is the principal feature of the Royal Festival Hall. The site was restricted, so it is raised on stilts above two foyers, on different levels, where concert-goers can stroll and view the river during intervals. The auditorium is sealed within an outer envelope which includes restaurants bars and a theatre.

Coventry Cathedral (554) is very much a product of its age. It is a modern building wherein have been employed modern methods of construction and

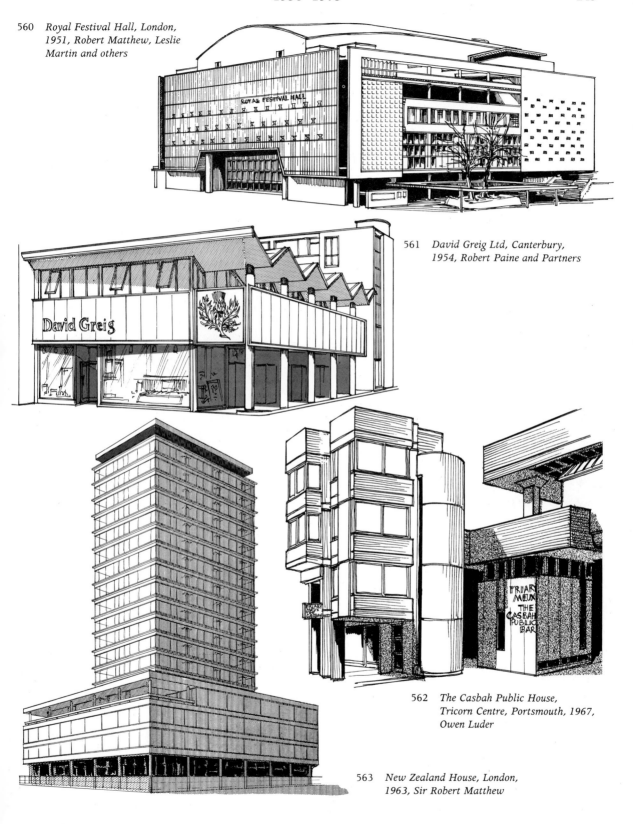

560 *Royal Festival Hall, London, 1951, Robert Matthew, Leslie Martin and others*

561 *David Greig Ltd, Canterbury, 1954, Robert Paine and Partners*

562 *The Casbah Public House, Tricorn Centre, Portsmouth, 1967, Owen Luder*

563 *New Zealand House, London, 1963, Sir Robert Matthew*

decoration. But, as the architect, *Sir Basil Spence*, has stated it is a traditional cathedral in plan, scale and materials. It is completely different from its Medieval and Renaissance predecessors yet its interior has that quality essential to all cathedral churches, the power to move and uplift the human spirit. On the exterior of this not large building of pinkish-grey sandstone the sole sculptural decoration is provided by *Sir Jacob Epstein's* bronze 25-feet high group of St Michael and the Devil. The work, which is one of the sculptor's last but finest, is ideally placed, set off by the great expanse of plain sandstone around it. Inside, of supreme quality, is the gloriously coloured 195-light baptistery window by *John Piper* and the two chapels. The focal centre, above the altar, is the tapestry of Christ by *Graham Sutherland*. The glass entrance screen, engraved by *John Hutton* (as at Guildford) gives a fairy-like quality to the end of the cathedral. It screens and protects from the outside but does not cut off or obscure. There is no full stop here, only a gossamer barrier between the new cathedral and the remains of the old.

In the years 1955–65 architecture became more modern and large scale. *New Zealand House* in *London* by *Sir Robert Matthew* is a good example of the tower block rising from its podium on Le Corbusier-type pilotis (563). The *Millbank Tower* (1963) by *Ronald Ward and Partners* is a loftier structure, it having been possible to retain the height of the original design due to the open site on the Thames embankment. The *B.B.C. Television Centre* is an interesting building by *Norman and Dawbarn*. This is circular in plan with a hollow centre and subsidiary blocks radiating from the external circle. It was the first attempt to provide studios purpose-built for television. The exterior is largely brick and glass; inside is a variety of colour and texture of which the highlight is the great abstract mural by *John Piper*.

Many new *hotels* have been built in the 1960s, especially in London. These are of varied design, in tall blocks and in long, low masses. In several instances the circular theme has been used; typical are the *Ariel Hotel* at London Airport, 1961, *Russell Diplock Associates* and the *Grand Metropolitan Hotel* in Knightsbridge, 1974, which is rather like a circular Centrepoint and by the same architect (*Seifert*).

More original than Coventry in its design and imaginative use of modern structural opportunities is the *Roman Catholic Cathedral of Liverpool*, built 1962–7 by *Sir Frederick Gibberd* to replace Lutyens' abandoned design.* It is constructed on circular plan – the centrally planned church of the Renaissance ideal – but this is no eclectic building. It is like an immense marquee with a glass lantern and metal crown above (564). The cathedral is built on the immense podium of its classical predecessor and has an outside sacrament chapel and altar where open air services are held. Inside, the cathedral emanates, by the handling of its spatial features and both the natural and artificial lighting, the spiritual quality to be felt in the great Medieval cathedrals. There is no white light. The natural lighting comes entirely from the lantern, of which the glass ranges through all the spectrum colours, and from the narrow strips of glass in the nave walls. Chapels are inserted into these walls all round, squeezed in between the great sloping buttresses which offset the thrust of the 2000-ton lantern. The lighting is rich and glowing, even on a dull day; in sunshine, it becomes magical. The altar is set in the centre of the grey-patterned floor. Round it are concentric rings of pews and, above, is suspended the delicate, metal baldacchino.

Sir Frederick Gibberd also designed the smaller but interestingly original new public library at *Redbridge* in London. This again is centrally planned, with high and top lighting.

The expansion of higher education since 1945 has led to a tremendous quantity of building for universities and technical colleges as well as new schools. Much of this work is pedestrian and, in the last decade, economy has dictated the architectural terms. Work of high quality at the *established universities* would include *Arts Faculty* buildings (1961) by *Casson* and *Conder* at *Cambridge*, also *Fitzwilliam House* (1961) by *Denys Lasdun* there (565) and, in more 'brutalist' form, the new *Churchill College* (1964) by *Richard Sheppard*. *Manchester University* pioneered the concept of a large, unified student community and there are some interesting buildings in the layout at Owen's Park student village.

Some original architectural designs have been carried out at *Durham University*. In the buildings fronting the A1 trunk road the façades have been kept

---

* This was designed by Lutyens in 1929 and intended to be an immense neo-classical cathedral. Due to the Second World War, the death of the architect and accelerating costs, the project was abandoned when only the crypt and sacristy had been built.

564 *Metropolitan Cathedral of Christ the
King, Liverpool, 1962–7, Sir Frederick
Gibberd*

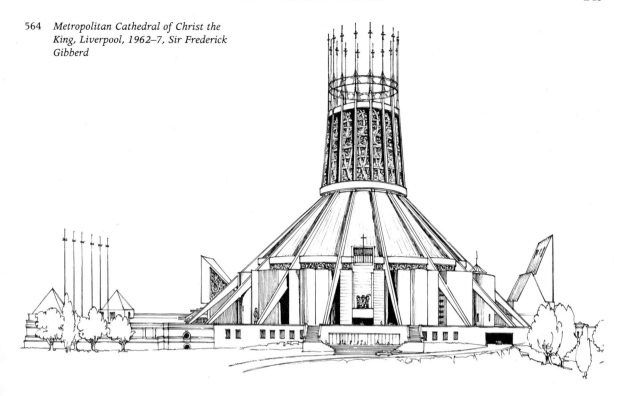

blind to cut out noise and dirt and advantage is taken of the natural lighting on the opposite elevation. Dunhelm House at the university is an interesting design reminiscent of Le Corbusier's Convent of La Tourette at Eveux-sur-l'Abresle. It is one of a number of buildings which, in the 1960s and 1970s, lean towards the 'brutalist' approach. Brutalism has not been a new replacement movement, indeed it was more an innovation of the 1950s than the 1960s, but the precepts of its exponents, usually the younger architects, took time before they were accepted and carried into practice, and then chiefly for public and university building. Such work is forceful and honest in its use of materials: concrete, slatted or boarded, brick, steel and/or glass. The main point is, that the materials should be used plainly and openly and should not be a disguise for something else. Brutalist form shows itself in powerful, simple, logical patterns, in massive, thrusting design. Although the theme owes much to Le Corbusier, it also stems from the pioneers of similar ideals in the 1920s and 1930s, such as Terragni of Italy and Mies Van der Rohe of Germany.

The *new universities* gave the greatest opportunities to the architect-planner. One of the earliest of these,

Sussex University, is built on a fine site of rolling country between the Downs and the sea at Falmer. The chief architect, *Sir Basil Spence*, has used a brick and concrete format, combining the two media skilfully in an arcaded style. This can be seen in the first building constructed, Falmer House, 1962–3, which has a central court in traditional British university pattern. The flattish arches are repeated, though the balance and proportion differs on each of the three floors (566). The architect's Meeting House is also interesting; of the two floors, the lower is designed for relaxation, the upper as a circular chapel. The work at Sussex is an example of 'brutalist' design in the more traditional materials.

York University has not only been constructed on a new site, but it has been extensively landscaped and the water-logged ground drained to provide a most attractive artificial lake around which the colleges are planned (567). The buildings are well and pleasantly designed and include some unusual structures such as the central hall with its roof suspended from an A-frame. Designed by *Sir Robert Matthew*, the university was begun in the early 1960s and work still continues.

Brutalist design has been used in public and

565 *Fitzwilliam House, Cambridge. Hall and library, Denys Lasdun*

566 *Courtyard, Falmer House, University of Sussex, founded 1961, Sir Basil Spence*

567 *University of York, founded 1961, Sir Robert Matthew*

568 *University of Salford, Manchester, 1961, Noel Hill*

general building. *Queen Elizabeth Concert Hall* on London's riverside is one stark and controversial example. An imaginative use of boarded concrete is to be seen in the *Tricorn Centre* at Portsmouth. Designed by *Owen Luder*, this town planning scheme is unashamedly plain, making no attempt to be elegant or finely finished. Its success is achieved by contrasts in shape and the play of light and shade one upon another and against the sky. Built on several levels, it is a breakaway from modern boxed-in architecture. It comprises a covered market with lorry space, a multi-storey car park, a piazza, a public house and flats. Typical of the interiors is the Casbah Public House (562), its ceiling decorated in black dull-surfaced material in square blocks and the walls wood-slatted and scarlet-painted. The scheme is warm and cosy, yet thoroughly modern.

Housing: Garden Cities, Flats, Housing Estates and New Towns

These are the four chief means by which individuals and corporate bodies both private and municipal, have sought to house a rapidly rising population in the twentieth century, in a manner which would be a social improvement upon the terrible conditions of the previous century. The ideas of such industrialists as Sir Titus Salt were carried to a further stage in the *garden cities* of the years 1900–40. The aim of a garden city was to create a new centre of population in a planned housing area which would also contain amenities such as churches, shops, schools and clubs and would produce a self-supporting community in the cleaner rural air with a higher proportion of open space per house than had been the case in nineteenth-century industrial towns.

Ebenezer Howard was one of the original proponents of the idea and published his plans in a book in 1898. He intended the land on which the town was built to be owned by or held in trust for its community and he wanted adequate land space to provide a rural belt between the town and other urban areas. It was an attempt to call a halt to the increasing urban sprawl of the great cities.

The Garden City Association was formed and a company established. The two examples which were built were *Welwyn* and *Letchworth*, both in Hertfordshire. Letchworth is larger, comprising about 4500 acres of which 1500 are used by the town and 3000

kept as a green belt. The factory area is apart from the town but readily accessible. In both towns the buildings are traditional, in brick, clapboard and half-timber and there is great variety in size and design of house from terraced cottages to large, detached villas. The houses have gardens and the roads are tree-lined. In the centre of the town are broad avenues with shops, council offices, a theatre and civic buildings (570).

At the same time a number of industrialists were establishing their own model housing estates adjacent to, but not an integral part of, their factory area. *Bourneville* stems from Cadbury and Rowntree built theirs at *York*. The most extensive and impressive was Lord Leverhulme's *Port Sunlight* in the Wirral of Cheshire. The Lever factory was built in 1888 and the housing estate has developed since then for the firm's employees. Architecturally the estate is successful. There is great variety of materials, styles and scale of buildings and no overall architectural monotony. A number of well known architects in the domestic field contributed to the scheme, such as *Sir Ernest George*. Most of the houses are simple in brick, stone, or half-timber with pargetting. There is also a church, an art gallery, schools, a cottage hospital, library, bank, fire station, post office and shops (573).

In municipal schemes the *London County Council* was the largest organisation in the field and a number of cottage estates were built. These were much more cramped than the garden cities, with a high density of population per acre and no green belt between one suburban estate and another. Also, these were dormitory suburbs and workers had to travel, often long distances, to their jobs.

It was after 1930 that the congestion in large cities became so acute that it was realised that flat accommodation represented the only way to solve the housing problem; the garden city had only touched the fringe of this. Two of the chief difficulties in designing good accommodation in flats are to permit adequate ingress of light and to cut out noise. Most council schemes did neither. The usual layout in the 1930s was for access by galleries, that is an open corridor along one façade of the block. Each corridor was reached by open staircases. There was no privacy from the noise of people approaching other flats and the gallery above cut out the light from the windows of the gallery below. Large numbers of these depressing, noisy blocks were built in these years.

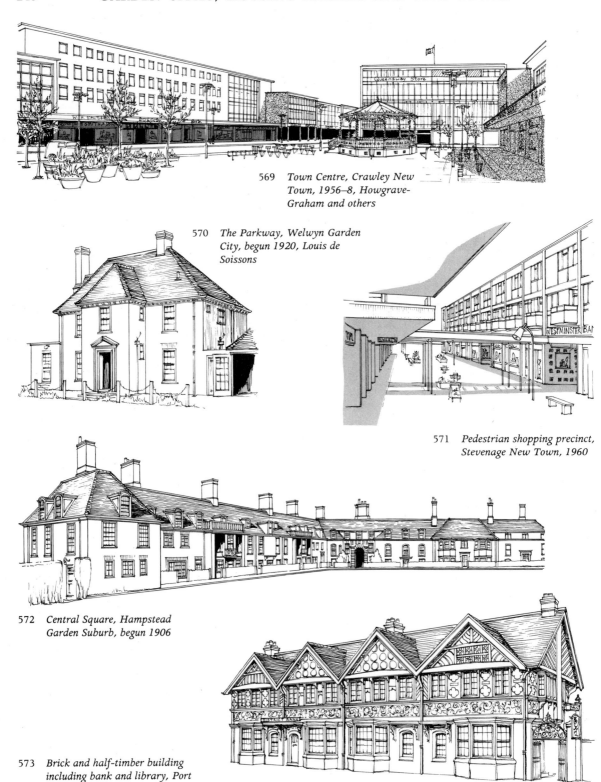

569   Town Centre, Crawley New
      Town, 1956–8, Howgrave-
      Graham and others

570   The Parkway, Welwyn Garden
      City, begun 1920, Louis de
      Soissons

571   Pedestrian shopping precinct,
      Stevenage New Town, 1960

572   Central Square, Hampstead
      Garden Suburb, begun 1906

573   Brick and half-timber building
      including bank and library, Port
      Sunlight Estate, Cheshire

Lutyens' low-cost flats at *Page Street* have been referred to (page 235 and 548). Of a high architectural standard and in luxury class but still of corridor access design, *Wells Coates* built the simple concrete *Isokon Flats* at Hampstead (574). In a balcony design in modern construction *Maxwell Fry* built *Kemsal House* in 1936. This was a low-cost block in Ladbroke Grove in *London* which was of advanced design for its time. *Tecton's Highpoint Flats* (page 241) were in the luxury class and are one of the earliest of the tower blocks (though small by post-war standards).

After 1945 the proportion of municipal housing increased, accelerated by the urgent demand created by war damage. The character of such housing had now altered and was both more enlightened and more catholic in interpretation. *London County Council*, having the largest housing problem on its hands, has, naturally, built some of the largest and most comprehensive of such schemes. The best of these is the *Alton Estate* at *Roehampton*. The open site is a magnificent one: on high ground with views in all directions, it adjoins Roehampton village and Wimbledon Common. Designed by the Housing Division of the L.C.C. Architects' Department under *Leslie Martin* and *Whitfield Lewis*, the estate is a mixed development with an informal layout incorporating eleven-storey blocks, four-storey maisonettes and two-tier terrace houses. The landscaping has been imaginatively carried out, taking full advantage of the natural beauties of the site; the only serious deficiency was the lack of foresight in considering provision for private cars.

Of different design, in a more heavily populated district of London, *Drake and Lasdun* evolved the 'cluster block' layout* in *Bethnal Green*. Here, four rectangular blocks are connected to a core by bridges. The structure, in reinforced concrete, has the advantage of easy ingress of light and air as well as being a more interesting building design (576). In the *Pimlico Housing Estate* in Churchill Gardens, *Powell and Moya* evolved an original heating system by using the exhaust heat from Battersea Power Station on the opposite side of the river to supply an estate of 1600 dwellings. The green glass tower, some 140 feet high, is the centre of the plant for the heating system.

---

* In recent years this interesting scheme has been emulated in Moscow as ideal for giving maximum light and air in crowded urban areas.

An interesting estate outside London which helped to pioneer the 'brutalist' architectural idiom, is the *Park Hill Estate* at *Sheffield*. Developed by the City Architects' Department, this is built on sloping ground so that at one end buildings are composed of 14 storeys and at the other of only four or five. The plan includes shops, pedestrian walks and play spaces. The structure is of reinforced concrete with brick panels. It is an imaginative and ingenious architectural scheme, but the extensive use of concrete in the South Yorkshire climate lacks colour and interest and has not weathered well.

The equivalent development after the Second World War to the Garden City theme after the First, was the *New Town* idea. With Lord Reith as its Chairman, the New Town Committee was set up in 1945 to suggest guiding principles upon which the theme might be developed. The New Towns Act of 1946, which followed, provided for 20 such towns to take the overspill from large cities, especially London, and that they should not adjoin the city in question. Planning was quickly implemented on the first sites: *Hatfield, Stevenage* and *Hemel Hempstead* in Hertfordshire, *Crawley* in Sussex, *Harlow* in Essex. Others, like *Cumbernauld* near Glasgow, followed later. The New Towns have been a success despite problems of resettling urban populations and providing interest and entertainment for the young. Each New Town comprises a town centre with large shops, car parks, civic and cultural buildings, amenities, schools and colleges. Adjacent residential areas have schools, churches, public houses, community centres and sports facilities. The architecture is entirely modern but varies greatly from one part of the country to another, using indigenous materials and methods of building. Probably the most successful examples are those set in the more rolling, varied landscapes such as Crawley in Sussex and Cumbernauld in Scotland (569, 571).

Houses

In the years up to 1918 large houses were still being built for well-to-do clients. Among the architects practising in this field *Sir Edwin Lutyens* was the foremost. Continuing in Shaw's and Voysey's tradition, Sir Edwin designed many such houses using different styles in brick, stone, wood and slate. They all have dignity, good proportions, restrained, elegant detail

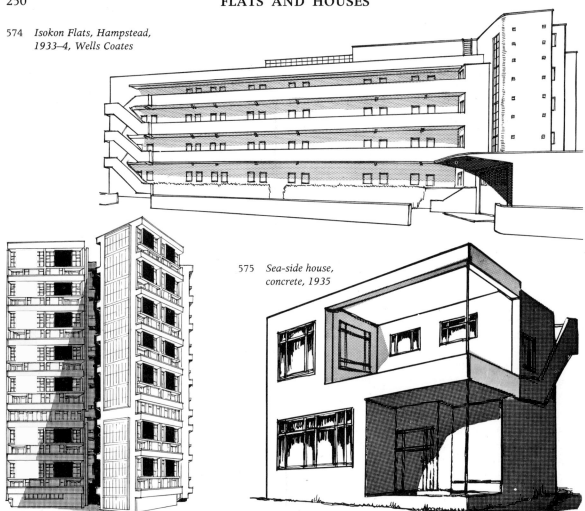

574 *Isokon Flats, Hampstead,*
1933–4, Wells Coates

575 *Sea-side house,*
concrete, 1935

576 *Claredale Street,*
Bethnal Green.
'Cluster' design,
1958, Drake and
Lasdun

577 *Drawing Room,*
1928–35

and a high standard of craftsmanship.

Interiors of the time were much plainer than Victorian ones, with less elaborate wallpapers and carpets, a smaller quantity of furniture and fewer ornaments. The Art Nouveau influence showed itself for a brief decade in wallpaper, furniture and stained-glass design.

The inter-war years produced few good houses from an architectural, aesthetic or comfort stand-point. It was a negative time, when reaction against over-decoration, overfurnishing and dark, rich in-teriors had set in and little that was positive took its place, with a resultant emptiness in exterior designs and interior decoration.

The bulk of domestic building was of a speculative nature and was put up on a vast scale in town suburbs. Mock Tudor or fifteenth-century beams, consisting of wood less than one inch thick, super-imposed upon brick and plaster, attempted to give the impression of character, originality and wealth. The term 'stockbroker Tudor' has now become one of disapprobation but, in their time, such houses in the desirable areas on the fringe of suburbia were eagerly sought after.

A few British architects in the 1930s followed the lead of the émigré Continental ones and designed houses on functionalist lines (575). *Maxwell Fry's* 'Sun House' in Frognal Way, Hampstead, 1935, is one of these, where the architect made full use of the new materials and modern structure in his flat roof and cantilevered balcony.

On the interior, the *dernier cri* in design was also for the plainest of décors (577). The walls were dis-tempered or papered in cream or white, carpets were unpatterned, chairs of functional design were covered in plain wool or velvet. An electric bar fire, set in a cream, stucco-finished fireplace, had replaced the old coal-burning grate, and electric light the gas mantle. Plainness was everywhere. Vacuity was accepted as simplicity and, though the ordinary person without intellectual pretensions did not go to such extremes even his drawing room scheme was carried out in cream or beige, neutrally if not emptily. The reaction from Victorianism was extreme; every attempt was made, if distemper was not used, to find a wallpaper with an indiscernible pattern and furnishings of like kind.

Since 1950 interiors have become more colourful again. Man-made fibres have made possible furnish-ing materials of bright, washable designs for curtains, chair covers and even carpets. An informal open-plan style has brought more variety to interior design and walls and ceilings can be painted, papered or even left in natural brick or stone. Modern home design and forms of heating have brought light and warmth to the contemporary home.

Glossary

The bold reference figures in brackets refer to line drawings in the glossary.

Abacus The top member of a capital, usually a square or curved-sided slab of stone or marble (**584, 586**).

Abutment Solid masonry acting as support against the thrust or lateral pressure of an arch (**581, 583**).

Acanthus A leaf form used in classical ornament (**586, 594**).

Acroteria Blocks resting on the vertex and lower extremities of a pediment to carry carved ornament (**584**).

Ambulatory A passage or aisle giving access between the choir, with high altar, and the apse of a church.

Antefixae Carved blocks set at regular intervals along the lower edge of a roof in classical architecture.

Anthemion A type of classical ornament based upon the honeysuckle flower (**594**).

Apse Semi-circular or polygonal termination to a church most commonly to be found in the eastern or transeptal elevations.

Arabesque Classical ornament in delicate, flowing forms, terminating in scrolls and decorated with flowers and leaves (**589**).

Arcade A series of arches open, or closed with masonry, supported on columns or piers.

Arch A structure of wedge-shaped blocks over an opening which support one another by mutual pressure (**578**).

Architrave The lowest member of the entablature (**584, 587, 588**).

Arcuated construction Where the structure is supported on arches.

Arris The vertical sharp edges between the flutes on a column (**584**).

Articulation The designing, defining and dividing up of a façade into vertical and horizontal architectural members

Ashlar Hewn and squared stones prepared for building.

Astragal A moulding at the top of the column and below the capital.

Astylar A classical façade without columns or pilasters.

Attic A term applied in Renaissance architecture to the upper storey of a structure above the cornice.

Bailey A court enclosed by inner or outer walls of a castle or by any of its defensive circuits.

Baldacchino A canopy supported on pillars set over an altar or throne.

Barbican Outer defence to a city or castle. Generally a double tower over a gate or bridge.

Barge board Ornamental carved wood boards on the exterior gable beams of a roof (**602**).

Barrel vault A continuous vault in semi-circular section, like a tunnel (**599**).

Bascule A type of drawbridge raised or lowered with counterpoise.

Basilica In Roman architecture a hall of justice and centre for commercial exchange. This type of structure was adapted by the early Christians for their church design. It was a rectangular building generally with an apse at one end. It was divided internally into nave and aisles by columns, not piers, and these supported a timber roof. The basilican plan continued in use for several centuries.

Bay Compartment or division in a building. Term applied particularly to cathedrals where bays are marked by vaulting shafts and pillars (**583**).

Bolection moulding A curved moulding generally used to raise one surface, such as a panel, above the remainder.

Caisson *see* Coffer.

Cantilever A specially shaped beam or other member (e.g. staircase tread) supported securely at one end and carrying a load at the other free end or with the load distributed uniformly along the beam. A cantilever bracket is used to support a cornice or balcony, etc. of considerable projection. The cantilever principle is frequently adopted in designs of large bridges, e.g. the Forth Railway Bridge, near Edinburgh.

Capital The crowning feature of a column or pilaster **584, 586, 587**).

Cartouche Ornament in the form of elaborate scrolled forms round shields, tablets or coats of arms.

Caryatid Sculptured female figure in the form of support or column.

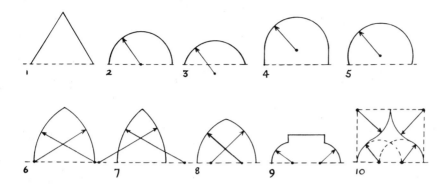

578 *The Arch*

1 Triangular	*7 Pointed – lancet*
2 Round – semicircular	*8 Pointed – obtuse*
3 Round – segmental	*9 Shouldered*
4 Round – stilted	*10 Ogee*
5 Round – horseshoe	*11 Four-centred*
6 Pointed – equilateral	

579   *Wall sets–off*

580   *Quoin stones*

581   *Buttress sets–off*

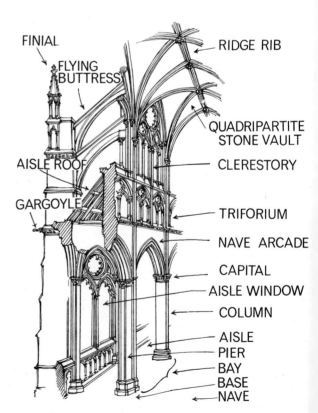

582   *Lintel*

583   *Gothic construction*

FINIAL

FLYING
BUTTRESS

RIDGE RIB

QUADRIPARTITE
STONE VAULT

CLERESTORY

AISLE ROOF

TRIFORIUM

GARGOYLE

NAVE ARCADE

CAPITAL
AISLE WINDOW
COLUMN
AISLE
PIER
BAY
BASE
NAVE

Ceiling cove Curved part of a ceiling where it joins the wall.

Centering A structure, usually made of timber, set up to support a dome, vault or ceiling until construction is complete.

Chamfer An angle which is cut off diagonally. The cut can be straight or concave.

Chevet Term given to circular or polygonal apse when surrounded by an ambulatory from which radiate chapels.

Chevron ornament Romanesque decoration in zig-zag form.

Cinquefoil Five-leaf tracery opening.

Clerestory The upper storey of a church generally pierced by a row of windows (583).

Coffer Panel or caisson sunk into a ceiling, dome or vault – often ornamented (585).

Collar beam Curved tying beam in a timber roof.

Corbel table A projecting section of wall supported on corbels (carved blocks of stone or wood) and generally forming a parapet.

Cornice The crowning member of the classical entablature (584, 588).

Coupled columns In classical architecture where the wall articulation is designed with the columns in pairs.

Crocket A projecting block of stone carved in Gothic foliage on the inclined sides of pinnacles and canopies (596).

Crossing The central area in a cruciform church where the transepts cross the nave and choir arm. Above this lofty space is generally set a tower, with or without a spire.

Cruciform A plan based upon the form of a cross.

Cupola A spherical roof covering a circular or polygonal form.

Curtain wall In modern architecture this term is in universal use and commonly describes an external non-loadbearing wall composed of repeated modular elements generally of glass in metal framing. These are prefabricated then erected on the site.

Cusp Point forming the foliations in Gothic tracery.

Cyma A moulding in a section of two contrasting curves – either cyma recta or cyma reversa – used especially in classical architecture (588, 594).

Dentil Classical form of ornament (587).

Domical vault A vault covering a square or polygonal compartment and shaped like a dome.

Drum The circular or poly-sided vertical walling supporting a dome.

Drum tower Round tower.

Echinus A curved, moulded member supporting the abacus of the Doric Order. The term is derived from the Greek *echinos* meaning sea urchin. The curve resembles the shell of the sea urchin (584).

Engaged column A column (in classical architecture) which is attached to the wall so that only a half to three-quarters of its circumference stands visible.

Entablature The top portion of an architectural order which consists of horizontal mouldings. These are divided into the architrave which surmounts the capital, then the frieze and last, and uppermost, the cornice (584, 588).

Entasis Taken from the Greek word for distension, is an outward curving along the outline of a column shaft. It is designed to counteract the optical illusion which gives to a shaft bounded by straight lines the appearance of being curved inwards, i.e. concave.

Fillet A narrow flat band which divides mouldings from one another; also separates column flutes (588).

Finial Ornament finishing off the apex of a roof, gable, pinnacle, newel, canopy, etc. (583).

Flute Vertical channelling in the shaft of a column (584, 587).

Frieze The central member of the classical entablature (584, 587, 588).

Frontispiece The two- or three-stage entrance feature applied to the principal façade of a court or building.

Giant order Used in later classical architecture wherein the order spans two storeys of the façade.

Greek cross plan A cruciform plan where the four arms of the cross are of equal length.

Guilloche Classical ornament in the form of an intertwined plait (594).

Guttae Small cones under the mutules and triglyphs of the Doric entablature (584, 590).

Hammerbeam Horizontal beam in timber roof situated as a tie beam but in two sections with main opening in the centre (605, 608).

Hammer post Rests on the inner side of the hammerbeam (605, 608).

Impost The horizontal stone or mouldings on top of a pier from which the arch springs (595).

Intercolumniation The space between columns.

Intersecting vault Where two vaults, either of semi-circular section or of pointed form, meet and intersect one another at right angles. Most usual instance is in the crossing of a church where the transepts cross nave and choir (601).

King post (also queen post) Vertical post extending from ridge to tie-beam centre to support the latter. Queen posts are in pairs (604).

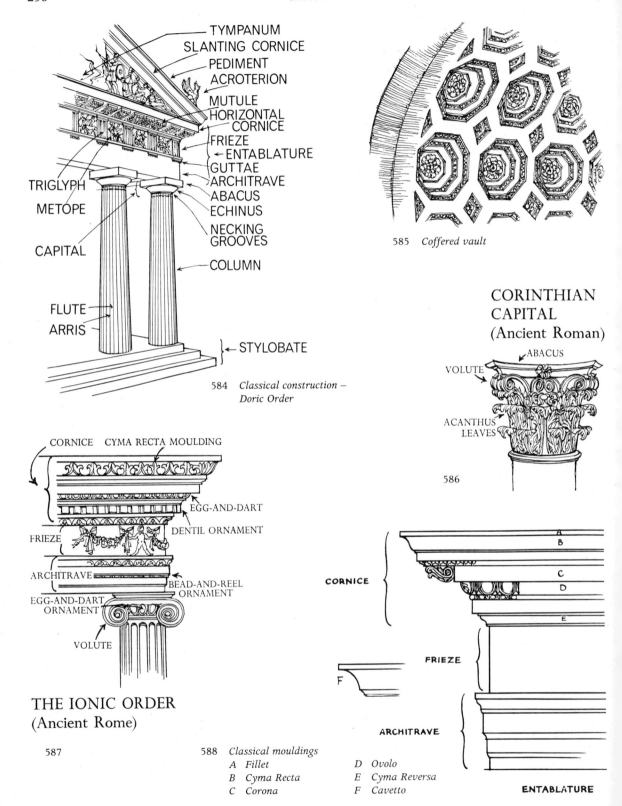

TYMPANUM
SLANTING CORNICE
PEDIMENT
ACROTERION
MUTULE
HORIZONTAL
CORNICE
FRIEZE
← ENTABLATURE
GUTTAE
ARCHITRAVE
ABACUS
ECHINUS
NECKING
GROOVES
COLUMN

TRIGLYPH
METOPE

CAPITAL

FLUTE
ARRIS

← STYLOBATE

584   *Classical construction –*
       Doric Order

585   *Coffered vault*

CORNICE   CYMA RECTA MOULDING

EGG-AND-DART
DENTIL ORNAMENT

FRIEZE

ARCHITRAVE
BEAD-AND-REEL
ORNAMENT

EGG-AND-DART
ORNAMENT

VOLUTE

THE IONIC ORDER
(Ancient Rome)

587

CORINTHIAN
CAPITAL
(Ancient Roman)

ABACUS
VOLUTE

ACANTHUS
LEAVES

586

CORNICE

FRIEZE

ARCHITRAVE

ENTABLATURE

588   *Classical mouldings*
       A *Fillet*
       B *Cyma Recta*   D *Ovolo*
       C *Corona*   E *Cyma Reversa*
                                F *Cavetto*

589 *Arabesque and griffin ornament*

590 *Greek Doric entablature*

KEY or FRET PATTERN

PATERA

591 *Classical ornament*

592 *Trefoil*

593 *Quatrefoil*

595 *Impost mouldings*

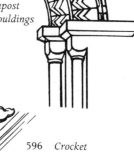

596 *Crocket*

597 *Oval patera*

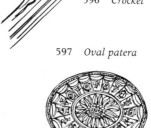

594 *Classical ornament*

EGG and DART

LEAF and DART

BAY LEAF GARLAND

GUILLOCHE

PATERA

FRET

ACANTHUS

CYMA RECTA
CYMA REVERSA

MOULDINGS

598 *Gothic mouldings*

← Bead and reel

← Anthemion

← Bead and reel

Lantern Structure for ventilation and light. Often surmounting a dome or tower.

Latin cross plan A cruciform plan where the nave is longer than the other three arms.

Lierne From the French *lier* = to tie. A short, intermediate rib in Gothic vaulting which is not a ridge rib nor rises from the impost (**609**).

Lintel The horizontal stone slab or timber beam spanning an opening and supported on columns or walls (**582**).

Lunette A semi-circular panel, often ornamented in the form of stone, wood or glass.

Machicolation A parapet in medieval fortified buildings with openings between supporting corbels for dropping missiles upon the enemy.

Metope The space between the triglyphs of a Doric frieze. Often decorated with sculptured groups or carved ornament (**584, 590**).

Module A unit of measurement based on proportion by which the parts of a classical order are regulated. Generally taken from the half-diameter of the column at its junction with the base. In modern architecture, a standard unit adopted for the convenience of mass production.

Monolith Single, standing stone.

Monolithic column One whose shaft is of one piece of stone or marble in contrast to one made up in hollow drums.

Mullion Vertical bar dividing the lights in a window.

Mutule Blocks attached under Doric cornices from which the guttae depend (**584, 590**).

Necking The space between the astragal of a column shaft and the actual capital.

Ogee moulding A moulding incorporating a convex and a concave curve.

Order In classical architecture the order comprises the column and the entablature which it supports. The column is divided into base, shaft and capital (**584**).

Pediment The triangular feature in classical architecture which resembles the Gothic gable. Supported on the entablature over porticoes, windows and doors (**584**).

Pendentive Spherical triangles formed by the intersecting of the dome by two pairs of opposite arches, themselves carried on four piers or columns.

Peristyle A row of columns surrounding a temple, court or cloister, also the space so enclosed.

Piano nobile An Italian Renaissance term meaning literally the 'noble floor'. In classical building it is the first and principal floor.

Pier A solid mass of masonry between windows, also support for a bridge and masonry from which an arch springs (**583**).

Pilaster A column of rectangular section often engaged in the wall.

Piloti A term in modern architecture taken from the French word for pile or stake. Introduced by Le Corbusier in his designs of flats and houses supported on columns or piles.

Plinth Lowest member of base or wall; sometimes divided into stages (**598**).

Podium A continuous projecting base or pedestal.

Portcullis A strong, heavy frame or grating of oak or iron, made to slide up and down in vertical grooves at the sides of a castle gateway.

Quatrefoil Four-leaf tracery opening (**593**).

Quoin External angle of a building (**580**).

Relieving arch A relieving or discharging arch or slab is constructed to prevent the weight of masonry above it from crushing the lintel stone below.

Ridge crest Exterior ridge or upper angle of roof.

Ridge pole, purlin or piece A baulk of timber extending along the internal ridge of a roof on which the upper ends of the rafters rest (**604**).

Rotunda Building of circular ground plan often surmounted by a dome; a circular hall or room.

Rubble work Stones of irregular shape and size used although generally roughly in cube or block form.

Rustication A treatment of masonry with sunk joints and roughened surfaces. Used in classical architecture.

Set-off Sloping or horizontal member connecting the lower and thicker part of a wall or buttress with the receding upper part (**579, 581**).

Shaft The column of an order between capital and base (**584, 587**).

Shingle Oak tile.

Spandrel Triangular space formed between an arch and the rectangles of outer mouldings as in a doorway. Generally decorated by carving or mosaic (**605, 608**).

Solar Medieval term for an upper room, usually the private sitting room of the owner of the house.

Squinch Arches placed diagonally across the internal angles of a tower or base of drum to convert the square form into an octagonal base to support an octagonal spire or circular drum.

Starling Pointed mass of masonry or wood projecting from the pier of a bridge.

Stilted arch An arch having its springing line higher than the level of the impost mouldings. It is then connected to these mouldings by vertical sections of walling or stilts (**578**).

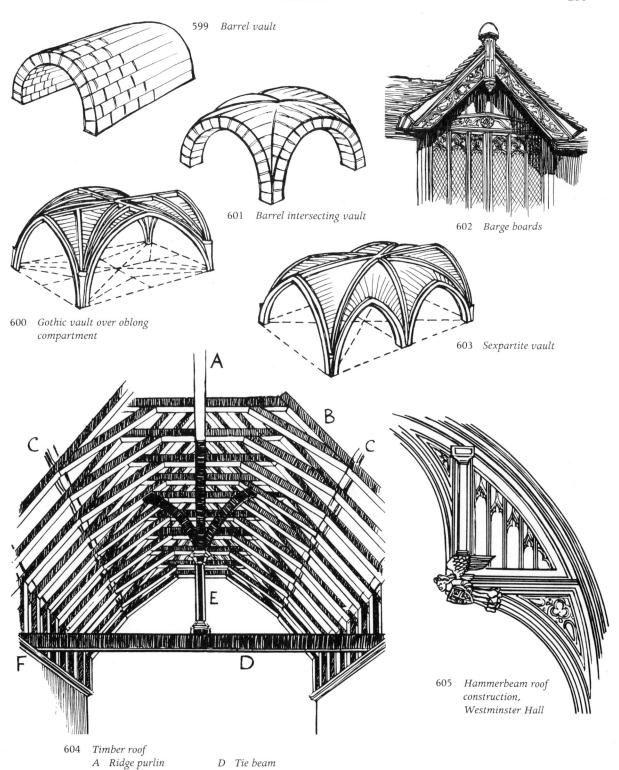

599 *Barrel vault*

601 *Barrel intersecting vault*

602 *Barge boards*

600 *Gothic vault over oblong compartment*

603 *Sexpartite vault*

604 *Timber roof*
  A *Ridge purlin*   D *Tie beam*
  B *Rafter*   E *King post*
  C *Purlin*   F *Wall plate*

605 *Hammerbeam roof construction, Westminster Hall*

606   *Groined vault*

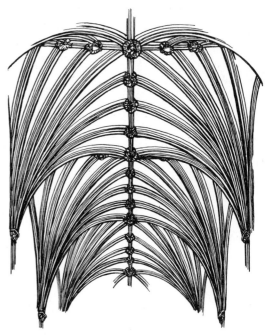

607   *Ribbed vault*

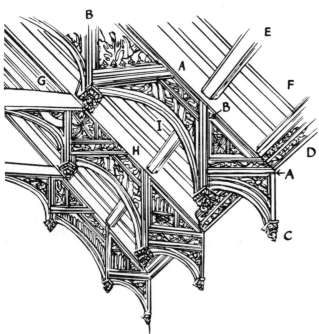

608   *Double hammerbeam roof*

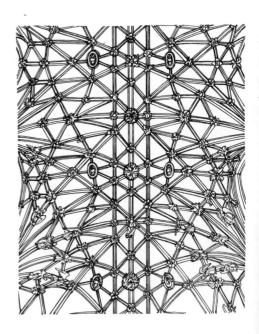

609   *Lierne vault*

Strapwork A form of ornament using straps or lines of decoration intertwined and forming panels. The straps are flat with raised fillet edges. Used on ceilings or walls, especially in early Mannerist type Renaissance work in Flanders, Poland and Britain.

String course A moulding or projecting course set horizontally along the elevation of a building.

Stucco A plaster used for coating wall surfaces for moulding into architectural decoration or sculpture.

Stylobate A basement, generally of three steps, supporting a row of columns in Greek temple design (**584**).

Swag A drop type of decoration composed of ribbons, flowers and fruit.

Tie beam A horizontal or slightly arched beam connecting the principal rafters of a roof (**604**).

Tierceron A third rib in Gothic vaulting.

Trabeated construction A structure composed of horizontal lintels and vertical posts as in Greek architecture (**584**).

Tracery The ornamental stonework in the head of a Gothic window.

Transept The arms of a cruciform church set at right angles to the nave and choir. Transepts are generally aligned north and south.

Transom Horizontal bar of wood or stone across a window or a door top.

Trefoil Three-leaf decoration used in Gothic architecture, particularly in window tracery and panelling (**592**).

Triforium The central, or first floor stage, of a Medieval church between the nave arcade and the clerestory. The triforium is usually arcaded and may have a passage behind at first floor level extending continuously round the church (**583**).

Triglyph The blocks, cut with vertical channels, which are set at regular intervals in the frieze of the Doric Order (**584, 590**)

Tympanum The triangular space between the sloping and horizontal cornices of a classical pediment (**584**).

Undercroft The chamber partly or wholly below ground generally in a Medieval building. In a church this would be a crypt, in a house or castle it would be used for storage.

Vault Arched covering in stone, brick or wood (**583, 599–601, 603, 606–7, 609**).

Vaulting bay The rectangular or square area bounded by columns or piers and covered by a ribbed or groined vault (**583**).

Vaulting boss A carved decorative feature set at intervals in a ribbed vault to hide the junctions between one rib and another (**607, 609**).

Vault springing The point at which the vault ribs spring upwards from the capital, corbel or arch impost (**583. 607**).

Volute A spiral or scroll to be seen in Ionic, Corinthian and Composite capitals (**586, 587**).

Voussoir The wedge-shaped stones which compose an arch.

Wall plate Horizontal timber extending lengthwise on top of the wall immediately under a timber roof (**604**).

Wattle-and-daub Walling made from vertical timber stakes woven horizontally with branches and reeds. The whole is then surfaced with mud.

Bibliography

A select list of books recommended for further reading

General

ALLSOPP, B., *A General History of Architecture*, Sir Isaac Pitman and Sons Ltd, 1960

ALLSOPP, B., BOOTON, H. W. and CLARK, U., *The Great Tradition of Western Architecture*, A. and C. Black, 1966

BATSFORD, H. and FRY, C., *The English Cottage*, B. T. Batsford Ltd, 1950; *The Cathedrals of England*, B. T. Batsford Ltd, 1960

BRAUN, H., *The Story of the English House*, B. T. Batsford Ltd, 1940; *Elements of English Architecture*, David and Charles, 1973; *English Abbeys*, Faber and Faber Ltd, 1971

CAMESASCA, E., *History of the House*, Collins, 1971

CLIFTON-TAYLOR, A., *The Pattern of English Building*, Faber and Faber Ltd, 1972; *The Cathedrals of England*, Thames and Hudson, 1967

COLVIN, H. M., *The Biographical Dictionary of English Architects 1660–1840*, John Murray Ltd, 1954

COOK, G. H., *The English Cathedral*, Phoenix House Ltd, 1957

COOK, O. and SMITH, E., *English Abbeys and Priories*, Thames and Hudson, 1960

CRUDEN, S., *Scottish Abbeys*, H.M. Stationery Office, 1960

COX, C. and FORD, C. B., *The English Parish Church*, B. T. Batsford Ltd, 1954

CROSSLEY, F. H., *Timber Building in England from Early Times to the end of the Seventeenth Century*, B. T. Batsford Ltd, 1951; *The English Abbey*, B. T. Batsford Ltd, 1949

DUNBAR, J. G., *The Historic Architecture of Scotland*, B. T. Batsford Ltd, 1966

DUTTON, R., *The English Country House*, B. T. Batsford Ltd, 1949

FLETCHER, B., *A History of Architecture*, The Athlone Press, 1975

GIBBERD, F., *The Architecture of England*, The Architectural Press, 1965

GLOAG, J., *Guide to Western Architecture*, George Allen and Unwin Ltd, 1958

GLOAG, J. and BRIDGWATER, D., *A History of Cast Iron in Architecture*, George Allen and Unwin Ltd, 1948

HARRIS, J. and LEVER, J., *Illustrated Glossary of Architecture 850–1830*, Faber and Faber, 1964

HARVEY, J., *The English Cathedral*, B. T. Batsford Ltd, 1956

HUTTON, G. and SMITH, E., *English Parish Churches*, Thames and Hudson, 1957

ISON, L. and W., *English Church Architecture Through the Ages*, Arthur Barker Ltd, 1972

JORDAN, R. FURNEAUX, *A Picture History of the English House*, Edward Hulton, 1960

KERSTING, A. F. and DUTTON, R., *English Country Houses in Colour*, B. T. Batsford Ltd, 1958

KIDSON, P. and MURRAY, P., *A History of English Architecture*, George G. Harrap and Co., 1962

LINNELL, C. L. S. and KERSTING, A. F., *English Cathedrals in Colour*, B. T. Batsford Ltd, 1960

LITTLE, B., *English Historic Architecture*, B. T. Batsford Ltd, 1964

MANSBRIDGE, J., *Graphic History of Architecture*, B. T. Batsford Ltd, 1967

MARÉ, E. de, *The Bridges of Britain*, B. T. Batsford Ltd, 1954

MEYER, P. and HURLIMANN, M., *English Cathedrals*, Thames and Hudson, 1950

NELLIST, J. B., *British Architecture and its Background*, Macmillan and Co. Ltd, 1967

OGILVIE, V., *The English Public School*, B. T. Batsford Ltd, 1957

O'NEIL, B. H. ST J., *Castles*, H.M. Stationery Office, 1954

PETZCH, H., *Architecture in Scotland*, Longman Group Ltd, 1971

PEVSNER, N., *Buildings of England*, Penguin Books Ltd

POTHORN, H., *Styles of Architecture*, B. T. Batsford Ltd, 1971

PUGIN, A. W. N., *The True Principles of Pointed Architecture* (Reprint of first edition of 1841), Academy Editions, 1973

RUSKIN, J., *The Stones of Venice*, William Collins Sons and Co., 1960; *The Seven Lamps of Architecture*, The Noonday Press, U.S.A. (new edition), 1961

SIMPSON, W. D., *Castles in England and Wales*, B. T. Batsford Ltd, 1969

SORRELL, A., *British Castles*, B. T. Batsford Ltd, 1974

VALE, E. and KERSTING, A. F., *A Portrait of English Churches*, B. T. Batsford Ltd, 1956

WARE, D., *A Short Dictionary of British Architects*, George Allen and Unwin, 1967

YARWOOD, D., *English Houses*, B. T. Batsford Ltd, 1966

Saxon and Romanesque

ALLSOPP, B., *Romanesque Architecture*, Arthur Barker Ltd, 1971

BLAIR, P. H., *An Introduction to Anglo-Saxon England*, Cambridge University Press, 1956

CONANT, K. J., *Carolingian and Romanesque Architecture*, Penguin Books, 1966

FISHER, E. A., *The Greater Anglo-Saxon Churches*, Faber and Faber Ltd, 1962

STOLL, R., *Architecture and Sculpture in Early Britain*, Thames and Hudson, 1967

Medieval and Gothic

BRAUN, H., *An Introduction to English Mediaeval Architecture*, Faber and Faber Ltd, 1951

BROWN, R. A., *English Medieval Castles*, B. T. Batsford Ltd, 1954

COOK, G. H., *English Monasteries in the Middle Ages*, Phoenix House Ltd, 1961

FRANKL, P., *Gothic Architecture*, Penguin Books, 1962

HARVEY, J., *The Gothic World*, B. T. Batsford Ltd, 1950; *The Master Builders*, Thames and Hudson 1971; *Henry Yevele*, B. T. Batsford Ltd, 1944; *Gothic England*, B. T. Batsford Ltd, 1948; *The Mediaeval Architect*, Wayland Publishers, 1972

RICKMAN, T., *An attempt to Discriminate the Styles of Architecture in England from the Conquest to the Reformation*, John Henry and James Parker, 1862

STEWART, C., *Gothic Architecture* (Simpson's History of Architectural Development), Longman Green and Co. Ltd

WEBB, G., *Architecture in Britain in the Middle Ages*, Penguin Books, 1956

WRIGHT, J., *Brick Building in England, Middle Ages to 1550*, John Baker, 1972

Elizabethan to Wren 1550–1700

ALLSOPP, B., *A History of Renaissance Architecture*, Sir Isaac Pitman and Sons Ltd, 1959

BRIGGS, M. S., *Wren the Incomparable*, George Allen and Unwin Ltd, 1953

DOWNES, K., *Christopher Wren*, Allen Lane, the Penguin Press, 1971

DUTTON, R., *The Age of Wren*, B. T. Batsford Ltd, 1951

FURST, V., *The Architecture of Sir Christopher Wren*, Percy Lund Humphries and Co., 1956

GIROUARD, M., *Robert Smythson and the Architecture of the Elizabethan Era*, Country Life Ltd, 1966

HIND, A. M., *Wenceslaus Hollar and his Views of London and Windsor in the Seventeenth Century*, The Bodley Head Press Ltd, 1922

HUGHES, J. Q. and LYNTON, N., *Renaissance Architecture* (Simpson's History of Architectural Development), Longmans Green and Co. Ltd, 1965

LEES-MILNE, J., *The Age of Inigo Jones*, B. T. Batsford Ltd, 1953; *Tudor Renaissance*, B. T. Batsford Ltd, 1951

PEVSNER, N., *Studies in Art, Architecture and Design* (2 vols.), Thames and Hudson, 1969

SEKLER, E., *Wren and his Place in European Architecture*, Faber and Faber Ltd, 1956

SITWELL, S., *British Architects and Craftsmen 1600–1830*, B. T. Batsford Ltd, 1948

WHIFFEN, M., *Stuart and Georgian Churches 1603–1837*, B. T. Batsford Ltd, 1948

WHINNEY, M., *Wren*, Thames and Hudson, 1971

The Eighteenth Century

ADAM, R. and J., *The Works in Architecture of Robert and James Adam*, Alec Tiranti Ltd, 1959

DAVIS, T., *John Nash*, David and Charles, 1973

DOWNES, K., *Hawksmoor*, Thames and Hudson, 1969

EDWARDS, A. T., *Sir William Chambers*, Ernest Benn Ltd, 1924

FLEMING, J., *Robert Adam and his Circle*, John Murray Ltd, 1962

HARRIS, J., *Sir William Chambers*, A. Zwemmer Ltd, 1970

HUSSEY, C., *English Country Houses, Early Georgian 1715–60*, Country Life Ltd, 1955; *English Country Houses, Mid-Georgian 1760–1800*, Country Life Ltd, 1956; *English Country Houses, Late Georgian 1800–1840*, Country Life Ltd, 1958

JOURDAIN, M., *The Work of William Kent*, Country Life Ltd, 1948

LEES-MILNE, J., *The Age of Adam*, B. T. Batsford Ltd, 1947

STROUD, D., *George Dance Architect 1741–1825*, Faber and Faber Ltd, 1971; *Henry Holland*, Country Life Ltd, 1966

SUMMERSON, J., *Architecture in Britain 1530–1830*, Penguin Books, 1969

WITTKOWER, R., *Palladio and English Palladianism*, Thames and Hudson, 1974

YARWOOD, D., *Robert Adam*, J. M. Dent and Sons Ltd, 1970

The Nineteenth Century

BARMAN, C., *An Introduction to Railway Architecture*, Art and Technics Ltd, 1950

BLOMFIELD, R., *Richard Norman Shaw*, B. T. Batsford Ltd, 1940

CLARK, K., *The Gothic Revival*, John Murray Ltd, 1962

COOK, J. M., *Victorian Architecture*, Johnson Reprint Co. Ltd, 1971

FERRIDAY, P., *Victorian Architecture*, Jonathan Cape, 1963

GOODHART-RENDEL, H. S., *English Architecture since the Regency*, Constable and Co., 1953

HITCHCOCK, H. RUSSELL, *Early Victorian Architecture in Britain* (2 Vols), Architectural Press Ltd, 1954; *Architecture, Nineteenth and Twentieth Centuries*, Penguin Books, 1958

HOBHOUSE, H., *Thomas Cubitt the Master Builder*, Macmillan, 1971

HOWARTH, T., *Nineteenth and Twentieth Century Architecture*, Longmans Green and Co. Ltd, 1959

MEEKS, C. L. V., *The Railway Station*, Architectural Press Ltd, 1957

PILCHER, D., *The Regency Style*, B. T. Batsford Ltd, 1948

POPE-HENNESSY, J. and WILD, H., *The Houses of Parliament*, B. T. Batsford Ltd, 1945

PUGIN, A. W. N., *Contrasts* (Repub.) Leicester University Press, 1969; *Specimens of Gothic Architecture* (2 Vols), M. A. Nattali, 1825

RICHARDS, J. M. and MARÉ, E. de, *The Functional Tradition in Early Industrial Buildings*, Architectural Press Ltd, 1958

STANTON, P., *Pugin*, Thames and Hudson, 1971

STROUD, D., *The Architecture of Sir John Soane*, Studio, 1961

TURNOR, R., *Nineteenth Century Architecture in Britain*, B. T. Batsford Ltd, 1950

Twentieth Century and Modern

BANHAM, R., *The New Brutalism*, The Architectural Press, 1966; *Guide to Modern Architecture*, The Architectural Press, 1962

BENNETT, T. P., *Architectural Design in Concrete*, Ernest Benn Ltd, 1927

BIRKS, T. and HOLFORD, M., *Building the New Universities*, David and Charles, 1972

BUTLER, A. S. G., *The Architecture of Sir Edwin Lutyens* (3 Vols), Country Life Ltd, 1950

DANNATT, T., *Modern Architecture in Britain*, B. T. Batsford Ltd, 1959

GROPIUS, W., *Scope of Total Architecture*, George Allen and Unwin, 1956

HATTRELL, W. S., *Hotels, Restaurants and Bars*, B. T. Batsford Ltd, 1962

HARVEY, W. A., *The Model Village and its Cottages, Bournville*, B. T. Batsford Ltd, 1906

HOWARTH, T., *Charles Rennie Mackintosh and the Modern Movement*, Routledge and Kegan Paul Ltd, 1952

HUSSEY, C., *The Life of Sir Edwin Lutyens*, Country Life Ltd, 1942

LE CORBUSIER, *Towards a New Architecture*, The Architectural Press, 1970; *The City of Tomorrow*, The Architectural Press, 1971

PEHNT, W., *Encyclopaedia of Modern Architecture*, Thames and Hudson, 1963

PEVSNER, N., *The Sources of Modern Architecture and Design*, Thames and Hudson, 1968

PRICE, B., *Technical Colleges and Colleges of Further Education*, B. T. Batsford Ltd, 1959

RICHARDS, J. M., *An Introduction to Modern Architecture*, Penguin Books, 1956

WHITTICK, A., *European Architecture in the Twentieth Century*, Leonard Hill Books, 1974; *Erich Mendelsohn*, Leonard Hill Ltd, 1956

WEBB, M., *Architecture in Britain Today*, Country Life Books, 1969

Regional

BOOTH, P. and TAYLOR, N., *Cambridge New Architecture*, Leonard Hill, 1970

COBB, G., *The Old Churches of London*, B. T. Batsford Ltd, 1948

COOK, G. H., *Portrait of St. Alban's Cathedral*, Phoenix House Ltd., 1951; *Old St. Paul's Cathedral*, Phoenix House Ltd, 1955; *Portrait of Canterbury Cathedral*, Phoenix House Ltd, 1949; *Portrait of Durham Cathedral*, Phoenix House Ltd, 1948

COURLANDER, K., *Richmond*, B. T. Batsford Ltd, 1953

EDWARDS, T., *Bristol*, B. T. Batsford Ltd, 1951

GODFREY, W. H., *A History of Architecture in and around London*, Phoenix House Ltd, 1962

HICKMAN, D., *Birmingham*, Studio Vista, 1970

ISON, W., *The Georgian Buildings of Bristol*, Faber and Faber Ltd, 1969; *The Georgian Buildings of Bath*, Faber and Faber Ltd, 1969

JESSUP, R. F. and F. W., *The Cinque Ports*, B. T. Batsford Ltd, 1952

JOWITT, R. L. P., *Salisbury*, B. T. Batsford Ltd, 1951

KERSTING, A. F. and DICK, M., *Portrait of Oxford*, B. T. Batsford Ltd, 1956

KERSTING, A. F. and LITTLE, B., *Portrait of Cambridge*, B. T. Batsford Ltd, 1955

LAMBERT, S., *New Architecture of London*, The Architectural Association, 1963

LINDLEY, K., *Sea-side Architecture*, Hugh Evelyn, 1973

LITTLE, B., *Birmingham Buildings*, David and Charles, 1971; *Cheltenham*, B. T. Batsford Ltd, 1952; *The Three Choirs Cities*, B. T. Batsford Ltd, 1952

MARGETSON, S., *Regency London*, Cassell, 1971

RODGERS, J., *York*, B. T. Batsford Ltd, 1951

SHEPHERD, T. H. and ELMES, J., *Metropolitan Improvements*, Jones and Co. 1828

SMITH, R. A. L., *Bath*, B. T. Batsford Ltd, 1948

SPENCE, B., *Phoenix at Coventry*, G. Bles Ltd, 1962

SUMMERSON, J., *Georgian London*, Barrie and Jenkins Ltd, 1962

Index

Buildings are generally listed under the names of towns or villages and persons under the surname. Illustration references are printed in bold type.